OF OTHER WORLDS

ESSAYS AND STORIES

BOOKS BY C. S. LEWIS

The Pilgrim's Regress
The Problem of Pain
The Screwtape Letters *and* Screwtape Proposes a Toast
Broadcast Talks
The Abolition of Man
Christian Behaviour
Beyond Personality
The Great Divorce
George MacDonald: An Anthology
Miracles
Transposition and Other Addresses
Mere Christianity
Surprised by Joy: The Shape of My Early Life
Reflections on the Psalms
The World's Last Night and Other Essays
The Four Loves
Letters to Malcolm: Chiefly on Prayer
Poems
Of Other Worlds: Essays and Stories
Letters of C. S. Lewis
Narrative Poems
A Mind Awake
On Stories: And Other Essays on Literature
Spirits in Bondage: A Cycle of Lyrics
The Business of Heaven: Daily Readings from C. S. Lewis
Present Concerns
All My Road Before Me: The Diary of C. S. Lewis, 1922–1927

FOR CHILDREN
THE CHRONICLES OF NARNIA:
The Lion, the Witch and the Wardrobe
Prince Caspian
The Voyage of the *Dawn Treader*
The Silver Chair
The Horse and His Boy
The Magician's Nephew
The Last Battle

FICTION
Out of the Silent Planet
Perelandra
That Hideous Strength
Till We Have Faces: A Myth Retold
The Dark Tower and Other Stories
Boxen: The Imaginary World of the Young C. S. Lewis

C. S. LEWIS

OF OTHER WORLDS

ESSAYS AND STORIES

A Harvest Book • Harcourt, Inc.

San Diego   New York   London

Library of Congress Cataloging-in-Publication Data
Lewis, Clive Staples, 1898–1963.
Of other worlds.
(A Harvest Book)
Includes bibliographical references
I. Title.
[PR6023.E92603   1975]   823'.9'12   75-6785
ISBN 0-15-602767-4

Printed in the United States of America
First Harvest edition 1975

D F H J I G E

PREFACE

'You can't get a cup of tea large enough or a book long enough to suit me,' said C. S. Lewis. And he meant it, for at that moment I was pouring his tea into a very large Cornish-ware cup and he was reading *Bleak House*.

This little anecdote suggests, I think, a theme for this book: the excellence of Story. And especially those kinds of story we call fairy tales and science fiction, both of which were dear to Lewis. In the nine essays printed here he discusses certain literary qualities which he feels critics neglect. Also—something rare with Lewis—he talks a little about his 'Chronicles of Narnia'[1] and his science fiction trilogy. Indeed, I have felt it so important to preserve in a permanent form all that Lewis has written about his own fiction that I have considered their publication, despite the overlapping in several of the pieces, justified. Following the essays are three science fiction short stories (as far as I know, the only short stories of Lewis's ever to be published) as well as the first five chapters of a novel which Lewis was writing at the time of his death.

Lewis's boyhood stories, written (I think) between the ages of about six and fifteen, were about his invented Animal-Land and the anthropomorphic beasts which inhabit it. His brother had, as his own country, India. In order that it might be a shared world, India was lifted out of its place in the real world and made into an island. Then, the mood of the systematizer being strong in both boys, Animal-Land was united with India to form the single state of Boxen. Soon the maps of Boxen included the principal train and steamship routes. The capital city of Murray had its own newspaper, *The Murray Evening Telegraph*. And so, out of an attic full of commonplace children's toys came a world

---

[1] Seven fairy tales which, according to Lewis, should be read in the following order: *The Magician's Nephew* (1955), *The Lion, the Witch and the Wardrobe* (1950), *The Horse and His Boy* (1954), *Prince Caspian* (1951), *The Voyage of the 'Dawn Treader'* (1952), *The Silver Chair* (1953), *The Last Battle* (1956).

as consistent and self-sufficient as that of the *Iliad* and the Barsetshire novels.

There are a good many stories and histories of Boxen extant (but unpublished) written in ruled exercise books in a large, neat handwriting and illustrated with his own drawings and water-colours. As the early legends of King Arthur and his Court grew to include romances of individual knights of the Round Table, so a systematic reading of Boxoniana from beginning to end (which, believe it or not, covers over seven hundred years) reveals a similar kind of growth. Lewis's interest was at first primarily that of tracing the history of Boxen; but once it became a finished creation, he turned to writing novels in which the principal characters—some little more than names in the histories—spring into prominence.

Lewis's masterpiece, and obviously the character he liked best, is Lord John Big. This noble frog is already the Little-Master, i.e. the Prime Minister, when we meet him in *Boxen: or Scenes from Boxonian City Life* (in two volumes complete with List of Contents, List of Illustrations, and Frontispiece). Later he has his own history: *The Life of Lord John Big of Bigham by C. S. Lewis in 3 Volumes* published by the 'Leeborough Press'. It is obvious, no doubt, from the titles that Lewis liked even the *making* of books. Drawn on the fly-leaf of one little book is the head of a spectacled mouse between the words 'Trade Mark'.

There is much to admire about Boxen. Lord Big is indeed a frog of powerful personality, and I find him almost as unforgettable as Reepicheep the Mouse and Puddleglum the Marshwiggle of the Narnia stories (who were, by the way, Lewis's favourites). There is not the slightest bit of evidence on a single page of the juvenilia that the author had to labour to find 'filling' for his really good plots: the stories seem to write themselves. And the humour, which is inseparable from the story itself, is unmistakably of the Lewis kind.

But, as Lewis himself admits,[1] Boxen is empty of poetry and romance. It would, I believe, astonish the readers of the Narnia books to know how really prosaic it is. This is (I think) chiefly because of his desire to be very 'grown-up'. He says himself, 'When I began writing stories in exercise books I tried to put

[1] *Surprised by Joy: The Shape of my Early Life* (1955), p. 22.

off all the things I really wanted to write about till at least the second page—I thought it wouldn't be like a grown-up book if it became interesting at once.'[1] Most of all, the Boxoniana are blighted by, of all things, politics—something which Lewis came to detest later in his life. It did, after all, hold him so long in bondage. The characters in *Scenes from Boxonian City Life* all relish a place in the 'Clique' though none of them, not even the author, appears to have any clear idea what a 'clique' is. Which is not surprising for, as Lewis wanted his characters to be 'grown-up', he naturally interested them in 'grown-up' affairs. And politics, his brother says, was a topic he almost always heard his elders discussing. There are, by the by, *no* children in any of these stories.

A sentence in a piece of juvenilia which points to the future chronicler of Narnia and lover of 'faery land' is to be found in *The Life of Lord John Big of Bigham* where Lewis puts into the mouth of the Little-Master these words: 'Say what he will, in every man's heart of hearts there is a deep-rooted objection to change—a love of old customs because of their age which neither time nor eternity can efface.'

One other comparison remains. Lewis, as a boy, seems to have had little feeling for the real nature of beasts as such. In the Boxen stories they are little more than 'dressed animals', and without the advantage of the illustrations one might find it difficult to remember that Lord Big is a frog, James Bar a bear, Macgoullah a horse, and so on. But it is as 'servants, playfellows, jesters' that we meet them in Narnia where there are 'wagging tails, and barking, and loose slobbery mouths and noses of dogs thrust into your hand' (*The Silver Chair*, p. 115). When Prince Caspian visits the tree-house of the Three Bulgy Bears, he is answered from within by a 'woolly sort of voice'; and when the bears come out 'blinking their eyes' they greet the Prince with 'very wet, snuffly kisses' and offer him some honey (*Prince Caspian*, p. 67). And Bree, who is as fond as any horse of sugar-lumps, rises up from his roll in the grass, 'blowing hard and covered with bits of braken' (*The Horse and His Boy*, p. 187).

There are, however, a few places in the juvenilia in which we

[1] 'Peace Proposals for Brother Every and Mr Bethell', *Theology*, vol. XLI (Dec. 1940), p. 344.

vii

find that winsome commingling of beast and man—what Lewis might call 'Eden's courtesy'—and which is so characteristic of his fairy tales. Viscount Puddiphat, a music-hall artist, is being wakened by his valet (the italics are mine):

> On a certain spring morning, the viscount's valet had entered his master['s] bedchamber with a cup of chocolate, and the ironed morning paper. No sooner had his step resounded on the floor than *a mass of feathers stirred in the large bed, and the owl raised himself on his elbow, with blinking eyes.*

The faerie element is absent from Animal-Land but this, in itself, does not prove that Lewis had to conceal his interest in fairy stories. After all, there are differences of *kind* and it would do harm to force them into competition. Lewis wrote another romance (unpublished) about Dr Ransom which falls, chronologically, between *Out of the Silent Planet* and *Perelandra*. Contrary to what might be expected, it does not have a theological theme. However, one truth that strikes me from comparing Boxen and Narnia is this: Boxen was invented by a boy who wanted to be 'grown-up'; the 'noble and joyous' tales of Narnia were created by one liberated from this desire. One wonders what different fruits Lewis's literary gifts would have borne had he not overcome the modern bugbear that fantastic literature is—in a contemptuous sense—'childish'. We can of course never know this: the important thing is that he did overcome it.

In introducing these essays and stories I should, at the same time, like to thank all those who have allowed me to reprint some of the papers in this book. (1) 'On Stories' was first published in *Essays Presented to Charles Williams* (1947) by the Oxford University Press. It was originally read, in a slightly fuller form, to a Merton College undergraduate literary society as 'The Kappa Element in Fiction'. 'Kappa' stood for κρύπτον—the 'hidden element'. (2) 'On Three Ways of Writing for Children' was read to the Library Association and published in their *Proceedings, Papers and Summaries of Discussions at the Bournemouth Conference 29th April to 2nd May 1952.* (3) 'Sometimes Fairy Stories May Say Best What's to be Said' first appeared in *The New York Times Book Review, Children's Book Section* (18

November 1956). (4) 'On Juvenile Tastes' is reprinted from the *Church Times, Children's Book Supplement* (28 November 1958) and (5) 'It All Began with a Picture . . .' is reprinted here from the *Radio Times, Junior Radio Times*, vol. CXLVIII (15 July 1960).

(6) 'On Critics' appears in print for the first time, as does (7) 'On Science Fiction', a talk given to the Cambridge University English Club on 24 November 1955. (8) 'A Reply to Professor Haldane', also published for the first time, is a rejoinder to Professor J. B. S. Haldane's article 'Auld Hornie, F.R.S.', *Modern Quarterly*, N.S., vol. I, No. 4 (Autumn 1946) in which he criticizes Lewis's science fiction trilogy: *Out of the Silent Planet, Perelandra,* and *That Hideous Strength.* I have not, however, thought it necessary to reprint Professor Haldane's article for Lewis makes the argument quite clear. Besides, the chief value of Lewis's reply is not in its polemical nature, but in the valuable light he throws on his own books. (9) 'Unreal Estates' is an informal conversation about science fiction between Lewis, Kingsley Amis, and Brian Aldiss. It was recorded on tape by Brian Aldiss in Lewis's rooms in Magdalene College, on 4 December 1962. It was first published under the title 'The Establishment must die and rot . . .' in *SF Horizons*, No. 1 (Spring 1964) and later as 'Unreal Estates' in *Encounter*, vol. XXIV (March 1965).

(10) 'The Shoddy Lands', a short story, first appeared in *The Magazine of Fantasy and Science Fiction*, vol. X (February 1956). (11) Lewis's next story, 'Ministering Angels', was set off by Dr Robert S. Richardson's article 'The Day after We Land on Mars' which was published in *The Saturday Review* (28 May 1955). Dr Richardson's article contains the prediction that 'If space travel and colonization of the planets eventually become possible on a fairly large scale, it seems probable that we may be forced into first tolerating and finally openly accepting an attitude toward sex that is taboo in our present social framework. . . . To put it bluntly, may it not be necessary for the success of the project to send some nice girls to Mars at regular intervals to relieve tensions and promote morale?'[1] Lewis

[1] Robert S. Richardson. 'The Day after We Land on Mars', *The Saturday Review*, vol. XXXVIII (28 May 1955), p. 28.

Preface

takes it from there in 'Ministering Angels' which was originally published in *The Magazine of Fantasy and Science Fiction*, vol. XIII (January 1958). (12) 'Forms of Things Unknown' is published for the first time.

(13) *After Ten Years* is an unfinished novel which Lewis began in 1959. Though he never abandoned the idea of finishing it, he could not think of how to continue the story. Lewis became very ill in 1960 and lived in comparative discomfort until his death in 1963. This may partially account for his inability to 'see pictures'—which was his usual way of writing stories. He usually wrote several drafts of a scholarly work such as *The Discarded Image*, although one draft was often sufficient for a work of fiction. And, as far as I know, he wrote only the single draft of *After Ten Years* which is published here for the first time. Lewis did not divide the fragment into parts (or give it a title); but, as each 'chapter' appears to have been written at a different time, I have decided to retain these rather natural divisions. The reader should be warned that Chapter V does not really follow Chapter IV. Lewis was anticipating the end of the novel, and had he completed it, there would have been many chapters between numbers IV and V.

Lewis discussed this work with Mr Roger Lancelyn Green, the author and formerly a pupil of Lewis's, and Dr Alastair Fowler, Fellow of Brasenose College, and I have asked them to write about the conversation they had with him. The nature of the story makes it important, however, that the reader should save Mr Green's and Dr Fowler's notes until last.

I have to thank Dr and Mrs Austin Farrer, Mr Owen Barfield, and Professor John Lawlor for the help they have given me in preparing this volume. I am also grateful to Mr Roger Lancelyn Green and Dr Alastair Fowler for their notes on *After Ten Years*. A large share of thanks also goes to my friend, Mr Daryl R. Williams, for his careful proof-reading. And it is to Major W. H. Lewis that I owe the pleasure of editing his brother's essays and stories.

Wadham College, Oxford.   WALTER HOOPER
October, 1965.

CONTENTS

Part I
ESSAYS

ON STORIES

It is astonishing how little attention critics have paid to Story considered in itself. Granted the story, the style in which it should be told, the order in which it should be disposed, and (above all) the delineation of the characters, have been abundantly discussed. But the Story itself, the series of imagined events, is nearly always passed over in silence, or else treated exclusively as affording opportunities for the delineation of character. There are indeed three notable exceptions. Aristotle in the *Poetics* constructed a theory of Greek tragedy which puts Story in the centre and relegates character to a strictly subordinate place. In the Middle Ages and the early Renaissance, Boccaccio and others developed an allegorical theory of Story to explain the ancient myths. And in our own time Jung and his followers have produced their doctrine of Archetypes. Apart from these three attempts the subject has been left almost untouched, and this has had a curious result. Those forms of literature in which Story exists merely as a means to something else—for example, the novel of manners where the story is there for the sake of the characters, or the criticism of social conditions—have had full justice done to them; but those forms in which everything else is there for the sake of the story have been given little serious attention. Not only have they been despised, as if they were fit only for children, but even the kind of pleasure they give has, in my opinion, been misunderstood. It is the second injustice which I am most anxious to remedy. Perhaps the pleasure of Story comes as low in the scale as modern criticism puts it. I do not think so myself, but on that point we may agree to differ. Let us, however, try to see clearly what kind of pleasure it is: or rather, what different kinds of pleasure it may be. For I suspect that a very hasty assumption has been made on this subject. I think that books which are read merely 'for the story' may be enjoyed in two very different ways. It is partly a division of books (some stories can be read only in the one spirit and some only in the other) and partly a division of readers (the same story can be read in different ways).

What finally convinced me of this distinction was a conversation which I had a few years ago with an intelligent American pupil. We were talking about the books which had delighted our boyhood. His favourite had been Fenimore Cooper whom (as it happens) I have never read. My friend described one particular scene in which the hero was half-sleeping by his bivouac fire in the woods while a Redskin with a tomahawk was silently creeping on him from behind. He remembered the breathless excitement with which he had read the passage, the agonized suspense with which he wondered whether the hero would wake up in time or not. But I, remembering the great moments in my own early reading, felt quite sure that my friend was misrepresenting his experience, and indeed leaving out the real point. Surely, surely, I thought, the sheer excitement, the suspense, was not what had kept him going back and back to Fenimore Cooper. If that were what he wanted any other 'boy's blood' would have done as well. I tried to put my thought into words. I asked him whether he were sure that he was not over-emphasizing and falsely isolating the importance of the danger simply as danger. For though I had never read Fenimore Cooper I had enjoyed other books about 'Red Indians'. And I knew that what I wanted from them was not simply 'excitement'. Dangers, of course, there must be: how else can you keep a story going? But they must (in the mood which led one to such a book) be Redskin dangers. The 'Redskinnery' was what really mattered. In such a scene as my friend had described, take away the feathers, the high cheek-bones, the whiskered trousers, substitute a pistol for a tomahawk, and what would be left? For I wanted not the momentary suspense but that whole world to which it belonged—the snow and the snow-shoes, beavers and canoes, war-paths and wigwams, and Hiawatha names. Thus I; and then came the shock. My pupil is a very clear-headed man and he saw at once what I meant and also saw how totally his imaginative life as a boy had differed from mine. He replied that he was perfectly certain that 'all that' had made no part of his pleasure. He had never cared one brass farthing for it. Indeed—and this really made me feel as if I were talking to a visitor from another planet—in so far as he had been dimly aware of 'all that', he had resented it as a distraction from the main issue. He would, if anything, have preferred to the Redskin some more ordinary danger such as a crook with a revolver.

To those whose literary experiences are at all like my own the distinction which I am trying to make between two kinds of pleasure will probably be clear enough from this one example. But to make it doubly clear I will add another. I was once taken to see a film version of *King Solomon's Mines*. Of its many sins —not least the introduction of a totally irrelevant young woman in shorts who accompanied the three adventurers wherever they went—only one here concerns us. At the end of Haggard's book, as everyone remembers, the heroes are awaiting death entombed in a rock chamber and surrounded by the mummified kings of that land. The maker of the film version, however, apparently thought this tame. He substituted a subterranean volcanic eruption, and then went one better by adding an earthquake. Perhaps we should not blame him. Perhaps the scene in the original was not 'cinematic' and the man was right, by the canons of his own art, in altering it. But it would have been better not to have chosen in the first place a story which could be adapted to the screen only by being ruined. Ruined, at least, for me. No doubt if sheer excitement is all you want from a story, and if increase of dangers increases excitement, then a rapidly changing series of two risks (that of being burned alive and that of being crushed to bits) would be better than the single prolonged danger of starving to death in a cave. But that is just the point. There must be a pleasure in such stories distinct from mere excitement or I should not feel that I had been cheated in being given the earthquake instead of Haggard's actual scene. What I lose is the whole sense of the deathly (quite a different thing from simple danger of death)—the cold, the silence, and the surrounding faces of the ancient, the crowned and sceptred, dead. You may, if you please, say that Rider Haggard's effect is quite as 'crude' or 'vulgar' or 'sensational' as that which the film substituted for it. I am not at present discussing that. The point is that it is extremely different. The one lays a hushing spell on the imagination; the other excites a rapid flutter of the nerves. In reading that chapter of the book curiosity or suspense about the escape of the heroes from their death-trap makes a very minor part of one's experience. The trap I remember for ever: how they got out I have long since forgotten.

It seems to me that in talking of books which are 'mere stories'—books, that is, which concern themselves principally with the imagined event and not with character or society—nearly everyone makes the assumption that 'excitement' is the only pleasure they ever give or are intended to give. *Excitement*, in this sense, may be defined as the alternate tension and appeasement of imagined anxiety. This is what I think untrue. In some such books, and for some readers, another factor comes in.

To put it at the very lowest, I know that something else comes in for at least one reader—myself. I must here be autobiographical for the sake of being evidential. Here is a man who has spent more hours than he cares to remember in reading romances, and received from them more pleasure perhaps than he should. I know the geography of Tormance better than that of Tellus. I have been more curious about travels from Uplands to Utterbol and from Morna Moruna to Koshtra Belorn than about those recorded in Hakluyt. Though I saw the trenches before Arras I could not now lecture on them so tactically as on the Greek wall, and Scamander and the Scaean Gate. As a

6

social historian I am sounder on Toad Hall and the Wild Wood
or the cave-dwelling Selenites or Hrothgar's court or Vorti-
gern's than on London, Oxford, and Belfast. If to love Story is
to love excitement then I ought to be the greatest lover of excitement alive. But the fact is that what is said to be the most
'exciting' novel in the world, *The Three Musketeers*, makes no
appeal to me at all. The total lack of atmosphere repels me.
There is no country in the book—save as a storehouse of inns
and ambushes. There is no weather. When they cross to London there is no feeling that London differs from Paris. There
is not a moment's rest from the 'adventures': one's nose is kept
ruthlessly to the grindstone. It all means nothing to me. If that
is what is meant by Romance, then Romance is my aversion
and I greatly prefer George Eliot or Trollope. In saying this I
am not attempting to criticize *The Three Musketeers*. I believe
on the testimony of others that it is a capital story. I am sure
that my own inability to like it is in me a defect and a misfortune. But that misfortune is evidence. If a man sensitive and
perhaps over-sensitive to Romance likes least that Romance
which is, by common consent, the most 'exciting' of all, then it
follows that 'excitement' is not the only kind of pleasure to be
got out of Romance. If a man loves wine and yet hates one of
the strongest wines, then surely the sole source of pleasure in
wine cannot be the alcohol?

If I am alone in this experience then, to be sure, the present
essay is of merely autobiographical interest. But I am pretty
sure that I am not absolutely alone. I write on the chance that
some others may feel the same and in the hope that I may help
them to clarify their own sensations.

In the example of *King Solomon's Mines* the producer of the
film substituted at the climax one kind of danger for another
and thereby, for me, ruined the story. But where excitement is
the only thing that matters kinds of danger must be irrelevant.
Only degrees of danger will matter. The greater the danger and
the narrower the hero's escape from it, the more exciting the
story will be. But when we are concerned with the 'something

else' this is not so. Different kinds of danger strike different chords from the imagination. Even in real life different kinds of danger produce different kinds of fear. There may come a point at which fear is so great that such distinctions vanish, but that is another matter. There is a fear which is twin sister to awe, such as a man in war-time feels when he first comes within sound of the guns; there is a fear which is twin sister to disgust, such as a man feels on finding a snake or scorpion in his bedroom. There are taut, quivering fears (for one split second hardly distinguishable from a kind of pleasurable thrill) that a man may feel on a dangerous horse or a dangerous sea; and again, dead, squashed, flattened, numbing fears, as when we think we have cancer or cholera. There are also fears which are not of *danger* at all: like the fear of some large and hideous, though innocuous, insect or the fear of a ghost. All this, even in real life. But in imagination, where the fear does not rise to abject terror and is not discharged in action, the qualitative difference is much stronger.

I can never remember a time when it was not, however vaguely, present to my consciousness. *Jack the Giant-Killer* is not, in essence, simply the story of a clever hero surmounting danger. It is in essence the story of such a hero surmounting *danger from giants*. It is quite easy to contrive a story in which, though the enemies are of normal size, the odds against Jack are equally great. But it will be quite a different story. The whole quality of the imaginative response is determined by the fact that the enemies are giants. That heaviness, that monstrosity, that uncouthness, hangs over the whole thing. Turn it into music and you will feel the difference at once. If your villain is a giant your orchestra will proclaim his entrance in one way: if he is any other kind of villain, in another. I have seen landscapes (notably in the Mourne Mountains) which, under a particular light, made me feel that at any moment a giant might raise his head over the next ridge. Nature has that in her which compels us to invent giants: and only giants will do. (Notice that Gawain was in the north-west corner of England when

8

'etins aneleden him', giants came *blowing* after him on the high fells. Can it be an accident that Wordsworth was in the same places when he heard 'low breathings coming after him'?) The dangerousness of the giants is, though important, secondary. In some folk-tales we meet giants who are not dangerous. But they still affect us in much the same way. A *good* giant is legitimate: but he would be twenty tons of living, earth-shaking oxymoron. The intolerable pressure, the sense of something older, wilder, and more earthy than humanity, would still cleave to him.

But let us descend to a lower instance. Are pirates, any more than giants, merely a machine for threatening the hero? That sail which is rapidly overhauling us may be an ordinary enemy: a Don or a Frenchman. The ordinary enemy may easily be made just as lethal as the pirate. At the moment when she runs up the Jolly Roger, what exactly does this do to the imagination? It means, I grant you, that if we are beaten there will be no quarter. But that could be contrived without piracy. It is not the mere increase of danger that does the trick. It is the whole image of the utterly lawless enemy, the men who have cut adrift from all human society and become, as it were, a species of their own—men strangely clad, dark men with earrings, men with a history which they know and we don't, lords of unspecified treasure in undiscovered islands. They are, in fact, to the young reader almost as mythological as the giants. It does not cross his mind that a man—a mere man like the rest of us—might be a pirate at one time of his life and not at another, or that there is any smudgy frontier between piracy and privateering. A pirate is a pirate, just as a giant is a giant.

Consider, again, the enormous difference between being shut out and being shut in: if you like, between agoraphobia and claustrophobia. In *King Solomon's Mines* the heroes were shut in: so, more terribly, the narrator imagined himself to be in Poe's *Premature Burial*. Your breath shortens while you read it. Now remember the chapter called 'Mr Bedford Alone' in H. G. Wells's *First Men in the Moon*. There Bedford finds himself shut out on the surface of the Moon just as the long lunar day is drawing to its close—and with the day go the air and all heat. Read it from the terrible moment when the first tiny snowflake startles him into a realization of his position down to the point at which he reaches the 'sphere' and is saved. Then ask yourself whether what you have been feeling is simply suspense. 'Over me, around me, closing in on me, embracing me ever nearer was the Eternal . . . the infinite and final Night of space.' That is the idea which has kept you enthralled. But if we were concerned only with the question whether Mr Bedford will live or freeze, that idea is quite beside the purpose. You can die of cold between Russian Poland and new Poland, just as well as by going to the Moon, and the pain will be equal. For the purpose of killing Mr Bedford 'the infinite and final Night of space' is almost entirely otiose: what is by cosmic standards an infinitesimal change of temperature is sufficient to kill a man and absolute zero can do no more. That airless outer darkness is important not for what it can do to Bedford but for what it does to us: to trouble us with Pascal's old fear of those eternal silences which have gnawed at so much religious faith and shattered so many humanistic hopes: to evoke with them and through them all our racial and childish memories of exclusion and desolation: to present, in fact, as an intuition one permanent aspect of human experience.

And here, I expect, we come to one of the differences between life and art. A man really in Bedford's position would probably not feel very acutely that sidereal loneliness. The immediate issue of death would drive the contemplative object out of his mind: he would have no interest in the many degrees of increasing cold lower than the one which made his survival impossible. That is one of the functions of art: to present what the narrow and desperately practical perspectives of real life exclude.

I have sometimes wondered whether the 'excitement' may not be an element actually hostile to the deeper imagination. In inferior romances, such as the American magazines of 'scientifiction' supply, we often come across a really suggestive idea.

But the author has no expedient for keeping the story on the move except that of putting his hero into violent danger. In the hurry and scurry of his escapes the poetry of the basic idea is lost. In a much milder degree I think this has happened to Wells himself in the *War of the Worlds*. What really matters in this story is the idea of being attacked by something utterly 'outside'. As in *Piers Plowman* destruction has come upon us 'from the planets'. If the Martian invaders are merely dangerous — if we once become mainly concerned with the fact that they can *kill* us—why, then, a burglar or a bacillus can do as much. The real nerve of the romance is laid bare when the hero first goes to look at the newly fallen projectile on Horsell Common. 'The yellowish-white metal that gleamed in the crack between the lid and the cylinder had an unfamiliar hue. *Extra-terrestrial* had no meaning for most of the onlookers.' But *extra-terrestrial* is the key word of the whole story. And in the later horrors, excellently as they are done, we lose the feeling of it. Similarly in the Poet Laureate's *Sard Harker* it is the journey across the Sierras that really matters. That the man who has heard that noise in the cañon—'He could not think what it was. It was not sorrowful nor joyful nor terrible. It was great and strange. It was like the rock speaking'—that this man should be later in danger of mere murder is almost an impertinence.

It is here that Homer shows his supreme excellence. The landing on Circe's island, the sight of the smoke going up from amidst those unexplored woods, the god meeting us ('the messenger, the slayer of Argus')—what an anti-climax if all these had been the prelude only to some ordinary risk of life and limb! But the peril that lurks here, the silent, painless, unendurable change into brutality, is worthy of the setting. Mr de la Mare too has surmounted the difficulty. The threat launched in the opening paragraphs of his best stories is seldom fulfilled in any identifiable event: still less is it dissipated. Our fears are never, in one sense, realized: yet we lay down the story feeling that they, and far more, were justified. But perhaps the most remarkable achievement in this kind is that of Mr David

Lindsay's *Voyage to Arcturus*. The experienced reader, noting the threats and promises of the opening chapter, even while he gratefully enjoys them, feels sure that they cannot be carried out. He reflects that in stories of this kind the first chapter is nearly always the best and reconciles himself to disappointment; Tormance, when we reach it, he forbodes, will be less interesting than Tormance seen from the Earth. But never will he have been more mistaken. Unaided by any special skill or even any sound taste in language, the author leads us up a stair of unpredictables. In each chapter we think we have found his final position; each time we are utterly mistaken. He builds whole worlds of imagery and passion, any one of which would have served another writer for a whole book, only to pull each of them to pieces and pour scorn on it. The physical dangers, which are plentiful, here count for nothing: it is we ourselves and the author who walk through a world of spiritual dangers which makes them seem trivial. There is no recipe for writing of this kind. But part of the secret is that the author (like Kafka) is recording a lived dialectic. His Tormance is a region of the spirit. He is the first writer to discover what 'other planets' are really good for in fiction. No merely physical strangeness or merely spatial distance will realize that idea of otherness which is what we are always trying to grasp in a story about voyaging through space: you must go into another dimension. To construct plausible and moving 'other worlds' you must draw on the only real 'other world' we know, that of the spirit.

Notice here the corollary. If some fatal progress of applied science ever enables us in fact to reach the Moon, that real journey will not at all satisfy the impulse which we now seek to gratify by writing such stories. The real Moon, if you could reach it and survive, would in a deep and deadly sense be just like anywhere else. You would find cold, hunger, hardship, and danger; and after the first few hours they would be *simply* cold, hunger, hardship, and danger as you might have met them on Earth. And death would be simply death among those bleached craters as it is simply death in a nursing home at

Sheffield. No man would find an abiding strangeness on the Moon unless he were the sort of man who could find it in his own back garden. 'He who would bring home the wealth of the Indies must carry the wealth of the Indies with him.'

Good stories often introduce the marvellous or supernatural, and nothing about Story has been so often misunderstood as this. Thus, for example, Dr Johnson, if I remember rightly, thought that children liked stories of the marvellous because they were too ignorant to know that they were impossible. But children do not always like them, nor are those who like them always children; and to enjoy reading about fairies—much more about giants and dragons—it is not necessary to believe in them. Belief is at best irrelevant; it may be a positive disadvantage. Nor are the marvels in good Story ever mere arbitrary fictions stuck on to make the narrative more sensational. I happened to remark to a man who was sitting beside me at dinner the other night that I was reading Grimm in German of an evening but never bothered to look up a word I didn't know, 'so that it is often great fun' (I added) 'guessing what it was that the old woman gave to the prince which he afterwards lost in the wood'. 'And specially difficult in a fairy-tale,' said he, 'where everything is arbitrary and therefore the object might be anything at all.' His error was profound. The logic of a fairy-tale is as strict as that of a realistic novel, though different.

Does anyone believe that Kenneth Grahame made an arbitrary choice when he gave his principal character the form of a toad, or that a stag, a pigeon, a lion, would have done as well? The choice is based on the fact that the real toad's face has a grotesque resemblance to a certain kind of human face— a rather apoplectic face with a fatuous grin on it. This is, no doubt, an accident in the sense that all the lines which suggest the resemblance are really there for quite different biological reasons. The ludicrous quasi-human expression is therefore changeless: the toad cannot stop grinning because its 'grin' is not really a grin at all. Looking at the creature we thus see, isolated and fixed, an aspect of human vanity in its funniest and most pardonable form; following that hint Grahame creates Mr Toad—an ultra-Jonsonian 'humour'. And we bring back the wealth of the Indies; we have henceforward more amusement in, and kindness towards, a certain kind of vanity in real life.

But why should the characters be disguised as animals at all? The disguise is very thin, so thin that Grahame makes Mr Toad on one occasion 'comb the dry leaves out of his *hair*'. Yet it is quite indispensable. If you try to rewrite the book with all the characters humanized you are faced at the outset with a dilemma. Are they to be adults or children? You will find that they can be neither. They are like children in so far as they have no responsibilities, no struggle for existence, no domestic cares. Meals turn up; one does not even ask who cooked them. In Mr Badger's kitchen 'plates on the dresser grinned at pots on the shelf'. Who kept them clean? Where were they bought? How were they delivered in the Wild Wood? Mole is very snug in his subterranean home, but what was he living *on*? If he is a *rentier* where is the bank, what are his investments? The tables in his forecourt were 'marked with rings that hinted at beer mugs'. But where did he get the beer? In that way the life of all the characters is that of children for whom everything is provided and who take everything for granted. But in other ways it is the life of adults. They go where they like and do what they please, they arrange their own lives.

To that extent the book is a specimen of the most scandalous escapism: it paints a happiness under incompatible conditions— the sort of freedom we can have only in childhood and the sort we can have only in maturity—and conceals the contradiction by the further pretence that the characters are not human beings at all. The one absurdity helps to hide the other. It might be expected that such a book would unfit us for the harshness of reality and send us back to our daily lives unsettled and discontented. I do not find that it does so. The happiness which it presents to us is in fact full of the simplest and most attainable things—food, sleep, exercise, friendship, the face of nature, even (in a sense) religion. That 'simple but sustaining meal' of 'bacon and broad beans and a macaroni pudding' which Rat gave to his friends has, I doubt not, helped down many a real nursery dinner. And in the same way the whole story, paradoxically enough, strengthens our relish for real life. This excursion into the preposterous sends us back with renewed pleasure to the actual.

It is usual to speak in a playfully apologetic tone about one's adult enjoyment of what are called 'children's books'. I think the convention a silly one. No book is really worth reading at the age of ten which is not equally (and often far more) worth reading at the age of fifty—except, of course, books of information. The only imaginative works we ought to grow out of are those which it would have been better not to have read at all. A mature palate will probably not much care for *crème de menthe*: but it ought still to enjoy bread and butter and honey.

Another very large class of stories turns on fulfilled prophecies—the story of Oedipus, or *The Man who would be King*, or *The Hobbit*. In most of them the very steps taken to prevent the fulfilment of the prophecy actually bring it about. It is foretold that Oedipus will kill his father and marry his mother. In order to prevent this from happening he is exposed on the mountain: and that exposure, by leading to his rescue and thus to his life among strangers in ignorance of his real parentage, renders possible both the disasters. Such stories produce (at least in me) a feeling of awe, coupled with a certain sort of bewilderment such as one often feels in looking at a complex pattern of lines that pass over and under one another. One sees, yet does not quite see, the regularity. And is there not good occasion both for awe and bewilderment? We have just had set before our imagination something that has always baffled the intellect: we have *seen* how destiny and free will can be combined, even how free will is the *modus operandi* of destiny. The story does what no theorem can quite do. It may not be 'like real life' in the superficial sense: but it sets before us an image of what reality may well be like at some more central region.

Of Other Worlds

It will be seen that throughout this essay I have taken my examples indiscriminately from books which critics would (quite rightly) place in very different categories—from American 'scientifiction' and Homer, from Sophocles and *Märchen*, from children's stories and the intensely sophisticated art of Mr de la Mare. This does not mean that I think them of real literary merit. But if I am right in thinking that there is another enjoyment in Story besides the excitement, then popular romance even on the lowest level becomes rather more important than we had supposed. When you see an immature or uneducated person devouring what seem to you merely sensational stories, can you be sure what kind of pleasure he is enjoying? It is, of course, no good asking *him*. If he were capable of analysing his own experience as the question requires him to do, he would be neither uneducated nor immature. But because he is inarticulate we must not give judgement against him. He may be seeking only the recurring tension of imagined anxiety. But he may also, I believe, be receiving certain profound experiences which are, for him, not acceptable in any other form.

Mr Roger Lancelyn Green, writing in *English* not long ago, remarked that the reading of Rider Haggard had been to many a sort of religious experience. To some people this will have seemed simply grotesque. I myself would strongly disagree with it if 'religious' is taken to mean 'Christian'. And even if we take it in a sub-Christian sense, it would have been safer to say that such people had first met in Haggard's romances elements which they would meet again in religious experience if they ever came to have any. But I think Mr Green is very much nearer the mark than those who assume that no one has ever read the romances except in order to be thrilled by hair-breadth escapes. If he had said simply that something which the educated receive from poetry can reach the masses through stories of adventure, and almost in no other way, then I think he would have been right. If so, nothing can be more disastrous than the view that the cinema can and should replace popular written fiction. The elements which it excludes are precisely those which give the untrained mind its only access to the imaginative world. There is death in the camera.

As I have admitted, it is very difficult to tell in any given case whether a story is piercing to the unliterary reader's deeper imagination or only exciting his emotions. You cannot tell even by reading the story for yourself. Its badness proves very little. The more imagination the reader has, being an untrained reader, the more he will do for himself. He will, at a mere hint from the author, flood wretched material with suggestion and never guess that he is himself chiefly making what he enjoys. The nearest we can come to a test is by asking whether he often *re-reads* the same story.

It is, of course, a good test for every reader of every kind of book. An unliterary man may be defined as one who reads books once only. There is hope for a man who has never read Malory or Boswell or *Tristram Shandy* or Shakespeare's *Sonnets*: but what can you do with a man who says he 'has read' them, meaning he has read them once, and thinks that this settles the matter? Yet I think the test has a special application to the matter in hand. For excitement, in the sense defined above, is just what must disappear from a second reading. You cannot, except at the first reading, be really curious about what happened. If you find that the reader of popular romance—however uneducated a reader, however bad the romances—goes back to his old favourites again and again, then you have pretty good evidence that they are to him a sort of poetry.

The re-reader is looking not for actual surprises (which can come only once) but for a certain surprisingness. The point has often been misunderstood. The man in Peacock thought that he had disposed of 'surprise' as an element in landscape gardening when he asked what happened if you walked through the garden for the second time. Wiseacre! In the only sense that matters the surprise works as well the twentieth time as the first. It is the *quality* of unexpectedness, not the *fact* that delights us. It is even better the second time. Knowing that the 'surprise' is coming we can now fully relish the fact that this path through the shrubbery doesn't *look* as if it were suddenly going to bring us out on the edge of the cliff. So in literature. We do not enjoy a story fully at the first reading. Not till the curiosity, the sheer narrative lust, has been given its sop and laid asleep, are we at leisure to savour the real beauties. Till then, it is like wasting great wine on a ravenous natural thirst which merely wants cold wetness. The children understand this well when they ask for the same story over and over again, and in the same words. They want to have again the 'surprise' of discovering that what seemed Little-Red-Riding-Hood's grandmother is really the wolf. It is better when you know it is coming: free from the shock of actual surprise you can attend better to the intrinsic surprisingness of the *peripeteia*.

I should like to be able to believe that I am here in a very small way contributing (for criticism does not always come later than practice) to the encouragement of a better school of prose story in England: of story that can mediate imaginative life to the masses while not being contemptible to the few. But perhaps this is not very likely. It must be admitted that the art of Story as I see it is a very difficult one. What its central difficulty is I have already hinted when I complained that in the *War of the Worlds* the idea that really matters becomes lost or blunted as the story gets under way. I must now add that there is a perpetual danger of this happening in all stories. To be stories at all they must be series of events: but it must be understood that this series—the *plot*, as we call it—is only really a net whereby to catch something else. The real theme may be, and perhaps usually is, something that has no sequence in it, something other than a process and much more like a state or quality. Giantship, otherness, the desolation of space, are examples that have crossed our path. The titles of some stories illustrate the point very well. *The Well at the World's End*—can a man write a story to that title? Can he find a series of events following one another in time which will really catch and fix and bring home to us all that we grasp at on merely hearing the six words? Can a man write a story on Atlantis—or is it better to leave the word to work on its own? And I must confess that the net very seldom does succeed in catching the bird. Morris in *The Well at the World's End* came near to success—quite near enough to make the book worth many readings. Yet, after all, the best moments of it come in the first half.

But it does sometimes succeed. In the works of the late E. R. Eddison it succeeds completely. You may like or dislike his invented worlds (I myself like that of *The Worm Ouroboros* and strongly dislike that of *Mistress of Mistresses*) but there is here no quarrel between the theme and the articulation of the story. Every episode, every speech, helps to incarnate what the author is imagining. You could spare none of them. It takes the whole story to build up that strange blend of renaissance luxury and northern hardness. The secret here is largely the style, and especially the style of the dialogue. These proud, reckless, amorous people create themselves and the whole atmosphere of their world chiefly by talking. Mr de la Mare also succeeds, partly by style and partly by never laying the cards on the table. Mr David Lindsay, however, succeeds while writing a style which is at times (to be frank) abominable. He succeeds because his real theme is, like the plot, sequential, a thing in time, or quasi-time: a passionate spiritual journey. Charles Williams had the same advantage, but I do not mention his stories much here because they are hardly pure story in the sense we are now considering. They are, despite their free use of the supernatural, much closer to the novel; a believed religion, detailed character drawing, and even social satire all come in. *The Hobbit* escapes the danger of degenerating into mere plot and excitement by a very curious shift of tone. As the humour and homeliness of the early chapters, the sheer 'Hobbitry', dies away we pass insensibly into the world of epic. It is as if the battle of Toad Hall had become a serious *heimsökn* and Badger had begun to talk like Njal. Thus we lose one theme but find another. We kill—but not the same fox.

It may be asked why anyone should be encouraged to write a form in which the means are apparently so often at war with the end. But I am hardly suggesting that anyone who can write great poetry should write stories instead. I am rather suggesting what those whose work will in any case be a romance should aim at. And I do not think it unimportant that good work in this kind, even work less than perfectly good, can come where poetry will never come.

Shall I be thought whimsical if, in conclusion, I suggest that this internal tension in the heart of every story between the theme and the plot constitutes, after all, its chief resemblance to life? If Story fails in that way does not life commit the same blunder? In real life, as in a story, something must happen. That is just the trouble. We grasp at a state and find only a succession of events in which the state is never quite embodied. The grand idea of finding Atlantis which stirs us in the first chapter of the adventure story is apt to be frittered away in mere excitement when the journey has once been begun. But so, in real life, the idea of adventure fades when the day-to-day details begin to happen. Nor is this merely because actual hardship and danger shoulder it aside. Other grand ideas—homecoming, reunion with a beloved—similarly elude our grasp. Suppose there is no disappointment; even so—well, you are here. But now, something must happen, and after that something else. All that happens may be delightful: but can any such series quite embody the sheer state of being which was what we wanted? If the author's plot is only a net, and usually an imperfect one, a net of time and event for catching what is not really a process at all, is life much more? I am not sure, on second thoughts, that the slow fading of the magic in *The Well at the World's End* is, after all, a blemish. It is an image of the truth. Art, indeed, may be expected to do what life cannot do: but so it has done. The bird has escaped us. But it was at least entangled in the net for several chapters. We saw it close and enjoyed the plumage. How many 'real lives' have nets that can do as much?

In life and art both, as it seems to me, we are always trying to catch in our net of successive moments something that is not successive. Whether in real life there is any doctor who can teach us how to do it, so that at last either the meshes will become fine enough to hold the bird, or we be so changed that we can throw our nets away and follow the bird to its own country, is not a question for this essay. But I think it is sometimes done—or very, very nearly done—in stories. I believe the effort to be well worth making.

ON THREE WAYS OF WRITING FOR CHILDREN

I think there are three ways in which those who write for children may approach their work; two good ways and one that is generally a bad way.

I came to know of the bad way quite recently and from two unconscious witnesses. One was a lady who sent me the MS of a story she had written in which a fairy placed at a child's disposal a wonderful gadget. I say 'gadget' because it was not a magic ring or hat or cloak or any such traditional matter. It was a machine, a thing of taps and handles and buttons you could press. You could press one and get an ice cream, another and get a live puppy, and so forth. I had to tell the author honestly that I didn't much care for that sort of thing. She replied, 'No more do I, it bores me to distraction. But it is what the modern child wants.' My other bit of evidence was this. In my own first story I had described at length what I thought a rather fine high tea given by a hospitable faun to the little girl who was my heroine. A man, who has children of his own, said, 'Ah, I see how you got to that. If you want to please grown-up readers you give them sex, so you thought to yourself, "That won't do for children, what shall I give them instead? I know! The little blighters like plenty of good eating."' In reality, however, I myself like eating and drinking. I put in what I would have liked to read when I was a child and what I still like reading now that I am in my fifties.

The lady in my first example, and the married man in my second, both conceived writing for children as a special department of 'giving the public what it wants'. Children are, of course, a special public and you find out what they want and give them that, however little you like it yourself.

On Three Ways of Writing for Children

The next way may seem at first to be very much the same, but I think the resemblance is superficial. This is the way of Lewis Carroll, Kenneth Grahame, and Tolkien. The printed story grows out of a story told to a particular child with the living voice and perhaps *ex tempore*. It resembles the first way because you are certainly trying to give that child what it wants. But then you are dealing with a concrete person, this child who, of course, differs from all other children. There is no question of 'children' conceived as a strange species whose habits you have 'made up' like an anthropologist or a commercial traveller. Nor, I suspect, would it be possible, thus face to face, to regale the child with things calculated to please it but regarded by yourself with indifference or contempt. The child, I am certain, would see through that. In any personal relation the two participants modify each other. You would become slightly different because you were talking to a child and the child would become slightly different because it was being talked to by an adult. A community, a composite personality, is created and out of that the story grows.

The third way, which is the only one I could ever use myself, consists in writing a children's story because a children's story is the best art-form for something you have to say: just as a composer might write a Dead March not because there was a public funeral in view but because certain musical ideas that had occurred to him went best into that form. This method could apply to other kinds of children's literature besides stories. I have been told that Arthur Mee never met a child and never wished to: it was, from his point of view, a bit of luck that boys liked reading what he liked writing. This anecdote may be untrue in fact but it illustrates my meaning.

Within the species 'children's story' the sub-species which happened to suit me is the fantasy or (in a loose sense of that word) the fairy tale. There are, of course, other sub-species. E. Nesbit's trilogy about the Bastable family is a very good specimen of another kind. It is a 'children's story' in the sense that children can and do read it: but it is also the only form in which E. Nesbit could have given us so much of the humours of childhood. It is true that the Bastable children appear, successfully treated from the adult point of view, in one of her grown-up novels, but they appear only for a moment. I do not think she would have kept it up. Sentimentality is so apt to creep in if we write at length about children as seen by their elders. And the reality of childhood, as we all experienced it, creeps out. For we all remember that our childhood, as lived, was immeasurably different from what our elders saw. Hence Sir Michael Sadler, when I asked his opinion about a certain new experimental school, replied, 'I never give an opinion on any of those experiments till the children have grown up and can tell us *what really happened.*' Thus the Bastable trilogy, however improbable many of its episodes may be, provides even adults, in one sense, with more realistic reading about children than they could find in most books addressed to adults. But also, conversely, it enables the children who read it to do something much more mature than they realize. For the whole book is a character study of Oswald, an unconsciously satiric self-portrait, which every intelligent child can fully appreciate: but no child would sit down to read a character study in any other form. There is another way in which children's stories mediate this psychological interest, but I will reserve that for later treatment.

In this short glance at the Bastable trilogy I think we have stumbled on a principle. Where the children's story is simply the right form for what the author has to say, then of course readers who want to hear that, will read the story or re-read it, at any age. I never met *The Wind in the Willows* or the Bastable books till I was in my late twenties, and I do not think I have enjoyed them any the less on that account. I am almost inclined to set it up as a canon that a children's story which is enjoyed only by children is a bad children's story. The good ones last. A waltz which you can like only when you are waltzing is a bad waltz.

This canon seems to me most obviously true of that particular type of children's story which is dearest to my own taste, the fantasy or fairy tale. Now the modern critical world uses 'adult' as a term of approval. It is hostile to what it calls 'nostalgia' and contemptuous of what it calls 'Peter Pantheism'. Hence a man who admits that dwarfs and giants and talking beasts and witches are still dear to him in his fifty-third year is now less likely to be praised for his perennial youth than scorned and pitied for arrested development. If I spend some little time defending myself against these charges, this is not so much because it matters greatly whether I am scorned and pitied as because the defence is germane to my whole view of the fairy tale and even of literature in general. My defence consists of three propositions.

1. I reply with a *tu quoque*. Critics who treat *adult* as a term of approval, instead of as a merely descriptive term, cannot be adult themselves. To be concerned about being grown up, to admire the grown up because it is grown up, to blush at the suspicion of being childish; these things are the marks of childhood and adolescence. And in childhood and adolescence they are, in moderation, healthy symptoms. Young things ought to want to grow. But to carry on into middle life or even into early manhood this concern about being adult is a mark of really arrested development. When I was ten, I read fairy tales in secret and would have been ashamed if I had been found doing so. Now that I am fifty I read them openly. When I became a man I put away childish things, including the fear of childishness and the desire to be very grown up.

2. The modern view seems to me to involve a false conception of growth. They accuse us of arrested development because we have not lost a taste we had in childhood. But surely arrested development consists not in refusing to lose old things but in failing to add new things? I now like hock, which I am sure I should not have liked as a child. But I still like lemon-squash. I call this growth or development because I have been enriched: where I formerly had only one pleasure, I now have two. But if I had to lose the taste for lemon-squash before I acquired

the taste for hock, that would not be growth but simple change. I now enjoy Tolstoy and Jane Austen and Trollope as well as fairy tales and I call that growth: if I had had to lose the fairy tales in order to acquire the novelists, I would not say that I had grown but only that I had changed. A tree grows because it adds rings: a train doesn't grow by leaving one station behind and puffing on to the next. In reality, the case is stronger and more complicated than this. I think my growth is just as apparent when I now read the fairy tales as when I read the novelists, for I now enjoy the fairy tales better than I did in childhood: being now able to put more in, of course I get more out. But I do not here stress that point. Even if it were merely a taste for grown-up literature added to an unchanged taste for children's literature, addition would still be entitled to the name 'growth', and the process of merely dropping one parcel when you pick up another would not. It is, of course, true that the process of growing does, incidentally and unfortunately, involve some more losses. But that is not the essence of growth, certainly not what makes growth admirable or desirable. If it were, if to drop parcels and to leave stations behind were the essence and virtue of growth, why should we stop at the adult? Why should not *senile* be equally a term of approval? Why are we not to be congratulated on losing our teeth and hair? Some critics seem to confuse growth with the cost of growth and also to wish to make that cost far higher than, in nature, it need be.

3. The whole association of fairy tale and fantasy with childhood is local and accidental. I hope everyone has read Tolkien's essay on Fairy Tales, which is perhaps the most important contribution to the subject that anyone has yet made. If so, you will know already that, in most places and times, the fairy tale has not been specially made for, nor exclusively enjoyed by, children. It has gravitated to the nursery when it became unfashionable in literary circles, just as unfashionable furniture gravitated to the nursery in Victorian houses. In fact, many children do not like this kind of book, just as many children do

26

not like horsehair sofas: and many adults do like it, just as many adults like rocking chairs. And those who do like it, whether young or old, probably like it for the same reason. And none of us can say with any certainty what that reason is. The two theories which are most often in my mind are those of Tolkien and of Jung.

According to Tolkien[1] the appeal of the fairy story lies in the fact that man there most fully exercises his function as a 'subcreator'; not, as they love to say now, making a 'comment upon life' but making, so far as possible, a subordinate world of his own. Since, in Tolkien's view, this is one of man's proper functions, delight naturally arises whenever it is successfully performed. For Jung, fairy tale liberates Archetypes which dwell in the collective unconscious, and when we read a good fairy tale we are obeying the old precept 'Know thyself'. I would venture to add to this my own theory, not indeed of the Kind as a whole, but of one feature in it: I mean, the presence of beings other than human which yet behave, in varying degrees, humanly: the giants and dwarfs and talking beasts. I believe these to be at least (for they may have many other sources of power and beauty) an admirable hieroglyphic which conveys psychology, types of character, more briefly than novelistic presentation and to readers whom novelistic presentation could not yet reach. Consider Mr Badger in *The Wind in the Willows*—that extraordinary amalgam of high rank, coarse manners, gruffness, shyness, and goodness. The child who has once met Mr Badger has ever afterwards, in its bones, a knowledge of humanity and of English social history which it could not get in any other way.

Of course as all children's literature is not fantastic, so all fantastic books need not be children's books. It is still possible, even in an age so ferociously anti-romantic as our own, to write fantastic stories for adults: though you will usually need to have made a name in some more fashionable kind of literature

[1] J. R. R. Tolkien, 'On Fairy-Stories', *Essays Presented to Charles Williams* (1947), p. 66 ff.

before anyone will publish them. But there may be an author who at a particular moment finds not only fantasy but fantasy-for-children the exactly right form for what he wants to say. The distinction is a fine one. His fantasies for children and his fantasies for adults will have very much more in common with one another than either has with the ordinary novel or with what is sometimes called 'the novel of child life'. Indeed the same readers will probably read both his fantastic 'juveniles' and his fantastic stories for adults. For I need not remind such an audience as this that the neat sorting-out of books into age-groups, so dear to publishers, has only a very sketchy relation with the habits of any real readers. Those of us who are blamed when old for reading childish books were blamed when children for reading books too old for us. No reader worth his salt trots along in obedience to a time-table. The distinction, then, is a fine one: and I am not quite sure what made me, in a particular year of my life, feel that not only a fairy tale, but a fairy tale addressed to children, was exactly what I must write—or burst. Partly, I think, that this form permits, or compels you to leave out things I wanted to leave out. It compels you to throw all the force of the book into what was done and said. It checks what a kind, but discerning critic called 'the expository demon' in me. It also imposes certain very fruitful necessities about length.

If I have allowed the fantastic type of children's story to run away with this discussion, that is because it is the kind I know and love best, not because I wish to condemn any other. But the patrons of the other kinds very frequently want to condemn it. About once every hundred years some wiseacre gets up and tries to banish the fairy tale. Perhaps I had better say a few words in its defence, as reading for children.

It is accused of giving children a false impression of the world they live in. But I think no literature that children could read gives them less of a false impression. I think what profess to be realistic stories for children are far more likely to deceive them. I never expected the real world to be like the fairy tales. I think that I did expect school to be like the school stories. The fantasies did not deceive me: the school stories did. All stories in which children have adventures and successes which are possible, in the sense that they do not break the laws of nature, but almost infinitely improbable, are in more danger than the fairy tales of raising false expectations.

Almost the same answer serves for the popular charge of escapism, though here the question is not so simple. Do fairy tales teach children to retreat into a world of wish-fulfilment— 'fantasy' in the technical psychological sense of the word— instead of facing the problems of the real world? Now it is here that the problem becomes subtle. Let us again lay the fairy tale side by side with the school story or any other story which is labelled a 'Boy's Book' or a 'Girl's Book', as distinct from a 'Children's Book'. There is no doubt that both arouse, and imaginatively satisfy, wishes. We long to go through the looking glass, to reach fairy land. We also long to be the immensely popular and successful schoolboy or schoolgirl, or the lucky boy or girl who discovers the spy's plot or rides the horse that none of the cowboys can manage. But the two longings are very different. The second, especially when directed on something so close as school life, is ravenous and deadly serious. Its fulfilment on the level of imagination is in very truth compensatory: we run to it from the disappointments and humiliations of the real world: it sends us back to the real world undivinely discontented. For it is all flattery to the ego. The pleasure consists in picturing oneself the object of admiration. The other longing, that for fairy land, is very different. In a sense a child does not long for fairy land as a boy longs to be the hero of the first eleven. Does anyone suppose that he really and prosaically longs for all the dangers and discomforts of a fairy tale?—really wants dragons in contemporary England? It is not so. It would be much truer to say that fairy land arouses a longing for he knows not what. It stirs and troubles him (to his life-long enrichment) with the dim sense of something beyond his reach and, far from dulling or emptying the actual world, gives it a new dimension of depth. He does not despise real woods because he has read of enchanted woods: the reading makes all real woods a little enchanted. This is a special kind of longing. The boy reading the school story of the type I have in mind desires success and is unhappy (once the book is over) because he can't get it: the boy reading the fairy tale desires and is happy in the very fact of desiring. For his mind has not been concentrated on himself, as it often is in the more realistic story.

I do not mean that school stories for boys and girls ought not to be written. I am only saying that they are far more liable to become 'fantasies' in the clinical sense than fantastic stories are. And this distinction holds for adult reading too. The dangerous fantasy is always superficially realistic. The real victim of wishful reverie does not batten on the *Odyssey*, *The Tempest*, or *The Worm Ouroboros*: he (or she) prefers stories about millionaires, irresistible beauties, posh hotels, palm beaches and bedroom scenes—things that really might happen, that ought to happen, that would have happened if the reader had had a fair chance. For, as I say, there are two kinds of longing. The one is an *askesis*, a spiritual exercise, and the other is a disease.

A far more serious attack on the fairy tale as children's literature comes from those who do not wish children to be frightened. I suffered too much from night-fears myself in childhood to undervalue this objection. I would not wish to heat the fires of that private hell for any child. On the other hand, none of my fears came from fairy tales. Giant insects were my specialty, with ghosts a bad second. I suppose the ghosts came directly or indirectly from stories, though certainly not from fairy stories, but I don't think the insects did. I don't know anything my parents could have done or left undone which would have saved me from the pincers, mandibles, and eyes of those many-legged abominations. And that, as so many people have pointed out, is the difficulty. We do not know what will or will not frighten a child in this particular way. I say 'in this particular way' for we must here make a distinction. Those who say that children must not be frightened may mean two things. They may mean (1) that we must not do anything likely to give the child those haunting, disabling, pathological fears against which ordinary courage is helpless: in fact, *phobias*. His mind must, if possible, be kept clear of things he can't bear to think of. Or they may mean (2) that we must try to keep out of his mind the knowledge that he is born into a world of death, violence, wounds, adventure, heroism and cowardice, good and evil. If they mean the first I agree with them: but not if they mean the second. The second would indeed be to give children a false impression and feed them on escapism in the bad sense. There is something ludicrous in the idea of so educating a generation which is born to the Ogpu and the atomic bomb. Since it is so likely that they will meet cruel enemies, let them at least have heard of brave knights and heroic courage. Otherwise you are making their destiny not brighter but darker. Nor do most of us find that violence and bloodshed, in a story, produce any haunting dread in the minds of children. As far as that goes, I side impenitently with the human race against the modern reformer. Let there be wicked kings and beheadings, battles and dungeons, giants and dragons, and let villains be soundly killed at the end of the book. Nothing will persuade me that this causes an ordinary child any kind or degree of fear beyond what it wants, and needs, to feel. For, of course, it wants to be a little frightened.

The other fears—the phobias—are a different matter. I do not believe one can control them by literary means. We seem to bring them into the world with us ready made. No doubt the particular image on which the child's terror is fixed can sometimes be traced to a book. But is that the source, or only the occasion, of the fear? If he had been spared that image, would not some other, quite unpredictable by you, have had the same effect? Chesterton has told us of a boy who was more afraid of the Albert Memorial than anything else in the world. I know a man whose great childhood terror was the India paper edition of the *Encyclopaedia Britannica*—for a reason I defy you to guess. And I think it possible that by confining your child to blameless stories of child life in which nothing at all alarming ever happens, you would fail to banish the terrors, and would succeed in banishing all that can ennoble them or make them endurable. For in the fairy tales, side by side with the terrible figures, we find the immemorial comforters and protectors, the radiant ones; and the terrible figures are not merely terrible, but sublime. It would be nice if no little boy in bed, hearing, or thinking he hears, a sound, were ever at all frightened. But if he is going to be frightened, I think it better that he should think of giants and dragons than merely of burglars. And I think St George, or any bright champion in armour, is a better comfort than the idea of the police.

I will even go further. If I could have escaped all my own night-fears at the price of never having known 'faerie', would I now be the gainer by that bargain? I am not speaking carelessly. The fears were very bad. But I think the price would have been too high.

But I have strayed far from my theme. This has been inevitable for, of the three methods, I know by experience only the third. I hope my title did not lead anyone to think that I was conceited enough to give you advice on how to write a story for children. There were two very good reasons for not doing that. One is that many people have written very much better stories than I, and I would rather learn about the art than set up to teach it. The other is that, in a certain sense, I have never exactly 'made' a story. With me the process is much more like bird-watching than like either talking or building. I see pictures. Some of these pictures have a common flavour, almost a common smell, which groups them together. Keep quiet and watch and they will begin joining themselves up. If you were very lucky (I have never been as lucky as all that) a whole set might join themselves so consistently that there you had a complete story: without doing anything yourself. But more often (in my experience always) there are gaps. Then at last you have to do some deliberate inventing, have to contrive reasons why these characters should be in these various places doing these various things. I have no idea whether this is the usual way of writing stories, still less whether it is the best. It is the only one I know: images always come first.

Before closing, I would like to return to what I said at the beginning. I rejected any approach which begins with the question 'What do modern children like?' I might be asked, 'Do you equally reject the approach which begins with the question "What do modern children need?"—in other words, with the moral or didactic approach?' I think the answer is Yes. Not because I don't like stories to have a moral: certainly not because I think children dislike a moral. Rather because I feel sure that the question 'What do modern children need?' will not lead you to a good moral. If we ask that question we are assuming too superior an attitude. It would be better to ask 'What moral do I need?' for I think we can be sure that what does not concern us deeply will not deeply interest our readers, whatever their age. But it is better not to ask the question at all. Let the pictures tell you their own moral. For the moral inherent in them will rise from whatever spiritual roots you have succeeded in striking during the whole course of your life. But if they don't show you any moral, don't put one in. For the moral you put in is likely to be a platitude, or even a falsehood, skimmed from the surface of your consciousness. It is impertinent to offer the children that. For we have been told on high authority that in the moral sphere they are probably at least as wise as we. Anyone who *can* write a children's story without a moral, had better do so: that is, if he is going to write children's stories at all. The only moral that is of any value is that which arises inevitably from the whole cast of the author's mind.

Indeed everything in the story should arise from the whole cast of the author's mind. We must write for children out of those elements in our own imagination which we share with children: differing from our child readers not by any less, or less serious, interest in the things we handle, but by the fact that we have other interests which children would not share

33

with us. The matter of our story should be a part of the habitual furniture of our minds. This, I fancy, has been so with all great writers for children, but it is not generally understood. A critic not long ago said in praise of a very serious fairy tale that the author's tongue 'never once got into his cheek'. But why on earth should it?—unless he had been eating a seed-cake. Nothing seems to me more fatal, for this art, than an idea that whatever we share with children is, in the privative sense, 'childish' and that whatever is childish is somehow comic. We must meet children as equals in that area of our nature where we are their equals. Our superiority consists partly in commanding other areas, and partly (which is more relevant) in the fact that we are better at telling stories than they are. The child as reader is neither to be patronized nor idolized: we talk to him as man to man. But the worst attitude of all would be the professional attitude which regards children in the lump as a sort of raw material which we have to handle. We must of course try to do them no harm: we may, under the Omnipotence, sometimes dare to hope that we may do them good. But only such good as involves treating them with respect. We must not imagine that we are Providence or Destiny. I will not say that a good story for children could never be written by someone in the Ministry of Education, for all things are possible. But I should lay very long odds against it.

Once in a hotel dining-room I said, rather too loudly, 'I loathe prunes.' 'So do I,' came an unexpected six-year-old voice from another table. Sympathy was instantaneous. Neither of us thought it funny. We both knew that prunes are far too nasty to be funny. That is the proper meeting between man and child as independent personalities. Of the far higher and more difficult relations between child and parent or child and teacher, I say nothing. An author, as a mere author, is outside all that. He is not even an uncle. He is a freeman and an equal, like the postman, the butcher, and the dog next door.

SOMETIMES FAIRY STORIES MAY SAY BEST WHAT'S TO BE SAID

In the sixteenth century when everyone was saying that poets (by which they meant all imaginative writers) ought 'to please and instruct', Tasso made a valuable distinction. He said that the poet, as poet, was concerned solely with pleasing. But then every poet was also a man and a citizen; in that capacity he ought to, and would wish to, make his work edifying as well as pleasing.

Now I do not want to stick very close to the renaissance ideas of 'pleasing' and 'instructing'. Before I could accept either term it might need so much redefining that what was left of it at the end would not be worth retaining. All I want to use is the distinction between the author as author and the author as man, citizen, or Christian. What this comes to for me is that there are usually two reasons for writing an imaginative work, which may be called Author's reason and the Man's. If only one of these is present, then, so far as I am concerned, the book will not be written. If the first is lacking, it can't; if the second is lacking, it shouldn't.

In the Author's mind there bubbles up every now and then the material for a story. For me it invariably begins with mental pictures. This ferment leads to nothing unless it is accompanied with the longing for a Form: verse or prose, short story, novel, play or what not. When these two things click you have the Author's impulse complete. It is now a thing inside him pawing to get out. He longs to see that bubbling stuff pouring into that Form as the housewife longs to see the new jam pouring into the clean jam jar. This nags him all day long and gets in the way of his work and his sleep and his meals. It's like being in love.

While the Author is in this state, the Man will of course have to criticize the proposed book from quite a different point of view. He will ask how the gratification of this impulse will fit in with all the other things he wants, and ought to do or be. Perhaps the whole thing is too frivolous and trivial (from the Man's point of view, not the Author's) to justify the time and pains it would involve. Perhaps it would be unedifying when it was done. Or else perhaps (at this point the Author cheers up) it looks like being 'good', not in a merely literary sense, but 'good' all around.

This may sound rather complicated but it is really very like what happens about other things. You are attracted by a girl; but is she the sort of girl you'd be wise, or right, to marry? You would like to have lobster for lunch; but does it agree with you and is it wicked to spend that amount of money on a meal? The Author's impulse is a desire (it is very like an itch), and of course, like every other desire, needs to be criticized by the whole Man.

Let me now apply this to my own fairy tales. Some people seem to think that I began by asking myself how I could say something about Christianity to children; then fixed on the fairy tale as an instrument; then collected information about child-psychology and decided what age group I'd write for; then drew up a list of basic Christian truths and hammered out 'allegories' to embody them. This is all pure moonshine. I couldn't write in that way at all. Everything began with images; a faun carrying an umbrella, a queen on a sledge, a magnificent lion. At first there wasn't even anything Christian about them; that element pushed itself in of its own accord. It was part of the bubbling.

Then came the Form. As these images sorted themselves into events (i.e., became a story) they seemed to demand no love interest and no close psychology. But the Form which excludes these things is the fairy tale. And the moment I thought of that I fell in love with the Form itself: its brevity, its severe restraints on description, its flexible traditionalism, its inflexible

36

hostility to all analysis, digression, reflections and 'gas'. I was now enamoured of it. Its very limitations of vocabulary became an attraction; as the hardness of the stone pleases the sculptor or the difficulty of the sonnet delights the sonneteer.

On that side (as Author) I wrote fairy tales because the Fairy Tale seemed the ideal Form for the stuff I had to say.

Then of course the Man in me began to have his turn. I thought I saw how stories of this kind could steal past a certain inhibition which had paralysed much of my own religion in childhood. Why did one find it so hard to feel as one was told one ought to feel about God or about the sufferings of Christ? I thought the chief reason was that one was told one ought to. An obligation to feel can freeze feelings. And reverence itself did harm. The whole subject was associated with lowered voices; almost as if it were something medical. But supposing that by casting all these things into an imaginary world, stripping them of their stained-glass and Sunday school associations, one could make them for the first time appear in their real potency? Could one not thus steal past those watchful dragons? I thought one could.

That was the Man's motive. But of course he could have done nothing if the Author had not been on the boil first.

You will notice that I have throughout spoken of Fairy Tales, not 'children's stories'. Professor J. R. R. Tolkien in *The Lord of the Rings*[1] has shown that the connection between fairy tales and children is not nearly so close as publishers and educationalists think. Many children don't like them and many adults do. The truth is, as he says, that they are now associated with children because they are out of fashion with adults; have in fact retired to the nursery as old furniture used to retire there, not because the children had begun to like it but because their elders had ceased to like it.

I was therefore writing 'for children' only in the sense that I excluded what I thought they would not like or understand;

[1] I think Lewis really meant Professor Tolkien's essay 'On Fairy-Stories' in *Essays Presented to Charles Williams* (1947), p. 58.

not in the sense of writing what I intended to be below adult attention. I may of course have been deceived, but the principle at least saves one from being patronizing. I never wrote down to anyone; and whether the opinion condemns or acquits my own work, it certainly is my opinion that a book worth reading only in childhood is not worth reading even then. The inhibitions which I hoped my stories would overcome in a child's mind may exist in a grown-up's mind too, and may perhaps be overcome by the same means.

The Fantastic or Mythical is a Mode available at all ages for some readers; for others, at none. At all ages, if it is well used by the author and meets the right reader, it has the same power: to generalize while remaining concrete, to present in palpable form not concepts or even experiences but whole classes of experience, and to throw off irrelevancies. But at its best it can do more; it can give us experiences we have never had and thus, instead of 'commenting on life', can add to it. I am speaking, of course, about the thing itself, not my own attempts at it.

'Juveniles', indeed! Am I to patronize sleep because children sleep sound? Or honey because children like it?

ON JUVENILE TASTES

Not long ago I saw in some periodical the statement that 'Children are a distinct race'. Something like this seems to be assumed today by many who write, and still more who criticize, what are called children's books or 'juveniles'. Children are regarded as being at any rate a distinct *literary* species, and the production of books that cater for their supposedly odd and alien taste has become an industry; almost a heavy one.

This theory does not seem to me to be borne out by the facts. For one thing, there is no literary taste common to all children. We find among them all the same types as among ourselves. Many of them, like many of us, never read when they can find any other entertainment. Some of them choose quiet, realistic, 'slice-of-life' books (say, *The Daisy Chain*) as some of us choose Trollope.

Some like fantasies and marvels, as some of us like the *Odyssey*, Boiardo, Ariosto, Spenser, or Mr Mervyn Peake. Some care for little but books of information, and so do some adults. Some of them, like some of us, are omnivorous. Silly children prefer success stories about school life as silly adults like success stories about grown-up life.

We can approach the matter in a different way by drawing up a list of books which, I am told, have been generally liked by the young. I suppose Aesop, *The Arabian Nights, Gulliver, Robinson Crusoe, Treasure Island, Peter Rabbit,* and *The Wind in the Willows* would be a reasonable choice. Only the last three were written for children, and those three are read with pleasure by many adults. I, who disliked *The Arabian Nights* as a child, dislike them still.

It may be argued against this that the enjoyment by children of some books intended for their elders does not in the least refute the doctrine that there is a specifically childish taste. They select (you may say) that minority of ordinary books which happens to suit them, as a foreigner in England may select those English dishes which come nearest to suiting his alien palate. And the specifically childish taste has been generally held to be that for the adventurous and the marvellous.

Now this, you may notice, implies that we are regarding as specifically childish a taste which in many, perhaps in most, times and places has been that of the whole human race. Those stories from Greek or Norse mythology, from Homer, from Spenser, or from folklore which children (but by no means all children) read with delight were once the delight of everyone.

Even the fairy tale *proprement dit* was not originally intended for children; it was told and enjoyed in (of all places) the court of Louis XIV. As Professor Tolkien has pointed out, it gravitated to the nursery when it went out of fashion among the grown-ups, just as old-fashioned furniture gravitated to the nursery. Even if all children and no adults now liked the marvellous—and neither is the case—we ought not to say that the peculiarity of children lies in their liking it. The peculiarity is that they *still* like it, even in the twentieth century.

It does not seem to me useful to say, 'What delighted the infancy of the species naturally still delights the infancy of the individual.' This involves a parallel between individual and species which we are in no position to draw. What age is Man? Is the race now in its childhood, its maturity, or its dotage? As we don't know at all exactly when it began, and have no notion when it will end, this seems a nonsense question. And who knows if it will ever be mature? Man may be killed in infancy.

Surely it would be less arrogant, and truer to the evidence, to say that the peculiarity of child readers is that they are not peculiar. It is we who are peculiar. Fashions in literary taste come and go among the adults, and every period has its own shibboleths. These, when good, do not improve the taste of children, and, when bad, do not corrupt it; for children read only to enjoy. Of course their limited vocabulary and general ignorance make some books unintelligible to them. But apart from that, juvenile taste is simply human taste, going on from age to age, silly with a universal silliness or wise with a universal wisdom, regardless of modes, movements, and literary revolutions.

This has one curious result. When the literary Establishment—the approved canon of taste—is so extremely jejune and narrow as it is today, much has to be addressed in the first instance to children if it is to get printed at all. Those who have a story to tell must appeal to the audience that still cares for story-telling.

The literary world of today is little interested in the narrative art as such; it is preoccupied with technical novelties and with 'ideas', by which it means not literary, but social or psychological, ideas. The ideas (in the literary sense) on which Miss Norton's *The Borrowers* or Mr White's *Mistress Masham's Repose* are built would not need to be embodied in 'juveniles' at most periods.

It follows that there are now two very different sorts of 'writers for children'. The wrong sort believe that children are 'a distinct race'. They carefully 'make up' the tastes of these odd creatures—like an anthropologist observing the habits of a savage tribe—or even the tastes of a clearly defined age-group within a particular social class within the 'distinct race'. They dish up not what they like themselves but what that race is supposed to like. Educational and moral, as well as commercial, motives may come in.

The right sort work from the common, universally human, ground they share with the children, and indeed with countless adults. They label their books 'For Children' because children are the only market now recognized for the books they, anyway, want to write.

IT ALL BEGAN WITH A PICTURE ...

The Editor has asked me to tell you how I came to write *The Lion, the Witch and the Wardrobe*. I will try, but you must not believe all that authors tell you about how they wrote their books. This is not because they mean to tell lies. It is because a man writing a story is too excited about the story itself to sit back and notice how he is doing it. In fact, that might stop the works; just as, if you start thinking about how you tie your tie, the next thing is that you find you can't tie it. And afterwards, when the story is finished, he has forgotten a good deal of what writing it was like.

One thing I am sure of. All my seven Narnian books, and my three science fiction books, began with seeing pictures in my head. At first they were not a story, just pictures. The *Lion* all began with a picture of a Faun carrying an umbrella and parcels in a snowy wood. This picture had been in my mind since I was about sixteen. Then one day, when I was about forty, I said to myself: 'Let's try to make a story about it.'

At first I had very little idea how the story would go. But then suddenly Aslan came bounding into it. I think I had been having a good many dreams of lions about that time. Apart from that, I don't know where the Lion came from or why He came. But once He was there He pulled the whole story together, and soon He pulled the six other Narnian stories in after Him.

So you see that, in a sense, I know very little about how this story was born. That is, I don't know where the pictures came from. And I don't believe anyone knows exactly how he 'makes things up'. Making up is a very mysterious thing. When you 'have an idea' could you tell anyone exactly *how* you thought of it?

ON CRITICISM

I want to talk about the ways in which an author who is also a critic may improve himself as a critic by reading the criticism of his own work. But I must narrow my subject a little further. It used to be supposed that one of the functions of a critic was to help authors to write better. His praise and censure were supposed to show them where and how they had succeeded or failed, so that next time, having profited by the diagnosis, they might cure their faults and increase their virtues. That was what Pope had in mind when he said, 'Make use of every friend—and every foe.' But that is not at all what I want to discuss. In that way the author–critic might no doubt profit, as a critic, by reviews of his critical work. I am considering how he could profit, as a critic, by reviews of his non-critical works: his poems, plays, stories, or what not; what he can learn about the art of criticism by seeing it practised on himself; how he can become a better, or less bad, critic of other men's imaginative works from the treatment of his own imaginative works. For I am going to contend that when your own work is being criticized you are, in one sense, in a specially advantageous position for detecting the goodness or badness of the critique.

This may sound paradoxical, but of course all turns on my reservation, *in one sense*. There is of course another sense in which the author of a book is of all men least qualified to judge the reviews of it. Obviously he cannot judge their evaluation of it, because he is not impartial. And whether this leads him, naïvely, to hail all laudatory criticism as good and damn all unfavourable criticism as bad, or whether (which is just as likely) it leads him, in the effort against that obvious bias, to lean over backwards till he under-rates all who praise and admires all

43

who censure him, it is equally a disturbing factor. Hence, if by criticism, you mean solely valuation, no man can judge critiques of his own work. In fact, however, most of what we call critical writing contains quite a lot of things besides evaluation. This is specially so both of reviews and of the criticism contained in literary history: for both these always should, and usually try to, inform their readers as well as direct their judgement. Now in so far as his reviewers do that, I contend that the author can see the defects and merits of their work better than anyone else. And if he is also a critic I think he can learn from them to avoid the one and emulate the other; how not to make about dead authors' books the same mistakes that have been made about his own.

I hope it will now be clear that in talking about what I think I have learned from my own critics I am not in any sense attempting what might be called an 'answer to critics'. That would, indeed, be quite incompatible with what I am actually doing. Some of the reviews I find most guilty of the critical vices I am going to mention were wholly favourable; one of the severest I ever had appeared to me wholly free from them. I expect every author has had the same experience. Authors no doubt suffer from self-love, but it need not always be voracious to the degree that abolishes all discrimination. I think fatuous praise from a manifest fool may hurt more than any depreciation.

One critical fault I must get out of the way at once because it forms no part of my real theme: I mean dishonesty. Strict honesty is not, so far as I can see, even envisaged as an ideal in the modern literary world. When I was a young, unknown writer on the eve of my first publication, a kind friend said to me, 'Will you have any difficulty about reviews? I could mention you to a few people. . . .' It is almost as if one said to an undergraduate on the eve of a Tripos, 'Do you know any of the examiners? I could put in a word for you.' Years later another man who had reviewed me with modest favour wrote to me (though a stranger) a letter in which he said that he had really

thought much more highly of my book than the review showed:
'but of course,' he said, 'if I'd praised it any more the So-and-
So would not have printed me at all.' Another time someone
had attacked me in a paper called X. Then he wrote a book
himself. The editor of X immediately offered it to me, of all
people, to review. Probably he only wanted to set us both by
the ears for the amusement of the public and the increase of his
sales. But even if we take the more favourable possibility—if
we assume that this editor had a sort of rough idea of what they
call sportsmanship, and said, 'A has gone for B, it's only fair to
let B have a go at A'—it is only too plain that he has no idea of
honesty towards the public out of whom he makes his living.
They are entitled, at the very least, to honest, that is, to impartial, unbiased criticism: and he cannot have thought that I
was the most likely person to judge this book impartially. What
is even more distressing is that whenever I tell this story someone replies—mildly, unemphatically—with the question, 'And
did you?' This seems to me insulting, because I cannot see
how an honest man could do anything but what I did: refuse
the editor's highly improper proposal. Of course they didn't
mean it as an insult. That is just the trouble. When a man
assumes my knavery with the intention of insulting me, it may
not matter much. He may only be angry. It is when he assumes
it without the slightest notion that anyone could be offended,
when he reveals thus lightly his ignorance that there ever were
any standards by which it could be insulting, that a chasm seems
to open at one's feet.

If I exclude this matter of honesty from my main subject it is
not because I think it unimportant. I think it very important
indeed. If there should ever come a time when honesty in
reviewers is taken for granted, I think men will look back on
the present state of affairs as we now look on countries or periods
in which judges or examiners commonly take bribes. My reason
for dismissing the matter briefly is that I want to talk about the
things I hope I have learned from my own reviewers, and this
is not one of them. I had been told long before I became an

author that one mustn't tell lies (not even by *suppressio veri* and *suggestio falsi*) and that we mustn't take money for doing a thing and then secretly do something quite different. I may add before leaving the point that one mustn't judge these corrupt reviewers too harshly. Much is to be forgiven to a man in a corrupt profession at a corrupt period. The judge who takes bribes in a time or place where all take bribes may, no doubt, be blamed: but not so much as a judge who had done so in a healthier civilization.

I now turn to my main subject.

The first thing I have learned from my reviewers is, not the necessity (we would all grant that in principle) but the extreme rarity of conscientiousness in that preliminary work which all criticism should presuppose. I mean, of course, a careful reading of what one criticizes. This may seem too obvious to dwell on. I put it first precisely because it is so obvious and also because I hope it will illustrate my thesis that in certain ways (not of course in others) the author is not the worst, but the best, judge of his critics. Ignorant as he may be of his book's value, he is at least an expert on its content. When you have planned and written and re-written the thing and read it twice or more in proof, you do know what is in it better than anyone else. I don't mean 'what is in it' in any subtle or metaphorical sense (there may, in that sense, be 'nothing in it') but simply what words are, and are not, printed on those pages. Unless you have been often reviewed you will hardly believe how few reviewers have really done their Prep. And not only hostile reviewers. For them one has some sympathy. To have to read an author who affects one like a bad smell or a toothache is hard work. Who can wonder if a busy man skimps this disagreeable task in order to get on as soon as possible to the far more agreeable exercise of insult and denigration. Yet we examiners do wade through the dullest, most loathsome, most illegible answers before we give a mark; not because we like it, not even because we think the answer is worth it, but because this is the thing we have accepted pay for doing. In fact, however, laudatory critics often show an equal ignorance of the text. They too had rather write than read. Sometimes, in both sorts of review, the ignorance is not due to idleness. A great many people start by thinking they know what you will say, and honestly believe they have read what they expected to read. But for whatever reason, it is certainly the case that if you are often reviewed you will find yourself repeatedly blamed and praised for saying what you never said and for not saying what you have said.

Now of course it is true that a good critic may form a correct estimate of a book without reading every word of it. That perhaps is what Sidney Smith meant when he said 'You should never read a book before you review it. It will only prejudice you.' I am not, however, speaking of evaluations based on an imperfect reading, but of direct factual falsehoods about what it contains or does not contain. Negative statements are of course particularly dangerous for the lazy or hurried reviewer. And here, at once, is a lesson for us all as critics. One passage out of the whole *Faerie Queene* will justify you in saying that Spenser sometimes does so-and-so: only an exhaustive reading and an unerring memory will justify the statement that he never does so. This everyone sees. What more easily escapes one is the concealed negative in statements apparently positive: for example in any statement that contains the predicate 'new'. One says lightly that something which Donne or Sterne or Hopkins did was new: thus committing oneself to the negative that no one had done it before. But this is beyond one's knowledge; taken rigorously, it is beyond anyone's knowledge. Again, things we are all apt to say about the growth or development of a poet may often imply the negative that he wrote nothing except what has come down to us—which no one knows. We have not seen the contents of his waste paper basket. If we had, what now looks like an abrupt change in his manner from poem A to poem B might turn out not to have been abrupt at all.

It would be wrong to leave this point without saying that, however it may be with reviewers, academic critics seem to me now better than they ever were before. The days when Macaulay could get away with the idea that the *Faerie Queene* contained the death of the Blatant Beast, or Dryden with the remark that Chapman translated the *Iliad* in Alexandrines, are over. On the whole we now do our homework pretty well. But not yet perfectly. About the more obscure works ideas still circulate from one critic to another which have obviously not been verified by actual reading. I have an amusing piece of private evidence in my possession. My copy of a certain voluminous poet formerly belonged to a great scholar. At first I thought I had found a treasure. The first and second page were richly, and most learnedly annotated in a neat, legible hand. There were fewer on the third; after that, for the rest of the first poem, there was nothing. Each work was in the same state: the first few pages annotated, the rest in mint condition. 'Thus far into the bowels of the land' each time, and no further. Yet he had written on these works.

That, then, is the first lesson the reviewers taught me. There is, of course, another lesson in it. Let no one try to make a living by becoming a reviewer except as a last resource. This fatal ignorance of the text is not always the fruit of laziness or malice. It may be mere defeat by an intolerable burden. To live night and day with that hopeless mountain of new books (mostly uncongenial) piling up on your desk, to be compelled to say something where you have nothing to say, to be always behindhand—indeed much is to be excused to one so enslaved. But of course to say that a thing is excusable is to confess that it needs excuse.

I now turn to something which interests me much more because the bottom sin I detect in the reviewers is one which I believe we shall all find it very difficult to banish from our own critical work. Nearly all critics are prone to imagine that they know a great many facts relevant to a book which in reality they don't know. The author inevitably perceives their ignorance because he (often he alone) knows the real facts. This critical vice may take many different forms.

48

On Criticism

1. Nearly all reviewers assume that your books were written in the same order in which they were published and all shortly before publication. There was a very good instance of this lately in the reviews of Tolkien's *Lord of the Rings*. Most critics assumed (this illustrates a different vice) that it must be a political allegory and a good many thought that the master Ring must 'be' the atomic bomb. Anyone who knew the real history of the composition knew that this was not only erroneous, but impossible; chronologically impossible. Others assumed that the mythology of his romance had grown out of his children's story *The Hobbit*. This, again, he and his friends knew to be mainly false. Now of course nobody blames the critics for not knowing these things: how should they? The trouble is that they don't know they don't know. A guess leaps into their minds and they write it down without even noticing that it is a guess. Here certainly the warning to us all as critics is very clear and alarming. Critics of *Piers Plowman* and the *Faerie Queene* make gigantic constructions about the history of these compositions. Of course we should all admit such constructions to be conjectural. And as conjectures, you may ask, are they not, some of them, probable? Perhaps they are. But the experience of being reviewed has lowered my estimate of their probability. Because, when you start by knowing the facts, you find that the constructions are very often wholly wrong. Apparently the chances of their being right are low, even when they are made along quite sensible lines. Of course I am not forgetting that the reviewer has (quite rightly) devoted less study to my book than the scholar has devoted to Langland or Spenser. But I should have expected that to be compensated for by other advantages which he has and the scholar lacks. After all, he lives in the same period as I, subjected to the same currents of taste and opinion, and has undergone the same kind of education. He can hardly help knowing—reviewers are good at this sort of thing and take an interest in it—quite a lot about my generation, my period, and the circles in which I probably move. He and I may even have common acquaintances. Surely he is

at least as well placed for guessing about me as any scholar is for guessing about the dead. Yet he seldom guesses right. Hence I cannot resist the conviction that similar guesses about the dead seem plausible only because the dead are not there to refute them; that five minutes conversation with the real Spenser or the real Langland might blow the whole laborious fabric into smithereens. And notice that in all these conjectures the reviewer's error has been quite gratuitous. He has been neglecting the thing he is paid to do, and perhaps could do, in order to do something different. His business was to give information about the book and to pass judgement on it. These guesses about its history are quite beside the mark. And on this point, I feel pretty sure that I write without bias. The imaginary histories written about my books are by no means always offensive. Sometimes they are even complimentary. There is nothing against them except that they're not true, and would be rather irrelevant if they were. *Mutato nomine de me.* I must learn not to do the like about the dead: and if I hazard a conjecture, it must be with full knowledge, and with a clear warning to my readers, that it is a long shot, far more likely to be wrong than right.

2. Another type of critic who speculates about the genesis of your book is the amateur psychologist. He has a Freudian theory of literature and claims to know all about your inhibitions. He knows what unacknowledged wishes you were gratifying. And here of course one cannot, in the same sense as before, claim to start by knowing all the facts. By definition you are unconscious of the things he professes to discover. Therefore the more loudly you disclaim them, the more right he must be: though, oddly enough, if you admitted them, that would prove him right too. And there is a further difficulty: one is not here so free from bias, for this procedure is almost entirely confined to hostile reviewers. And now that I come to think of it, I have seldom seen it practised on a dead author except by a scholar who intended, in some measure, to debunk him. That in itself is perhaps significant. And it would not be unreasonable to

point out that the evidence on which such amateur psychologists base their diagnosis would not be thought sufficient by a professional. They have not had their author on the sofa, nor heard his dreams, and had the whole case-history. But I am here concerned only with what the author can say about such reviews solely because he is the author. And surely, however ignorant he is of his unconscious, he knows something more than they about the content of his conscious mind. And he will find them wholly overlooking the (to him) perfectly obvious conscious motive for some things. If they mentioned this and then discounted it as the author's (or patient's) 'rationalization', they might be right. But it is clear that they have never thought of it. They have never seen why, from the very structure of your story, from the very nature of story telling in general, that episode or image (or something like it) had to come in at that point. It is in fact quite clear that there is one impulse in your mind of which, with all their psychology, they have never reckoned: the plastic impulse, the impulse to make a thing, to shape, to give unity, relief, contrast, pattern. But this, unhappily, is the impulse which chiefly caused the book to be written at all. They have, clearly, no such impulse themselves, and they do not suspect it in others. They seem to fancy that a book trickles out of one like a sigh or a tear or automatic writing. It may well be that there is much in every book which comes from the unconscious. But when it is your own book you know the conscious motives as well. You may be wrong in thinking that these often give the full explanation of this or that. But you can hardly believe accounts of the sea-bottom given by those who are blind to the most obvious objects on the surface. They could be right only by accident. And I, if I attempt any similar diagnosis about the dead, shall equally be right, if at all, only by accident.

The truth is that a very large part of what comes up from the unconscious and which, for that very reason, seems so attractive and important in the early stages of planning a book, is weeded out and jettisoned long before the job is done: just as people (if they are not bores) tell us of their dreams only those which are amusing or in some other way interesting by the standards of the waking mind.

3. I now come to the imaginary history of the book's composition in a much subtler form. Here I think critics, and of course we when we criticize, are often deceived or confused as to what they are really doing. The deception may lurk in the words themselves. You and I might condemn a passage in a book for being 'laboured'. Do we mean by this that it sounds laboured? Or are we advancing the theory that it was in fact laboured? Or are we sometimes not quite sure which we mean? If we mean the second, notice that we are ceasing to write criticism. Instead of pointing out the faults in the passage we are inventing a story to explain, causally, how it came to have those faults. And if we are not careful we may complete our story and pass on as if we had done all that was necessary, without noticing that we have never even specified the faults at all. We explain something by causes without saying what the something is. We can do the same when we think we are praising. We may say that a passage is unforced or spontaneous. Do we mean that it sounds as if it were, or that it actually was written effortlessly and *currente calamo*? And whichever we mean, would it not be more interesting and more within the critics' province to point out, instead, those merits in the passage which made us want to praise it at all?

The trouble is that certain critical terms—*inspired, perfunctory, painstaking, conventional*—imply a supposed history of composition. The critical vice I am talking about consists in yielding to the temptation they hold out and then, instead of telling us what is good and bad in a book, inventing stories about the process which led to the goodness and badness. Or are they misled by the double sense of the word *Why*? For of course the question 'Why is this bad?' may mean two things: (a) What do you mean by calling it bad? Wherein does its badness consist? Give me the Formal Cause. (b) How did it become bad? Why did he write so ill? Give me the Efficient Cause. The first seems to me the essentially critical question. The critics I am thinking of answer the second, and usually answer it wrong, and unfortunately regard this as a substitute for the answer to the first.

Thus a critic will say of a passage, 'This is an afterthought.' He is just as likely to be wrong as right. He may be quite right in thinking it bad. And he must presumably think he has discerned in it the sort of badness which one might expect to occur in an afterthought. Surely an exposure of that badness itself would be far better than an hypothesis about its origin? Certainly this is the only thing that would make the critique at all useful to the author. I as author may know that the passage diagnosed as an afterthought was in reality the seed from which the whole book grew. I should very much like to be shown what inconsistency or irrelevance or flatness makes it look like an afterthought. It might help me to avoid these errors next time. Simply to know what the critic imagines, and imagines wrongly, about the history of the passage is of no use. Nor is it of much use to the public. They have every right to be told of the faults in my book. But this fault, as distinct from an hypothesis (boldly asserted as fact) about its origin, is just what they do not learn.

Here is an example which is specially important because I am quite sure the judgement which the critic was really making was correct. In a book of essays of mine the critic said that one essay was written without conviction, was task-work, or that my heart was not in it, or something like that. Now this in itself was plumb-wrong. Of all the pieces in the book it was the one I most cared about and wrote with most ardour.[1] Where the critic was right was in thinking it the worst. Everyone agrees with him about that. I agree with him. But you see that neither the public nor I learns anything about that badness from his criticism. He is like a doctor who makes no diagnosis and prescribes no cure but tells you how the patient got the disease (still

[1] Lewis, I am quite certain, is talking about the essay on William Morris in *Rehabilitations and Other Essays* (1939).

unspecified) and tells you wrong because he is describing scenes and events on which he has no evidence. The fond parents ask, 'What is it? Is it scarlatina or measles or chicken-pox?' The doctor replies, 'Depend upon it, he picked it up in one of those crowded trains.' (The patient actually has not travelled by train lately.) They then ask, 'But what are we to do? How are we to treat him?' The doctor replies, 'You may be quite sure it was an infection.' Then he climbs into his car and drives away.

Notice here again the total disregard of writing as a skill, the assumption that the writer's psychological state always flows unimpeded and undisguised into the product. How can they not know that in writing as in carpentry or tennis-playing or prayer or love-making or cookery or administration or anything else there is both skill and also those temporary heightenings and lowerings of skill which a man describes by saying that he is in good or bad form, that his hand is 'in' or 'out', that this is one of his good days or his bad days?

Such is the lesson, but it is very difficult to apply. It needs great perseverance to force oneself, in one's own criticism, to attend always to the product before one instead of writing fiction about the author's state of mind or methods of work: to which of course one has no direct access. 'Sincere', for example, is a word we should avoid. The real question is what makes a thing *sound* sincere or not. Anyone who has censored letters in the army must know that semi-literate people, though not in reality less sincere than others, very seldom *sound* sincere when they use the written word. Indeed we all know from our own experience in writing letters of condolence that the occasions on which we really feel most are not necessarily those on which our letters would suggest this. Another day, when we felt far less, our letter may have been more convincing. And of course the danger of error is greater in proportion as our own experience in the form we are criticizing is less. When we are criticizing a kind of work we have never attempted ourselves, we must realise that we do not know how such things are written and what is difficult or easy to do in them and how particular faults are likely to occur. Many critics quite clearly have an idea of how they think they would proceed if they tried to write the sort of book you have written, and assume that you were doing that. They often reveal unconsciously why they never have written a book of that kind.

I don't mean at all that we must never criticize work of a kind we have never done. On the contrary we must do nothing but criticize it. We may analyse and weigh its virtues and defects. What we must not do is to write imaginary histories. I know that all beer in railway refreshment rooms is bad and I could to some extent say 'why' (in one sense of the word: that is, I could give the Formal Cause)—it is tepid, sour, cloudy, and weak. But to tell you 'why' in the other sense (the Efficient Cause) I should need to have been a brewer or a publican or both and to know how beer should be brewed and kept and handled.

I would gladly be no more austere than is necessary. I must admit that words which seem, in their literal sense, to imply a history of the composition may sometimes be used as merely elliptical pointers to the character of the work done. When a man says that something is 'forced' or 'effortless' he may not really be claiming to know how it was written but only indicating in a kind of short-hand a quality he supposes everyone will recognize. And perhaps to banish all expression of this kind from our criticism would be a counsel of perfection. But I am increasingly convinced of their danger. If we use them at all, we must do so with extreme caution. We must make it quite clear to ourselves and to our readers that we do not know and are not pretending to know how things were written. Nor would it be relevant if we did. What sounds forced would be no better if it had been dashed off without pains; what sounds inspired, no worse if it had been arduously put together *invita Minerva*.

I now turn to interpretation. Here of course all critics, and we among them, will make mistakes. Such mistakes are far more venial than the sort I have been describing, for they are not gratuitous. The one sort arise when the critic writes fiction instead of criticism; the other, in the discharge of a proper function. At least I assume that critics ought to interpret, ought to try to find out the meaning or intention of a book. When they fail the fault may lie with them or with the author or with both.

I have said vaguely 'meaning' or 'intention'. We shall have to give each word a fairly definite sense. It is the author who *intends*; the book *means*. The author's intention is that which, if it is realized, will in his eyes constitute success. If all or most readers, or such readers as he chiefly desires, laugh at a passage, and he is pleased with this result, then his intention was comic, or he intended to be comic. If he is disappointed and humiliated at it, then he intended to be grave, or his intention was serious. *Meaning* is a much more difficult term. It is simplest when used of an allegorical work. In the *Romance of the Rose* plucking the rosebud means enjoying the heroine. It is still fairly easy when used of a work with a conscious and definite 'lesson' in it. *Hard Times* means, among other things, that elementary state education is bosh; *Macbeth*, that your sin will find you out; *Waverley*, that solitude and abandonment to the imagination in youth render a man an easy prey to those who wish to exploit him; the *Aeneid*, that the *res Romana* rightly demands the sacrifice of private happiness. But we are already in deep waters, for of course each of these books means a good deal more. And what are we talking about when we talk, as we do, of the 'meaning' of *Twelfth Night, Wuthering Heights*, or *The Brothers Karamazov?* And especially when we differ and dispute as we do, about their real or true meaning? The nearest I have yet got to a definition is something like this: the meaning of a book is the series or system of emotions, reflections, and attitudes produced by reading it. But of course this product differs with different readers. The ideally false or wrong 'meaning' would be the product in the mind of the stupidest and least sensitive and most prejudiced reader after a single careless reading. The ideally true or right 'meaning' would be that shared (in some measure) by the largest number of the best readers after repeated and careful readings over several generations, different periods, nationalities, moods, degrees of alertness, private pre-occupa-

tions, states of health, spirits, and the like cancelling one another out when (this is an important reservation) they cannot
be fused so as to enrich one another. (This happens when one's
readings of a work at widely different periods of one's own life,
influenced by the readings that reach us indirectly through the
works of critics, all modify our present reading so as to improve
it.) As for the many generations, we must add a limit. These
serve to enrich the perception of the meaning only so long as
the cultural tradition is not lost. There may come a break or
change after which readers arise whose point of view is so alien
that they might as well be interpreting a new work. Medieval
readings of the *Aeneid* as an allegory and Ovid as a moralist, or
modern readings of the *Parlement of Foules* which make the
duck and goose its heroes, would be examples. To delay, even
if we cannot permanently banish such interpretations, is a large
part of the function of scholarly, as distinct from pure,
criticism; so doctors labour to prolong life though they know
they cannot make men immortal.

Of a book's meaning, in this sense, its author is not necessarily the best, and is never a perfect, judge. One of his intentions usually was that it should have a certain meaning: he
cannot be sure that it has. He cannot even be sure that the
meaning he intended it to have was in every way, or even at all,
better than the meaning which readers find in it. Here, therefore, the critic has great freedom to range without fear of contradiction from the author's superior knowledge.

Where he seems to me most often to go wrong is in the hasty
assumption of an allegorical sense; and as reviewers make this
mistake about contemporary works, so, in my opinion, scholars
now often make it about old ones. I would recommend to both,
and I would try to observe in my own critical practice, these
principles. First, that no story can be devised by the wit of man
which cannot be interpreted allegorically by the wit of some
other man. The Stoic interpretations of primitive mythology,
the Christian interpretations of the Old Testament, the medieval
interpretations of the classics, all prove this. Therefore (2) the

mere fact that you *can* allegorize the work before you is of itself no proof that it is an allegory. Of course you can allegorize it. You can allegorize anything, whether in art or real life. I think we should here take a hint from the lawyers. A man is not tried at the assizes until there has been shown to be a *prima-facie* case against him. We ought not to proceed to allegorize any work until we have plainly set out the reasons for regarding it as an allegory at all.

[Lewis, apparently, did not finish this essay for at the foot of the existing manuscript are the words:]

As regards other attributions of intention

One's own preoccupations

Quellenforschung. *Achtung*—dates

ON SCIENCE FICTION

Sometimes a village or small town which we have known all our lives becomes the scene of a murder, a novel, or a centenary, and then for a few months everyone knows its name and crowds go to visit it. A like thing happens to one's private recreations. I had been walking, and reading Trollope, for years when I found myself suddenly overtaken, as if by a wave from behind, by a boom in Trollope and a short-lived craze for what was called hiking. And lately I have had the same sort of experience again. I had read fantastic fiction of all sorts ever since I could read, including, of course, the particular kind which Wells practised in his *Time Machine, First Men in the Moon* and others. Then, some fifteen or twenty years ago, I became aware of a bulge in the production of such stories. In America whole magazines began to be exclusively devoted to them. The execution was usually detestable; the conceptions, sometimes worthy of better treatment. About this time the name *scientifiction,* soon altered to *science fiction,* began to be common. Then, perhaps five or six years ago, the bulge still continuing and even increasing, there was an improvement: not that very bad stories ceased to be the majority, but that the good ones became better and more numerous. It was after this that the *genre* began to attract the attention (always, I think, contemptuous) of the literary weeklies. There seems, in fact, to be a double paradox in its history: it began to be popular when it least deserved popularity, and to excite critical contempt as soon as it ceased to be wholly contemptible.

Of the articles I have read on the subject (and I expect I have missed many) I do not find that I can make any use. For one thing, most were not very well informed. For another, many were by people who clearly hated the kind they wrote about. It is very dangerous to write about a kind you hate. Hatred obscures all distinctions. I don't like detective stories and therefore all detective stories look much alike to me: if I wrote about them I should therefore infallibly write drivel. Criticism of kinds, as distinct from criticism of works, cannot of course be avoided: I shall be driven to criticize one sub-species of science fiction myself. But it is, I think, the most subjective and least reliable type of criticism. Above all, it should not masquerade as criticism of individual works. Many reviews are useless because, while purporting to condemn the book, they only reveal the reviewer's dislike of the kind to which it belongs. Let bad tragedies be censured by those who love tragedy, and bad detective stories by those who love the detective story. Then we shall learn their real faults. Otherwise we shall find epics blamed for not being novels, farces for not being high comedies, novels by James for lacking the swift action of Smollett. Who wants to hear a particular claret abused by a fanatical teetotaller, or a particular woman by a confirmed misogynist?

Moreover, most of these articles were chiefly concerned to account for the bulge in the output and consumption of science fiction on sociological and psychological grounds. This is of course a perfectly legitimate attempt. But here as elsewhere those who hate the thing they are trying to explain are not perhaps those most likely to explain it. If you have never enjoyed a thing and do not know what it feels like to enjoy it, you will hardly know what sort of people go to it, in what moods, seeking what sort of gratification. And if you do not know what sort of people they are, you will be ill-equipped to find out what conditions have made them so. In this way, one may say of a kind not only (as Wordsworth says of the poet) that 'you must love it ere to you it will seem worthy of your love', but that you must at least have loved it once if you are even to warn others against it. Even if it is a vice to read science fiction, those who cannot understand the very temptation to that vice will not be likely to tell us anything of value about it. Just as I, for instance, who have no taste for cards, could not find anything very useful to say by way of warning against deep play. They will be like the frigid preaching chastity, misers warning us against prodigality, cowards denouncing rashness. And because, as I have said, hatred assimilates all the hated objects, it will make you assume that all the things lumped together as science fiction are of the same sort, and that the psychology of all those who like to read any of them is the same. That is likely to make the problem of explaining the bulge seem simpler than it really is.

I myself shall not attempt to explain it at all. I am not interested in the bulge. It is nothing to me whether a given work makes part of it or was written long before it occurred. The existence of the bulge cannot make the kind (or kinds) intrinsically better or worse; though of course bad specimens will occur most often within it.

I will now try to divide this species of narrative into its sub-species. I shall begin with that sub-species which I think radically bad, in order to get it out of our way.

In this sub-species the author leaps forward into an imagined future when planetary, sidereal, or even galactic travel has become common. Against this huge backcloth he then proceeds to develop an ordinary love-story, spy-story, wreck-story, or crime-story. This seems to me tasteless. Whatever in a work of art is not used, is doing harm. The faintly imagined, and sometimes strictly unimaginable, scene and properties, only blur the real theme and distract us from any interest it might have had. I presume that the authors of such stories are, so to speak, Displaced Persons—commercial authors who did not really want to write science fiction at all, but who availed themselves of its popularity by giving a veneer of science fiction to their normal kind of work. But we must distinguish. A leap into the future, a rapid assumption of all the changes which are feigned to have occurred, is a legitimate 'machine' if it enables the author to develop a story of real value which could not have been told (or not so economically) in any other way. Thus John Collier in *Tom's A-Cold* (1933) wants to write a story of heroic action among people themselves semi-barbarous but supported by the surviving tradition of a literate culture recently overthrown. He could, of course, find an historical situation suitable to his purpose, somewhere in the early Dark Ages. But that would involve all manner of archaeological details which would spoil his book if they were done perfunctorily and perhaps distract our interest if they were done well. He is therefore, on my view, fully justified in positing such a state of affairs in England after the destruction of our present civilization. That enables him (and us) to assume a familiar climate, flora, and fauna. He is not interested in the process whereby the change came about. That is all over before the curtain rises. This supposition is equivalent to the rules of his game: criticism applies only to the quality of his play. A much more frequent use of the leap into the future, in our time, is satiric or prophetic: the author criticizes tendencies in the present by imagining them carried out ('produced', as Euclid would say) to their logical limit. *Brave New World* and *Nineteen Eighty-Four* leap to our minds. I can see no objection to such a 'machine'. Nor do I see much use in discussing, as someone did, whether books that use it can be called 'novels' or not. That is merely a question of definition. You may define the novel either so as to exclude or so as to include them. The best definition is that which proves itself most convenient. And of course to devise a definition for the purpose of excluding either *The Waves* in one direction or *Brave New World* in another, and then blame them for being excluded, is foolery.

I am, then, condemning not all books which suppose a future widely different from the present, but those which do so without a good reason, which leap a thousand years to find plots and passions which they could have found at home.

Having condemned that sub-species, I am glad to turn to another which I believe to be legitimate, though I have not the slightest taste for it myself. If the former is the fiction of the Displaced Persons, this might be called the fiction of Engineers. It is written by people who are primarily interested in space-travel, or in other undiscovered techniques, as real possibilities in the actual universe. They give us in imaginative form their guesses as to how the thing might be done. Jules Verne's *Twenty Thousand Leagues Under the Sea* and Wells's *Land Ironclads* were once specimens of this kind, though the coming of the real submarine and the real tank has altered their original interest. Arthur Clarke's *Prelude to Space* is another. I am too uneducated scientifically to criticize such stories on the mechanical side; and I am so completely out of sympathy with the projects they anticipate that I am incapable of criticizing them as stories. I am as blind to their appeal as a pacifist is to *Maldon* and *Lepanto*, or an aristocratophobe (if I may coin the word) to the *Arcadia*. But heaven forbid that I should regard the limitations of my sympathy as anything save a red light which warns me not to criticize at all. For all I know, these may be very good stories in their own kind.

I think it useful to distinguish from these Engineers' Stories a third sub-species where the interest is, in a sense, scientific, but speculative. When we learn from the sciences the probable nature of places or conditions which no human being has experienced, there is, in normal men, an impulse to attempt to imagine them. Is any man such a dull clod that he can look at the moon through a good telescope without asking himself what it would be like to walk among those mountains under that black, crowded sky? The scientists themselves, the moment they go beyond purely mathematical statements, can hardly avoid describing the facts in terms of their probable effect on the senses of a human observer. Prolong this, and give, along with that observer's sense experience, his probable emotions and thoughts, and you at once have a rudimentary science fiction. And of course men have been doing this for centuries. What would Hades be like if you could go there alive? Homer sends Odysseus there and gives his answer. Or again, what would it be like at the Antipodes? (For this was a question of the same sort so long as men believed that the torrid zone rendered them forever inaccessible.) Dante takes you there: he describes with all the gusto of the later scientifictionist how surprising it was to see the sun in such an unusual position. Better still, what would it be like if you could get to the centre of the earth? Dante tells you at the end of the *Inferno* where he and Virgil, after climbing down from the shoulders to the waist of Lucifer, find that they have to climb up from his waist to his feet, because of course they have passed the centre of gravitation. It is a perfect science fiction effect. Thus again Athanasius Kircher in his *Iter Extaticum Celeste* (1656) will take you to all the planets and most of the stars, presenting as vividly as he can what you would see and feel if this were possible. He, like Dante, uses supernatural means of transport. In Wells's *First Men in the Moon* we have means which are feigned to be natural. What keeps his story within this sub-species, and distinguishes it from those of the Engineers, is his choice of a quite impossible composition called cavorite. This impossibility is of course a merit, not a defect. A man of his ingenuity could easily have thought up something more plausible. But the more plausible, the worse. That would merely invite interest in actual possibilities of reaching the Moon, an interest foreign to his story. Never mind how they got there; we are imagining what it would be like. The first glimpse of the unveiled airless sky, the lunar landscape, the lunar levity, the incomparable solitude, then the growing terror, finally the overwhelming approach of the lunar night—it is for these things that the story (especially in its original and shorter form) exists.

How anyone can think this form illegitimate or contemptible passes my understanding. It may very well be convenient not to call such things novels. If you prefer, call them a very special form of novels. Either way, the conclusion will be much the same: they are to be tried by their own rules. It is absurd to condemn them because they do not often display any deep or sensitive characterization. They oughtn't to. It is a fault if they do. Wells's Cavor and Bedford have rather too much than too little character. Every good writer knows that the more unusual the scenes and events of his story are, the slighter, the more ordinary, the more typical his persons should be. Hence Gulliver is a commonplace little man and Alice a commonplace little girl. If they had been more remarkable they would have wrecked their books. The Ancient Mariner himself is a very ordinary man. To tell how odd things struck odd people is to have an oddity too much: he who is to see strange sights must not himself be strange. He ought to be as nearly as possible Everyman or Anyman. Of course, we must not confuse slight or typical characterization with impossible or unconvincing characterization. Falsification of character will always spoil a story. But character can apparently be reduced, simplified, to almost any extent with wholly satisfactory results. The greater ballads are an instance.

Of course, a given reader may be (some readers seem to be) interested in nothing else in the world except detailed studies of complex human personalities. If so, he has a good reason for not reading those kinds of work which neither demand nor admit it. He has no reason for condemning them, and indeed no qualification for speaking of them at all. We must not allow the novel of manners to give laws to all literature: let it rule its own domain. We must not listen to Pope's maxim about the proper study of mankind. The proper study of man is everything. The proper study of man as artist is everything which gives a foothold to the imagination and the passions.

But while I think this sort of science fiction legitimate, and capable of great virtues, it is not a kind which can endure copious production. It is only the first visit to the Moon or to Mars that is, for this purpose, any good. After each has been discovered in one or two stories (and turned out to be different in each) it becomes difficult to suspend our disbelief in favour of subsequent stories. However good they were they would kill each other by becoming numerous.

My next sub-species is what I would call the Eschatological. It is about the future, but not in the same way as *Brave New World* or *The Sleeper Awakes*. They were political or social. This kind gives an imaginative vehicle to speculations about the ultimate destiny of our species. Examples are Wells's *Time Machine*, Olaf Stapledon's *Last and First Men*, or Arthur Clarke's *Childhood's End*. It is here that a definition of science fiction which separates it entirely from the novel becomes imperative. The form of *Last and First Men* is not novelistic at all. It is indeed in a new form—the pseudo history. The pace, the concern with broad, general movements, the tone, are all those of the historiographer, not the novelist. It was the right form for the theme. And since we are here diverging so widely from the novel, I myself would gladly include in this sub-species a work which is not even narrative, Geoffrey Dennis's *The End of the World* (1930). And I would certainly include, from J. B. S. Haldane's *Possible Worlds* (1927), the brilliant, though to my mind depraved, paper called 'The Last Judgement'.

Work of this kind gives expression to thoughts and emotions which I think it good that we should sometimes entertain. It is sobering and cathartic to remember, now and then, our collective smallness, our apparent isolation, the apparent indifference of nature, the slow biological, geological, and astronomical processes which may, in the long run, make many of our hopes (possibly some of our fears) ridiculous. If *memento mori* is sauce for the individual, I do not know why the species should be spared the taste of it. Stories of this kind may explain the hardly disguised political rancour which I thought I detected in one article on science fiction. The insinuation was that those who read or wrote it were probably Fascists. What lurks behind such a hint is, I suppose, something like this. If we were all on board ship and there was trouble among the stewards, I can just conceive their chief spokesman looking with disfavour on anyone who stole away from the fierce debates in the saloon or pantry to take a breather on deck. For up there, he would taste the salt, he would see the vastness of the water, he would remember that the ship had a whither and a whence. He would remember things like fog, storms, and ice. What had seemed, in the hot, lighted rooms down below to be merely the scene for a political crisis, would appear once more as a tiny egg-shell moving rapidly through an immense darkness over an element in which man cannot live. It would not necessarily change his convictions about the rights and wrongs of the dispute down below, but it would probably show them in a new light. It could hardly fail to remind him that the stewards were taking for granted hopes more momentous than that of a rise in pay, and the passengers forgetting dangers more serious than that of having to cook and serve their own meals. Stories of the sort I am describing are like that visit to the deck. They cool us. They are as refreshing as that passage in E. M. Forster where the man, looking at the monkeys, realizes that most of the inhabitants of India do not care how India is governed. Hence the uneasiness which they arouse in those who, for whatever reason, wish to keep us wholly imprisoned in the immediate conflict. That perhaps is why people are so ready with the charge of 'escape'. I never fully understood it till my friend Professor Tolkien asked me the very simple question, 'What class of men would you expect to be most preoccupied with, and most hostile to, the idea of escape?' and gave the obvious answer: jailers. The charge of Fascism is, to be sure, mere mud-flinging. Fascists, as well as Communists, are jailers; both would assure us that the proper study of prisoners is prison. But there is perhaps this truth behind it: that those who brood much on the remote past or future, or stare long at the night sky, are less likely than others to be ardent or orthodox partisans.

I turn at last to that sub-species in which alone I myself am greatly interested. It is best approached by reminding ourselves of a fact which every writer on the subject whom I have read completely ignores. Far the best of the American magazines bears the significant title *Fantasy and Science Fiction*. In it (as also in many other publications of the same type) you will find not only stories about space-travel but stories about gods, ghosts, ghouls, demons, fairies, monsters, etc. This gives us our clue. The last sub-species of science fiction represents simply an imaginative impulse as old as the human race working under the special conditions of our own time. It is not difficult to see why those who wish to visit strange regions in search of such beauty, awe, or terror as the actual world does not supply have increasingly been driven to other planets or other stars. It is the result of increasing geographical knowledge. The less known the real world is, the more plausibly your marvels can be located near at hand. As the area of knowledge spreads, you need to go further afield: like a man moving his house further and further out into the country as the new building estates catch him up. Thus in Grimm's *Märchen*, stories told by peasants in wooded country, you need only walk an hour's journey into the next forest to find a home for your witch or ogre. The author of *Beowulf* can put Grendel's lair in a place of which he himself says *Nis þæt feor heonon Mil-gemearces*. Homer, writing for a maritime people has to take Odysseus several days' journey by sea before he meets Circe, Calypso, the Cyclops, or the Sirens. Old Irish has a form called the *immram*, a voyage among islands. Arthurian romance, oddly at first sight, seems usually content with the old *Märchen* machine of a neighbouring forest. Chrétien and his successors knew a great deal of real geography. Perhaps the explanation is that these romances are chiefly written by Frenchmen about Britain, and Britain in the past. *Huon of Bordeaux* places Oberon in the East. Spenser invents a country not in our universe at all; Sidney goes to an imaginary past in Greece. By the eighteenth century we have to move well out into the country. Paltock and Swift take us to remote seas, Voltaire to America. Rider Haggard had to go to unexplored Africa or Tibet; Bulwer Lytton, to the depths of the Earth. It might have been predicted that stories of this kind would, sooner or later, have to leave Tellus altogether. We know now that where Haggard put She and Kôr we should really find groundnut schemes or Mau Mau.

In this kind of story the pseudo-scientific apparatus is to be taken simply as a 'machine' in the sense which that word bore for the Neo-Classical critics. The most superficial appearance of plausibility—the merest sop to our critical intellect—will do. I am inclined to think that frankly supernatural methods are best. I took a hero once to Mars in a space-ship, but when I knew better I had angels convey him to Venus. Nor need the strange worlds, when we get there, be at all strictly tied to scientific probabilities. It is their wonder, or beauty, or suggestiveness that matter. When I myself put canals on Mars I believe I already knew that better telescopes had dissipated that old optical delusion. The point was that they were part of the Martian myth as it already existed in the common mind.

The defence and analysis of this kind are, accordingly, no different from those of fantastic or mythopoeic literature in general. But here sub-species and sub-sub-species break out in baffling multitude. The impossible—or things so immensely improbable that they have, imaginatively, the same status as the impossible—can be used in literature for many different purposes. I cannot hope to do more than suggest a few main types: the subject still awaits its Aristotle.

It may represent the intellect, almost completely free from emotion, at play. The purest specimen would be Abbott's *Flatland*, though even here some emotion arises from the sense (which it inculcates) of our own limitations—the consciousness that our own human awareness of the world is arbitrary and contingent. Sometimes such play gives a pleasure analogous to that of the conceit. I have unluckily forgotten both the name and author of my best example: the story of a man who is enabled to travel into the future, because himself, in that future when he shall have discovered a method of time travel, comes back to himself in the present (then, of course, the past) and fetches him.[1] Less comic, but a more strenuous game, is the very fine working out of the logical consequences of time-travel in Charles Williams's *Many Dimensions*: where, however, this element is combined with many others.

Secondly, the impossible may be simply a postulate to liberate farcical consequences, as in 'F. Anstey's' *Brass Bottle*. The garunda-stone in his *Vice Versa* is not so pure an example; a

[1] Lewis is thinking, I believe, of Robert A. Heinlein's 'By His Bootstraps' in *Spectrum: A Science Fiction Anthology* (1961).

serious moral and, indeed, something not far from pathos, come in—perhaps against the author's wish.

Sometimes it is a postulate which liberates consequences very far from comic, and, when this is so, if the story is good it will usually point a moral: of itself, without any didactic manipulation by the author on the conscious level. Stevenson's *Dr Jekyll and Mr Hyde* would be an example. Another is Marc Brandel's *Cast the First Shadow*, where a man, long solitary, despised, and oppressed, because he had no shadow, at last meets a woman who shares his innocent defect, but later turns from her in disgust and indignation on finding that she has, in addition, the loathsome and unnatural property of having no reflection. Readers who do not write themselves often describe such stories as allegories, but I doubt if it is as allegories that they arise in the author's mind.

In all these the impossibility is, as I have said, a postulate, something to be granted before the story gets going. Within that frame we inhabit the known world and are as realistic as anyone else. But in the next type (and the last I shall deal with) the marvellous is in the grain of the whole work. We are, throughout, in another world. What makes that world valuable is not, of course, mere multiplication of the marvellous either for comic effect (as in *Baron Munchausen* and sometimes in Ariosto and Boiardo) or for mere astonishment (as, I think, in the worst of the *Arabian Nights* or in some children's stories), but its quality, its flavour. If good novels are comments on life, good stories of this sort (which are very much rarer) are actual additions to life; they give, like certain rare dreams, sensations we never had before, and enlarge our conception of the range of possible experience. Hence the difficulty of discussing them at all with those who refuse to be taken out of what they call 'real life'—which means, perhaps, the groove through some far wider area of possible experience to which our senses and our biological, social, or economic interests usually confine us—or, if taken, can see nothing outside it but aching boredom or sickening monstrosity. They shudder and ask to go home.

Specimens of this kind, at its best, will never be common. I would include parts of the *Odyssey*, the *Hymn to Aphrodite*, much of the *Kalevala* and *The Faerie Queene*, some of Malory (but none of Malory's best work) and more of *Huon*, parts of Novalis's *Heinrich von Ofterdingen*, *The Ancient Mariner* and *Christabel*, Beckford's *Vathek*, Morris's *Jason* and the *Prologue* (little else) of the *Earthly Paradise*, MacDonald's *Phantastes*, *Lilith*, and *The Golden Key*, Eddison's *Worm Ouroboros*, Tolkien's *Lord of the Rings*, and that shattering, intolerable, and irresistible work, David Lindsay's *Voyage to Arcturus*. Also Mervyn Peake's *Titus Groan*. Some of Ray Bradbury's stories perhaps make the grade. W. H. Hodgson's *The Night Land* would have made it in eminence from the unforgettable sombre splendour of the images it presents, if it were not disfigured by a sentimental and irrelevant erotic interest and by a foolish, and flat archaism of style. (I do not mean that all archaism is foolish, and have never seen the modern hatred of it cogently defended. If archaism succeeds in giving us the sense of having entered a remote world, it justifies itself. Whether it is correct by philological standards does not then matter a rap.)

I am not sure that anyone has satisfactorily explained the keen, lasting, and solemn pleasure which such stories can give. Jung, who went furthest, seems to me to produce as his explanation one more myth which affects us in the same way as the rest. Surely the analysis of water should not itself be wet? I shall not attempt to do what Jung failed to do. But I would like to draw attention to a neglected fact: the astonishing intensity of the dislike which some readers feel for the mythopoeic. I first found it out by accident. A lady (and, what makes the story more piquant, she herself was a Jungian psychologist by profession) had been talking about a dreariness which seemed to be creeping over her life, the drying up in her of the power to feel pleasure, the aridity of her mental landscape. Drawing a bow at a venture, I asked, 'Have you any taste for fantasies and fairy tales?' I shall never forget how her muscles tightened, her hands clenched themselves, her eyes started as if with horror, and her voice changed, as she hissed out, 'I *loathe* them.' Clearly we here have to do not with a critical opinion but with something like a phobia. And I have seen traces of it elsewhere, though never quite so violent. On the other side, I know from my own experience, that those who like the mythopoeic like it with almost equal intensity. The two phenomena, taken together, should at least dispose of the theory that it is something trivial. It would seem from the reactions it produces, that the mythopoeic is rather, for good or ill, a mode of imagination which does something to us at a deep level. If some seem to go to it in almost compulsive need, others seem to be in terror of what they may meet there. But that is of course only suspicion. What I feel far more sure of is the critical *caveat* which I propounded a while ago. Do not criticize what you have no taste for without great caution. And above all, do not ever criticize what you simply can't stand. I will lay all the cards on the table. I have long since discovered my own private *phobia*, the thing I can't bear in literature, the thing which makes me profoundly uncomfortable, is the representation of anything like a quasi love affair between two children. It embarrasses and nauseates me. But of course I regard this not as a charter to write slashing reviews of books in which the hated theme occurs, but as a warning not to pass judgement on them at all. For my reaction is unreasonable: such child-loves quite certainly occur in real life and I can give no reason why they should not be represented in art. If they touch the scar of some early *trauma* in me, that is my misfortune. And I would venture to advise all who are attempting to become critics to adopt the same principle. A violent and actually resentful reaction to all books of a certain kind, or to situations of a certain kind, is a danger signal. For I am convinced that good adverse criticism is the most difficult thing we have to do. I would advise everyone to begin it under the most favourable conditions: this is, where you thoroughly know and heartily like the thing the author is trying to do, and have enjoyed many books where it was done well. Then you will have some chance of really showing that he has failed and perhaps even of showing why. But if our real reaction to a book is 'Ugh! I just can't bear this sort of thing,' then I think we shall not be able to diagnose whatever real faults it has. We may labour to conceal our emotion, but we shall end in a welter of emotive, unanalysed, vogue-words—'arch', 'facetious', 'bogus', 'adolescent', 'immature' and the rest. When we really know what is wrong we need none of these.

A REPLY TO PROFESSOR HALDANE

Before attempting a reply to Professor Haldane's *Auld Hornie,
F.R.S.*, in *The Modern Quarterly*, I had better note the one
point of agreement between us. I think, from the Professor's
complaint that my characters are 'like slugs in an experimental
cage who get a cabbage if they turn right and an electric shock
if they turn left', he suspects me of finding the sanctions of
conduct in reward and punishment. His suspicion is erroneous.
I share his detestation for any such view and his preference for
Stoic or Confucian ethics. Although I believe in an omnipotent
God I do not consider that His omnipotence could in itself
create the least obligation to obey Him. In my romances the
'good' characters are in fact rewarded. That is because I consider a happy ending appropriate to the light, holiday kind of
fiction I was attempting. The Professor has mistaken the
'poetic justice' of romance for an ethical theorem. I would go
further. Detestation for any ethic which worships success is one
of my chief reasons for disagreeing with most communists. In
my experience they tend, when all else fails, to tell me that I
ought to forward the revolution because 'it is bound to come'.
One dissuaded me from my own position on the shockingly
irrelevant ground that if I continued to hold it I should, in
good time, be 'mown down'—argued, as a cancer might argue
if it could talk, that he must be right because he could kill me.
I gladly recognize the difference between Professor Haldane
and such communists as that. I ask him, in return, to recognize
the difference between my Christian ethics and those, say, of
Paley. There are, on his side as well as on mine, Vichy-like
vermin who define the right side as the side that is going to win.
Let us put them out of the room before we begin talking.

A Reply to Professor Haldane

My chief criticism of the Professor's article is that, wishing to criticize my philosophy (if I may give it so big a name) he almost ignores the books in which I have attempted to set it out and concentrates on my romances. He was told in the preface to *That Hideous Strength* that the doctrines behind that romance could be found, stripped of their fictional masquerade, in *The Abolition of Man*. Why did he not go there to find them? The result of his method is unfortunate. As a philosophical critic the Professor would have been formidable and therefore useful. As a literary critic—though even there he cannot be dull—he keeps on missing the point. A good deal of my reply must therefore be concerned with removal of mere misunderstandings.

His attack resolves itself into three main charges. (1) That my science is usually wrong; (2) That I traduce scientists; (3) That on my view scientific planning 'can only lead to Hell' (and that therefore I am 'a most useful prop to the existing social order', dear to those who 'stand to lose by social changes' and reluctant, for bad motives, to speak out about usury).

(1) My science is usually wrong. Why, yes. So is the Professor's history. He tells us in *Possible Worlds* (1927) that 'five hundred years ago . . . it was not clear that celestial distances were so much greater than terrestrial'. But the astronomical textbook which the Middle Ages used, Ptolemy's *Almagest*, had clearly stated (I. v.) that in relation to the distance of the fixed stars the whole Earth must be treated as a mathematical point and had explained on what observations this conclusion was based. The doctrine was well known to King Alfred and even to the author of a 'popular' book like the *South English Legendary*. Again, in *Auld Hornie*, the Professor seems to think that Dante was exceptional in his views on gravitation and the rotundity of the Earth. But the most popular and orthodox authority whom Dante could have consulted, and who died a year or so before his birth, was Vincent of Beauvais. And in his *Speculum Naturale* (VII. vii.) we learn that if there were a hole right through the terrestrial globe (*terre globus*) and you dropped

75

a stone into that hole, it would come to rest at the centre. In other words, the Professor is about as good a historian as I am a scientist. The difference is that his false history is produced in works intended to be true, whereas my false science is produced in romances. I wanted to write about imaginary worlds. Now that the whole of our own planet has been explored other planets are the only place where you can put them. I needed for my purpose just enough popular astronomy to create in 'the common reader' a 'willing suspension of disbelief'. No one hopes, in such fantasies, to satisfy a real scientist, any more than the writer of a historical romance hopes to satisfy a real archaeologist. (Where the latter effort is seriously made, as in *Romola*, it usually spoils the book.) There is thus a great deal of scientific falsehood in my stories: some of it known to be false even by me when I wrote the books. The canals in Mars are there not because I believe in them but because they are part of the popular tradition; the astrological character of the planets for the same reason. The poet, Sidney says, is the only writer who never lies, because he alone never claims truth for his statements. Or, if 'poet' be too high a term to use in such a context, we can put it another way. The Professor has caught me carving a toy elephant and criticizes it as if my aim had been to teach zoology. But what I was after was not the elephant as known to science but our old friend Jumbo.

(2) I think Professor Haldane himself probably regarded his critique of my science as mere skirmishing; with his second charge (that I traduce scientists) we reach something more serious. And here, most unhappily, he concentrates on the wrong book—*That Hideous Strength*—missing the strong point of his own case. If any of my romances could be plausibly accused of being a libel on scientists it would be *Out of the Silent Planet*. It certainly is an attack, if not on scientists, yet on something which might be called 'scientism'—a certain outlook on the world which is causally connected with the popularization of the sciences, though it is much less common among real scientists than among their readers. It is, in a word,

the belief that the supreme moral end is the perpetuation of our own species, and that this is to be pursued even if, in the process of being fitted for survival, our species has to be stripped of all those things for which we value it—of pity, of happiness, and of freedom. I am not sure that you will find this belief formally asserted by any writer: such things creep in as assumed, and unstated, major premisses. But I thought I could feel its approach; in Shaw's *Back to Methuselah*, in Stapledon, and in Professor Haldane's 'Last Judgement' (in *Possible Worlds*). I had noted, of course, that the Professor dissociates his own ideal from that of his Venerites. He says that his own ideal is 'somewhere in between' them and a race 'absorbed in the pursuit of individual happiness'. The 'pursuit of individual happiness' is, I trust, intended to mean 'the pursuit by each individual of his own happiness at the expense of his neighbour's'. But it might also be taken to support the (to me meaningless) view that there is some other kind of happiness—that something other than an individual is capable of happiness or misery. I also suspected (was I wrong?) that the Professor's 'somewhere in between' came pretty near the Venerite end of the scale. It was against this outlook on life, this ethic, if you will, that I wrote my satiric fantasy, projecting in my Weston a buffoon-villain image of the 'metabiological' heresy. If anyone says that to make him a scientist was unfair, since the view I am attacking is not chiefly rampant among scientists, I might agree with him: though I think such a criticism would be over sensitive. The odd thing is that Professor Haldane thinks Weston 'recognisable as a scientist'. I am relieved, for I had doubts about him. If I were briefed to attack my own books I should have pointed out that though Weston, for the sake of the plot, has to be a physicist, his interests seem to be exclusively biological. I should also have asked whether it was credible that such a gas-bag could ever have invented a mouse-trap, let alone a space-ship. But then, I wanted farce as well as fantasy.

Perelandra, in so far as it does not merely continue its

predecessor, is mainly for my co-religionists. Its real theme would not interest Professor Haldane, I think, one way or the other. I will only point out that if he had noticed the very elaborate ritual in which the angels hand over the rule of that planet to the humans he might have realized that the 'angelocracy' pictured on Mars is, for me, a thing of the past: the Incarnation has made a difference. I do not mean that he can be expected to be interested in this view as such: but it might have saved us from at least one political red-herring.

That Hideous Strength he has almost completely misunderstood. The 'good' scientist is put in precisely to show that 'scientists' as such are not the target. To make the point clearer, he leaves my N.I.C.E. because he finds he was wrong in his original belief that 'it had something to do with science' (p. 83). To make it clearer yet, my principal character, the man almost irresistibly attracted by the N.I.C.E. is described (p. 226) as one whose 'education had been neither scientific nor classical—merely "Modern". The severities both of abstraction and of high human tradition had passed him by. . . . He was . . . a glib examinee in subjects that require no exact knowledge.' To make it doubly and trebly clear the rake's progress of Wither's mind is represented (p. 438) as philosophical, not scientific at all. Lest even this should not be enough, the hero (who is, by the way, to some extent a fancy portrait of a man I know, but not of me) is made to say that the sciences are 'good and innocent in themselves' (p. 248), though evil 'scientism' is creeping into them. And finally, what we are obviously up against throughout the story is not scientists but *officials*. If anyone ought to feel himself libelled by this book it is not the scientist but the civil servant: and, next to the civil servant, certain philosophers. Frost is the mouthpiece of Professor Waddington's ethical theories: by which I do not, of course, mean that Professor Waddington in real life is a man like Frost.

What, then, was I attacking? Firstly, a certain view about values: the attack will be found, undisguised, in *The Abolition of Man*. Secondly, I was saying, like St James and Professor

A Reply to Professor Haldane

Haldane, that to be a friend of 'the World' is to be an enemy of God. The difference between us is that the Professor sees the 'World' purely in terms of those threats and those allurements which depend on money. I do not. The most 'worldly' society I have ever lived in is that of schoolboys: most worldly in the cruelty and arrogance of the strong, the toadyism and mutual treachery of the weak, and the unqualified snobbery of both. Nothing was so base that most members of the school proletariat would not do it, or suffer it, to win the favour of the school aristocracy: hardly any injustice too bad for the aristocracy to practice. But the class system did not in the least depend on the amount of anyone's pocket money. Who needs to care about money if most of the things he wants will be offered by cringing servility and the remainder can be taken by force? This lesson has remained with me all my life. That is one of the reasons why I cannot share Professor Haldane's exaltation at the banishment of Mammon from 'a sixth of our planet's surface'. I have already lived in a world from which Mammon was banished: it was the most wicked and miserable I have yet known. If Mammon were the only devil, it would be another matter. But where Mammon vacates the throne, how if Moloch takes his place? As Aristotle said, 'Men do not become tyrants in order to keep warm.' All men, of course, desire pleasure and safety. But all men also desire power and all men desire the mere sense of being 'in the know' or the 'inner ring', of not being 'outsiders': a passion insufficiently studied and the chief theme of my story. When the state of society is such that money is the passport to all these prizes, then of course money will be the prime temptation. But when the passport changes, the desires will remain. And there are many other possible passports: position in an official hierarchy, for instance. Even now, the ambitious and worldly man would not inevitably choose the post with the higher salary. The pleasure of being 'high up and far within' may be worth the sacrifice of some income.

(3) Thirdly, was I attacking scientific planning? According to Professor Haldane 'Mr Lewis's idea is clear enough. The

application of science to human affairs can only lead to Hell.'
There is certainly no warrant for 'can only'; but he is justified
in assuming that unless I had thought I saw a serious and
widespread danger I would not have given planning so central
a place even in what I called 'a fairy tale' and a 'tall story'. But
if you must reduce the romance to a proposition, the proposition would be almost the converse of that which the Professor
supposes: not 'scientific planning will certainly lead to Hell',
but 'Under modern conditions any effective invitation to Hell
will certainly appear in the guise of scientific planning'—as
Hitler's régime in fact did. Every tyrant must begin by claiming
to have what his victims respect and to give what they want. The
majority in most modern countries respect science and want
to be planned. And, therefore, almost by definition, if any man
or group wishes to enslave us it will of course describe itself
as 'scientific planned democracy'. It may be true that any real
salvation must equally, though by hypothesis truthfully, describe itself as 'scientific planned democracy'. All the more
reason to look very carefully at anything which bears that
label.

My fears of such a tyranny will seem to the Professor either
insincere or pusillanimous. For him the danger is all in the
opposite direction, in the chaotic selfishness of individualism.
I must try to explain why I fear more the disciplined cruelty of
some ideological oligarchy. The Professor has his own explanation of this; he thinks I am unconsciously motivated by the
fact that I 'stand to lose by social change'. And indeed it would
be hard for me to welcome a change which might well consign
me to a concentration camp. I might add that it would be like-
wise easy for the Professor to welcome a change which might
place him in the highest rank of an omnicompetent oligarchy.
That is why the motive game is so uninteresting. Each side can
go on playing *ad nauseam*, but when all the mud has been flung
every man's views still remain to be considered on their merits.
I decline the motive game and resume the discussion. I do not
hope to make Professor Haldane agree with me. But I should

like him at least to understand why I think devil worship a real possibility.

I am a democrat. Professor Haldane thinks I am not, but he bases his opinion on a passage in *Out of the Silent Planet* where I am discussing, not the relations of a species to itself (politics) but the relations of one species to another. His interpretation, if consistently worked out, would attribute to me the doctrine that horses are fit for an equine monarchy though not for an equine democracy. Here, as so often, what I was really saying was something which the Professor, had he understood it, would have found simply uninteresting.

I am a democrat because I believe that no man or group of men is good enough to be trusted with uncontrolled power over others. And the higher the pretentions of such power, the more dangerous I think it both to the rulers and to the subjects. Hence Theocracy is the worst of all governments. If we must have a tyrant a robber baron is far better than an inquisitor. The baron's cruelty may sometimes sleep, his cupidity at some point be sated; and since he dimly knows he is doing wrong he may possibly repent. But the inquisitor who mistakes his own cruelty and lust of power and fear for the voice of Heaven will torment us infinitely because he torments us with the approval of his own conscience and his better impulses appear to him as temptations. And since Theocracy is the worst, the nearer any government approaches to Theocracy the worse it will be. A metaphysic, held by the rulers with the force of a religion, is a bad sign. It forbids them, like the inquisitor, to admit any grain of truth or good in their opponents, it abrogates the ordinary rules of morality, and it gives a seemingly high, super-personal sanction to all the very ordinary human passions by which, like other men, the rulers will frequently be actuated. In a word, it forbids wholesome doubt. A political programme can never in reality be more than probably right. We never know all the facts about the present and we can only guess the future. To attach to a party programme—whose highest real claim is to reasonable prudence—the sort of assent which we should reserve for demonstrable theorems, is a kind of intoxication.

This false certainty comes out in Professor Haldane's article. He simply cannot believe that a man could really be in doubt about usury. I have no objection to his thinking me wrong. What shocks me is his instantaneous assumption that the question is so simple that there could be no real hesitation about it. It is breaking Aristotle's canon—to demand in every enquiry that degree of certainty which the subject matter allows. And not *on your life* to pretend that you see further than you do.

Being a democrat, I am opposed to all very drastic and sudden changes of society (in whatever direction) because they never in fact take place except by a particular technique. That technique involves the seizure of power by a small, highly disciplined group of people; the terror and the secret police follow, it would seem, automatically. I do not think any group good enough to have such power. They are men of like passions with ourselves. The secrecy and discipline of their organisation will have already inflamed in them that passion for the inner ring which I think at least as corrupting as avarice; and their high ideological pretensions will have lent all their passions the dangerous prestige of the Cause. Hence, in whatever direction the change is made, it is for me damned by its *modus operandi*. The worst of all public dangers is the committee of public safety. The character in *That Hideous Strength* whom the Professor never mentions is Miss Hardcastle, the chief of the secret police. She is the common factor in all revolutions; and, as she says, you won't get anyone to do her job well unless they get some kick out of it.

I must, of course, admit that the actual state of affairs may sometimes be so bad that a man is tempted to risk change even by revolutionary methods; to say that desperate diseases require desperate remedies and that necessity knows no law. But to yield to this temptation is, I think, fatal. It is under that pretext that every abomination enters. Hitler, the Machiavellian Prince, the Inquisition, the Witch Doctor, all claimed to be necessary.

A Reply to Professor Haldane

From this point of view is it impossible that the Professor could come to understand what I mean by devil worship, as a symbol? For me it is not merely a symbol. Its relation to the reality is more complicated, and it would not interest Professor Haldane. But it is at least partly symbolical and I will try to give the Professor such an account of my meaning as can be grasped without introducing the supernatural. I have to begin by correcting a rather curious misunderstanding. When we accuse people of devil worship we do not usually mean that they knowingly worship the devil. That, I agree, is a rare perversion. When a rationalist accuses certain Christians, say, the seventeenth-century Calvinists, of devil worship, he does not mean that they worshipped a being whom they regarded as the devil; he means that they worshipped as God a being whose character the rationalist thinks diabolical. It is clearly in that sense, and that sense only, that my Frost worships devils. He adores the 'macrobes' because they are beings stronger, and therefore to him 'higher', than men: worships them, in fact, on the same grounds on which my communist friend would have me favour the revolution. No man at present is (probably) doing what I represent Frost as doing: but he is the ideal point at which certain lines of tendency already observable will meet if produced.

The first of these tendencies is the growing exaltation of the collective and the growing indifference to persons. The philosophical sources are probably in Rousseau and Hegel, but the general character of modern life with its huge impersonal organisations may be more potent than any philosophy. Professor Haldane himself illustrates the present state of mind very well. He thinks that if one were inventing a language for 'sinless beings who loved their neighbours as themselves' it would be appropriate to have no words for 'my', 'I', and 'other personal pronouns and inflexions'. In other words he sees no difference between two opposite solutions of the problem of selfishness: between love (which is a relation between persons) and the abolition of persons. Nothing but a *Thou* can be loved and a *Thou* can exist only for an *I*. A society in which no one was conscious of himself as a person over against other persons, where none could say 'I love you', would, indeed, be free from selfishness, but not through love. It would be 'unselfish' as a bucket of water is unselfish. Another good example comes in *Back to Methuselah*. There, as soon as Eve has learned that generation is possible, she says to Adam, 'You may die when I have made a new Adam. Not before. But then, as soon as you like.' The individual does not matter. And therefore when we really get going (shreds of an earlier ethic still cling to most minds) it will not matter what you do to an individual.

Secondly, we have the emergence of 'the Party' in the modern sense—the Fascists, Nazis or Communists. What distinguishes this from the political parties of the nineteenth century is the belief of its members that they are not merely trying to carry out a programme but are obeying an impersonal force: that Nature, or Evolution, or the Dialectic, or the Race, is carrying them on. This tends to be accompanied by two beliefs which cannot, so far as I see, be reconciled in logic but which blend very easily on the emotional level: the belief that the process which the Party embodies is inevitable, and the belief that the forwarding of this process is the supreme duty and abrogates all ordinary moral laws. In this state of mind men can become devil-worshippers in the sense that they can now *honour*, as well as obey, their own vices. All men at times obey their vices: but it is when cruelty, envy, and lust of power appear as the commands of a great super-personal force that they can be exercised with self-approval. The first symptom is in language. When to 'kill' becomes to 'liquidate' the process has begun. The pseudo-scientific word disinfects the thing of blood and tears, or pity and shame, and mercy itself can be regarded as a sort of untidiness.

[Lewis goes on to say: 'It is, at present, in their sense of serving a metaphysical force that the modern "Parties" approximate most closely to religions. Odinism in Germany, or the cult of Lenin's corpse in Russia are probably less important but there is quite a . . . '—and here the manuscript ends. One page (I think no more) is missing. It was probably lost soon after the essay was written, and without Lewis's knowledge, for he had, characteristically, folded the manuscript and scribbled the title 'Anti-Haldane' on one side with a pencil.]

UNREAL ESTATES

This informal conversation between Professor Lewis, Kingsley Amis, and Brian Aldiss was recorded on tape in Professor Lewis's rooms in Magdalene College a short while before illness forced him to retire. When drinks are poured, the discussion begins——

ALDISS: One thing that the three of us have in common is that we have all had stories published in the *Magazine of Fantasy and Science Fiction*, some of them pretty far-flung stories. I take it we would all agree that one of the attractions of science fiction is that it takes us to unknown places.

AMIS: Swift, if he were writing today, would have to take us out to the planets, wouldn't he? Now that most of our *terra incognita* is—real estate.

ALDISS: There is a lot of the eighteenth century equivalent of science fiction which is placed in Australia or similar unreal estates.

LEWIS: Exactly: Peter Wilkins and all that. By the way, is anyone ever going to do a translation of Kepler's *Somnium*?

AMIS: Groff Conklin told me he had read the book; I think it must exist in translation. But may we talk about the worlds you created? You chose the science fiction medium because you wanted to go to strange places? I remember with respectful and amused admiration your account of the space drive in *Out of the Silent Planet*. When Ransom and his friend get into the spaceship he says, 'How does this ship work?' and the man says, 'It operates by using some of the lesser known properties of——' what was it?

86

LEWIS: Solar radiation. Ransom was reporting words without a meaning to him, which is what a layman gets when he asks for a scientific explanation. Obviously it was vague, because I'm no scientist and not interested in the purely technical side of it.

ALDISS: It's almost a quarter of a century since you wrote that first novel of the trilogy.

LEWIS: Have I been a prophet?

ALDISS: You have to a certain extent; at least, the idea of vessels propelled by solar radiation is back in favour again. Cordwiner Smith used it poetically, James Blish tried to use it technically in *The Star Dwellers.*

LEWIS: In my case it was pure mumbo-jumbo, and perhaps meant primarily to convince me.

AMIS: Obviously when one deals with isolated planets or isolated islands one does this for a certain purpose. A setting in contemporary London or a London of the future couldn't provide one with the same isolation and the heightening of consciousness it engenders.

LEWIS: The starting point of the second novel, *Perelandra,* was my mental picture of the floating islands. The whole of the rest of my labours in a sense consisted of building up a world in which floating islands could exist. And then of course the story about an averted fall developed. This is because, as you know, having got your people to this exciting country, something must happen.

AMIS: That frequently taxes people very much.

ALDISS: But I am surprised that you put it this way round. I would have thought that you constructed *Perelandra* for the didactic purpose.

LEWIS: Yes, everyone thinks that. They are quite wrong.

AMIS: If I may say a word on Professor Lewis's side, there was a didactic purpose of course; a lot of very interesting profound things were said, but—correct me if I'm wrong— I'd have thought a simple sense of wonder, extraordinary things going on, were the motive forces behind the creation.

87

LEWIS: Quite, but something has got to happen. The story of this averted fall came in very conveniently. Of course it wouldn't have been that particular story if I wasn't interested in those particular ideas on other grounds. But that isn't what I started from. I've never started from a message or a moral, have you?

AMIS: No, never. You get interested in the situation.

LEWIS: The story itself should force its moral upon you. You find out what the moral is by writing the story.

AMIS: Exactly: I think that sort of thing is true of all kinds of fiction.

ALDISS: But a lot of science fiction has been written from the other point of view: those dreary sociological dramas that appear from time to time, started with a didactic purpose—to make a preconceived point—and they've got no further.

LEWIS: I suppose Gulliver started from a straight point of view? Or did it really start because he wanted to write about a lot of big and little men?

AMIS: Possibly both, as Fielding's parody of Richardson turned into *Joseph Andrews*. A lot of science fiction loses much of the impact it could have by saying, 'Well, here we are on Mars, we all know where we are, and we're living in these pressure domes or whatever it is, and life is really very much like it is on earth, except there is a certain climatic difference. . . .' They accept other men's inventions rather than forge their own.

LEWIS: It's only the first journey to a new planet that is of any interest to imaginative people.

AMIS: In your reading of science fiction have you ever come across a writer who's done this properly?

LEWIS: Well, the one you probably disapprove of because he's so very unscientific is David Lindsay, in *Voyage to Arcturus*. It's a remarkable thing, because scientifically it's nonsense, the style is appalling, and yet this ghastly vision comes through.

ALDISS: It didn't come through to me.

AMIS: Nor me. Still . . . Victor Gollancz told me a very interesting remark of Lindsay's about *Arcturus*; he said, 'I shall never appeal to a large public at all, but I think that as long as our civilization lasts one person a year will read me.' I respect that attitude.

LEWIS: Quite so. Modest and becoming. I also agree with something you said in a preface, I believe it was, that some science fiction really does deal with issues far more serious than those realistic fiction deals with; real problems about human destiny and so on. Do you remember that story about the man who meets a female monster landed from another planet with all its cubs hanging round it? It's obviously starving, and he offers them thing after thing to eat; they immediately vomit it up, until one of the young fastens on him, begins sucking his blood, and immediately begins to revive. This female creature is utterly unhuman, horrible in form; there's a long moment when it looks at the man—they're in a lonely place—and then very sadly it packs up its young, and goes back into its spaceship and goes away. Well now, you could not have a more serious theme than that. What is a footling story about some pair of human lovers compared with that?

AMIS: On the debit side, you often have these marvellous large themes tackled by people who haven't got the mental or moral or stylistic equipment to take them on. A reading of more recent science fiction shows that writers are getting more capable of tackling them. Have you read Walter Miller's *Canticle for Leibowitz*? Have you any comments on that?

LEWIS: I thought it was pretty good. I only read it once; mind you, a book's no good to me until I've read it two or three times—I'm going to read it again. It was a major work, certainly.

AMIS: What did you think about its religious feeling?

LEWIS: It came across very well. There were bits of the actual writing which one could quarrel with, but on the whole it was well imagined and well executed.

AMIS: Have you seen James Blish's novel *A Case of Conscience*? Would you agree that to write a religious novel that isn't concerned with details of ecclesiastical practice and the numbing minutiae of history and so on, science fiction would be the natural outlet for this?

LEWIS: If you have a religion it must be cosmic; therefore it seems to me odd that this *genre* was so late in arriving.

ALDISS: It's been around without attracting critical attention for a long time; the magazines themselves have been going since 1926, although in the beginning they appealed mainly to the technical side. As Amis says, people have come along who can write, as well as think up engineering ideas.

LEWIS: We ought to have said earlier that that's quite a different species of science fiction, about which I say nothing at all; those who were really interested in the technical side of it. It's obviously perfectly legitimate if it's well done.

AMIS: The purely technical and the purely imaginative overlap, don't they?

ALDISS: There are certainly the two streams, and they often overlap, for instance in Arthur Clarke's writings. It can be a rich mixture. Then there's the type of story that's not theological, but it makes a moral point. An example is the Sheckley story about Earth being blasted by radioactivity. The survivors of the human race have gone away to another planet for about a thousand years; they come back to reclaim Earth and find it full of all sorts of gaudy armour-plated creatures, vegetation, etc. One of the party says, 'We'll clear this lot out, make it habitable for man again.' But in the end the decision is, 'Well, we made a mess of the place when it was ours, let's get out and leave it to them.' This story was written about '49, when most people hadn't started thinking round the subject at all.

LEWIS: Yes, most of the earlier stories start from the op-

posite assumption that we, the human race, are in the
right, and everything else is ogres. I may have done a little
towards altering that, but the new point of view has come
very much in. We've lost our confidence, so to speak.

AMIS: It's all terribly self-critical and self-contemplatory
nowadays.

LEWIS: This is surely an enormous gain—a human gain, that
people should be thinking that way.

AMIS: The prejudice of supposedly educated persons towards this type of fiction is fantastic. If you pick up a
science fiction magazine, particularly *Fantasy and Science
Fiction*, the range of interests appealed to and I.Q.s employed, is pretty amazing. It's time more people caught on.
We've been telling them about it for some while.

LEWIS: Quite true. The world of serious fiction is very
narrow.

AMIS: Too narrow if you want to deal with a broad theme.
For instance, Philip Wylie in *The Disappearance* wants to
deal with the difference between men and women in a
general way, in twentieth century society, unencumbered
by local and temporary considerations; his point, as I
understand it, is that men and women, shorn of their social
roles, are really very much the same. Science fiction, which
can presuppose a major change in our environment, is the
natural medium for discussing a subject of that kind. Look
at the job of dissecting human nastiness carried out in
Golding's *Lord of the Flies*.

LEWIS: That can't be science fiction.

AMIS: I would dissent from that. It starts off with a characteristic bit of science fiction situation: that World War
III has begun, bombs dropped and all that. . . .

LEWIS: Ah, well, you're now taking the German view that
any romance about the future is science fiction. I'm not
sure that this is a useful classification.

AMIS: 'Science fiction' is such a hopelessly vague label.

LEWIS: And of course a great deal of it isn't *science* fiction.

Really it's only a negative criterion: anything which is not naturalistic, which is not about what we call the real world.

ALDISS: I think we oughtn't to try to define it, because it's a self-defining thing in a way. We know where we are. You're right, though, about *Lord of the Flies*. The atmosphere is a science fiction atmosphere.

LEWIS: It was a very terrestrial island; the best island, almost, in fiction. Its actual sensuous effect on you is terrific.

ALDISS: Indeed. But it's a laboratory case——

AMIS: —isolating certain human characteristics, to see how they would work out——

LEWIS: The only trouble is that Golding writes so well. In one of his other novels, *The Inheritors*, the detail of every sensuous impression, the light on the leaves and so on, was so good that you couldn't find out what was happening. I'd say it was almost too well done. All these little details you only notice in real life if you've got a high temperature. You couldn't see the wood for the leaves.

ALDISS: You had this in *Pincher Martin*; every feeling in the rocks, when he's washed ashore, is done with a hallucinatory vividness.

AMIS: It is, that's exactly the phrase. I think thirty years ago if you wanted to discuss a general theme you would go to the historical novel; now you would go to what I might describe in a prejudiced way as science fiction. In science fiction you can isolate the factors you want to examine. If you wanted to deal with the theme of colonialism, for instance, as Poul Anderson has done, you don't do it by writing a novel about Ghana or Pakistan——

LEWIS: Which involves you in such a mass of detail that you don't want to go into——

AMIS: You set up worlds in space which incorporate the characteristics you need.

LEWIS: Would you describe Abbott's *Flatland* as science fiction? There's so little effort to bring it into any sensuous—

well, you couldn't do it, and it remains an intellectual theorem. Are you looking for an ashtray? Use the carpet.

AMIS: I was looking for the Scotch, actually.

LEWIS: Oh, yes, do, I beg your pardon. . . . But probably the great work in science fiction is still to come. Futile books about the next world came before Dante, Fanny Burney came before Jane Austen, Marlowe came before Shakespeare.

AMIS: We're getting the prolegomena.

LEWIS: If only the modern highbrow critics could be induced to take it seriously . . .

AMIS: Do you think they ever can?

LEWIS: No, the whole present dynasty has got to die and rot before anything can be done at all.

ALDISS: Splendid!

AMIS: What's holding them up, do you think?

LEWIS: Matthew Arnold made the horrible prophecy that literature would increasingly replace religion. It has, and it's taken on all the features of bitter persecution, great intolerance, and traffic in relics. All literature becomes a sacred text. A sacred text is always exposed to the most monstrous exegesis; hence we have the spectacle of some wretched scholar taking a pure *divertissement* written in the seventeenth century and getting the most profound ambiguities and social criticisms out of it, which of course aren't there at all. . . . It's the discovery of the mare's nest by the pursuit of the red herring. (Laughter.) This is going to go on long after my lifetime; you may be able to see the end of it, I shan't.

AMIS: You think this is so integral a part of the Establishment that people can't overcome——

LEWIS: It's an industry, you see. What would all the people be writing *D. Phil.* theses on if this prop were removed?

AMIS: An instance of this mentality the other day: somebody referred to 'Mr Amis's I suspect rather affected enthusiasm for science fiction. . . .'

LEWIS: Isn't that maddening!

AMIS: You can't really like it.

LEWIS: You must be pretending to be a plain man or something. . . . I've met the attitude again and again. You've probably reached the stage too of having theses written on yourself. I received a letter from an American examiner asking, 'Is it true that you meant this and this and this?' A writer of a thesis was attributing to me views which I have explicitly contradicted in the plainest possible English. They'd be much wiser to write about the dead, who can't answer.

ALDISS: In America, I think science fiction is accepted on a more responsible level.

AMIS: I'm not so sure about that, you know, Brian, because when our anthology *Spectrum I* came out in the States we had less friendly and less understanding treatment from reviewers than we did over here.

LEWIS: I'm surprised at that, because in general all American reviewing is more friendly and generous than in England.

AMIS: People were patting themselves on the back in the States for not understanding what we meant.

LEWIS: This extraordinary pride in being exempt from temptations that you have not yet risen to the level of! Eunuchs boasting of their chastity! (Laughter).

AMIS: One of my pet theories is that serious writers as yet unborn or still at school will soon regard science fiction as a natural way of writing.

LEWIS: By the way, has any science fiction writer yet succeeded in inventing a third sex? Apart from the third sex we all know.

AMIS: Clifford Simak invented a set-up where there were seven sexes.

LEWIS: How rare happy marriages must have been then!

ALDISS: Rather worth striving for perhaps.

LEWIS: Obviously when achieved they'd be wonderful. (Laughter.)

ALDISS: I find I would much rather write science fiction than anything else. The dead weight is so much less there than in the field of the ordinary novel. There's a sense in which you're conquering a fresh country.

AMIS: Speaking as a supposedly realistic novelist, I've written little bits of science fiction and this is such a tremendous liberation.

LEWIS: Well, you're a very ill-used man; you wrote a farce and everyone thought it a damning indictment of Redbrick. I've always had great sympathy for you. They will not understand that a joke is a joke. Everything must be serious.

AMIS: 'A fever chart of society.'

LEWIS: One thing in science fiction that weighs against us very heavily is the horrible shadow of the comics.

ALDISS: I don't know about that. Titbits Romantic Library doesn't really weigh against the serious writer.

LEWIS: That's a fair analogy. All the novelettes didn't kill the ordinary legitimate novel of courtship and love.

ALDISS: There might have been a time when science fiction and comics were weighed together and found wanting, but that at least we've got past.

AMIS: I see the comic books that my sons read, and you have there a terribly vulgar reworking of the themes that science fiction goes in for.

LEWIS: Quite harmless, mind you. This chatter about the moral danger of the comics is absolute nonsense. The real objection is against the appalling draughtsmanship. Yet you'll find the same boy who reads them also reads Shakespeare or Spenser. Children are so terribly catholic. That's my experience with my stepchildren.

ALDISS: This is an English habit, to categorize: that if you read Shakespeare you can't read comics, that if you read science fiction you can't be serious.

AMIS: That's the thing that annoys me.

LEWIS: Oughtn't the word 'serious' to have an embargo slapped on it? 'Serious' ought to mean simply the opposite of comic, whereas now it means 'good' or 'Literature' with a capital L.

ALDISS: You can be serious without being earnest.

LEWIS: Leavis demands moral earnestness; I prefer morality.

AMIS: I'm with you every time on that one.

LEWIS: I mean I'd sooner live among people who don't cheat at cards than among people who are earnest about not cheating at cards. (Laughter.)

AMIS: More Scotch?

LEWIS: Not for me, thank you, help yourself. (Liquid noises.)

AMIS: I think all this ought to stay in, you know—all these remarks about drink.

LEWIS: There's no reason why we shouldn't have a drink. Look, you want to borrow Abbott's *Flatland*, don't you? I must go to dinner I'm afraid. (Hands over *Flatland*.) The original manuscript of the *Iliad* could not be more precious. It's only the ungodly who borroweth and payeth not again.

AMIS (reading): By A. Square.

LEWIS: But of course the word 'square' hadn't the same sense then.

ALDISS: It's like the poem by Francis Thompson that ends 'She gave me tokens three, a look, a word of her winsome mouth, and a sweet wild raspberry'; there again the meaning has changed. It really was a wild raspberry in Thompson's day. (Laughter.)

LEWIS: Or the lovely one about the Bishop of Exeter, who was giving the prizes at a girls' school. They did a performance of *A Midsummer Night's Dream*, and the poor man stood up afterwards and made a speech and said (piping voice): 'I was very interested in your delightful performance, and among other things I was very interested in seeing for the first time in my life a female Bottom.' (Guffaws.)

Part II
STORIES

THE SHODDY LANDS

Being, as I believe, of sound mind and in normal health, I am sitting down at 11 p.m. to record, while the memory of it is still fresh, the curious experience I had this morning.

It happened in my rooms in college, where I am now writing, and began in the most ordinary way with a call on the telephone. 'This is Durward,' the voice said. 'I'm speaking from the porter's lodge. I'm in Oxford for a few hours. Can I come across and see you?' I said yes, of course. Durward is a former pupil and a decent enough fellow; I would be glad to see him again. When he turned up at my door a few moments later I was rather annoyed to find that he had a young woman in tow. I loathe either men or women who speak as if they were coming to see you alone and then spring a husband or a wife, a fiancé or a fiancée on you. One ought to be warned.

The girl was neither very pretty nor very plain, and of course she ruined my conversation. We couldn't talk about any of the things Durward and I had in common because that would have meant leaving her out in the cold. And she and Durward couldn't talk about the things they (presumably) had in common because that would have left me out. He introduced her as Peggy and said they were engaged. After that, the three of us just sat and did social patter about the weather and the news.

I tend to stare when I am bored, and I am afraid I must have stared at that girl, without the least interest, a good deal. At any rate I was certainly doing so at the moment when the strange experience began. Quite suddenly, without any faintness or nausea or anything of that sort, I found myself in a wholly different place. The familiar room vanished; Durward and Peggy vanished. I was alone. And I was standing up.

My first idea was that something had gone wrong with my eyes. I was not in darkness, nor even in twilight, but everything seemed curiously blurred. There was a sort of daylight, but when I looked up I didn't see anything that I could very confidently call a sky. It might, just possibly, be the sky of a very featureless, dull, grey day, but it lacked any suggestion of distance. 'Nondescript' was the word I would have used to describe it. Lower down and closer to me, there were upright shapes, vaguely green in colour, but of a very dingy green. I peered at them for quite a long time before it occurred to me that they might be trees. I went nearer and examined them; and the impression they made on me is not easy to put into words. 'Trees of a sort,' or, 'Well, trees, if you call *that* a tree,' or, 'An attempt at trees,' would come near it. They were the crudest, shabbiest apology for trees you could imagine. They had no real anatomy, even no real branches; they were more like lamp-posts with great, shapeless blobs of green stuck on top of them. Most children could draw better trees from memory.

It was while I was inspecting them that I first noticed the light: a steady, silvery gleam some distance away in the Shoddy Wood. I turned my steps towards it at once, and then first noticed what I was walking on. It was comfortable stuff, soft and cool and springy to the feet; but when you looked down it was horribly disappointing to the eye. It was, in a very rough way, the colour of grass; the colour grass has on a very dull day when you look at it while thinking pretty hard about something else. But there were no separate blades in it. I stooped down and tried to find them; the closer one looked, the vaguer it seemed to become. It had in fact just the same smudged, unfinished quality as the trees: shoddy.

The full astonishment of my adventure was now beginning to descend on me. With it came fear, but, even more, a sort of disgust. I doubt if it can be fully conveyed to anyone who has not had a similar experience. I felt as if I had suddenly been banished from the real, bright, concrete, and prodigally complex world into some sort of second-rate universe that had all been put together on the cheap; by an imitator. But I kept on walking towards the silvery light.

Here and there in the shoddy grass there were patches of what looked, from a distance, like flowers. But each patch, when you came close to it, was as bad as the trees and the grass. You couldn't make out what species they were supposed to be. And they had no real stems or petals; they were mere blobs. As for the colours, I could do better myself with a shilling paintbox.

I should have liked very much to believe that I was dreaming, but somehow I knew I wasn't. My real conviction was that I had died. I wished—with a fervour that no other wish of mine has ever achieved—that I had lived a better life.

A disquieting hypothesis, as you see, was forming in my mind. But next moment it was gloriously blown to bits. Amidst all that shoddiness I came suddenly upon daffodils. Real daffodils, trim and cool and perfect. I bent down and touched them; I straightened my back again and gorged my eyes on their beauty. And not only their beauty but—what mattered to me even more at that moment—their, so to speak, honesty; real, honest, finished daffodils, live things that would bear examination.

But where, then, could I be? 'Let's get on to that light. Perhaps everything will be made clear there. Perhaps it is at the centre of this queer place.'

I reached the light sooner than I expected, but when I reached it I had something else to think about. For now I met the Walking Things. I have to call them that, for 'people' is just what they weren't. They were of human size and they walked on two legs; but they were, for the most part, no more like true men than the Shoddy Trees had been like trees. They were indistinct. Though they were certainly not naked, you couldn't make out what sort of clothes they were wearing, and though there was a pale blob at the top of each, you couldn't say they had faces. At least that was my first impression. Then I began to notice curious exceptions. Every now and then one of them became partially distinct; a face, a hat, or a dress would stand out in full detail. The odd thing was that the distinct clothes were always women's clothes, but the distinct faces were always those of men. Both facts made the crowd—at least, to a man of my type—about as uninteresting as it could possibly be. The male faces were not the sort I cared about; a flashy-looking crew—gigolos, fripoons. But they seemed pleased enough with themselves. Indeed they all wore the same look of fatuous admiration.

I now saw where the light was coming from. I was in a sort of street. At least, behind the crowd of Walking Things on each side, there appeared to be shop-windows, and from these the light came. I thrust my way through the crowd on my left—but my thrusting seemed to yield no physical contacts—and had a look at one of the shops.

Here I had a new surprise. It was a jeweller's, and after the vagueness and general rottenness of most things in that queer place, the sight fairly took my breath away. Everything in that window was perfect; every facet on every diamond distinct, every brooch and tiara finished down to the last perfection of intricate detail. It was good stuff too, as even I could see; there must have been hundreds of thousands of pounds' worth of it. 'Thank Heaven!' I gasped. 'But will it keep on?' Hastily I looked at the next shop. It *was* keeping on. This window contained women's frocks. I'm no judge, so I can't say how good they were. The great thing was that they were real, clear, palpable. The shop beyond this one sold women's shoes. And it was still keeping on. They were real shoes; the toe-pinching and very high-heeled sort which, to my mind, ruins even the prettiest foot, but at any rate real.

I was just thinking to myself that some people would not find this place half as dull as I did, when the queerness of the whole thing came over me afresh. 'Where the Hell,' I began, but immediately changed it to 'Where on earth'—for the other word seemed, in all the circumstances, singularly unfortunate—'Where on earth have I got to? Trees no good; grass no good; sky no good; flowers no good, except the daffodils; people no good; shops, first class. What can that possibly mean?'

The Shoddy Lands

The shops, by the way, were all women's shops, so I soon lost interest in them. I walked the whole length of that street, and then, a little way ahead, I saw sunlight.

Not that it was proper sunlight, of course. There was no break in the dull sky to account for it, no beam slanting down. All that, like so many other things in that world, had not been attended to. There was simply a patch of sunlight on the ground, unexplained, impossible (except that it was there), and therefore not at all cheering; hideous, rather, and disquieting. But I had little time to think about it; for something in the centre of that lighted patch—something I had taken for a small building—suddenly moved, and with a sickening shock I realized that I was looking at a gigantic human shape. It turned round. Its eyes looked straight into mine.

It was not only gigantic, but it was the only complete human shape I had seen since I entered that world. It was female. It was lying on sunlit sand, on a beach apparently, though there was no trace of any sea. It was very nearly naked, but it had a wisp of some brightly coloured stuff round its hips and another round its breasts; like what a modern girl wears on a real beach. The general effect was repulsive, but I saw in a moment or two that this was due to the appalling size. Considered abstractly, the giantess had a good figure; almost a perfect figure, if you like the modern type. The face—but as soon as I had really taken in the face, I shouted out.

'Oh, I say! There you are. Where's Durward? And where's this? What's happened to us?'

But the eyes went on looking straight at me and through me. I was obviously invisible and inaudible to her. But there was no doubt who she was. She was Peggy. That is, she was recognizable; but she was Peggy changed. I don't mean only the size. As regards the figure, it was Peggy improved. I don't think anyone could have denied that. As to the face, opinions might differ. I would hardly have called the change an improvement myself. There was no more—I doubt if there was as much—sense or kindness or honesty in this face than in the original Peggy's. But it was certainly more regular. The teeth in particular, which I had noticed as a weak point in the old Peggy, were perfect, as in a good denture. The lips were fuller. The complexion was so perfect that it suggested a very expensive doll. The expression I can best describe by saying that Peggy now looked exactly like the girl in all the advertisements.

If I had to marry either I should prefer the old, unimproved Peggy. But even in Hell I hoped it wouldn't come to that.

And, as I watched, the background—the absurd little bit of sea-beach—began to change. The giantess stood up. She was on a carpet. Walls and windows and furniture grew up around her. She was in a bedroom. Even I could tell it was a very expensive bedroom though not at all my idea of good taste. There were plenty of flowers, mostly orchids and roses, and these were even better finished than the daffodils had been. One great bouquet (with a card attached to it) was as good as any I have ever seen. A door which stood open behind her gave me a view into a bathroom which I should rather like to own, a bathroom with a sunk bath. In it there was a French maid fussing about with towels and bath salts and things. The maid was not nearly so finished as the roses, or even the towels, but what face she had looked more French than any real Frenchwoman's could.

The gigantic Peggy now removed her beach equipment and stood up naked in front of a full-length mirror. Apparently she enjoyed what she saw there; I can hardly express how much I didn't. Partly the size (it's only fair to remember that) but, still more, something that came as a terrible shock to me, though I suppose modern lovers and husbands must be hardened to it. Her body was (of course) brown, like the bodies in the sun-bathing advertisements. But round her hips, and again round her breasts, where the coverings had been, there were two bands of dead white which looked, by contrast, like leprosy. It made me for the moment almost physically sick. What staggered me was that she could stand and admire it. Had she no idea how it would affect ordinary male eyes? A very disagreeable conviction grew in me that this was a subject of no interest to her; that all her clothes and bath salts and two-piece swimsuits, and indeed the voluptuousness of her every look and gesture, had not, and never had had, the meaning which every man would read, and was intended to read, into them. They were a huge overture to an opera in which she had no interest at all; a coronation procession with no Queen at the centre of it; gestures, gestures about nothing.

And now I became aware that two noises had been going for a long time; the only noises I ever heard in that world. But they were coming from outside, from somewhere beyond that low, grey covering which served the Shoddy Lands instead of a sky. Both the noises were knockings; patient knockings, infinitely remote, as if two outsiders, two excluded people, were knocking on the walls of that world. The one was faint, but hard; and with it came a voice saying, 'Peggy, Peggy, let me in.' Durward's voice, I thought. But how shall I describe the other knocking? It was, in some curious way, soft; 'soft as wool and sharp as death,' soft but unendurably heavy, as if at each blow some enormous hand fell on the outside of the Shoddy Sky and covered it completely. And with that knocking came a voice at whose sound my bones turned to water: 'Child, child, child, let me in before the night comes.'

Before the night comes—instantly common daylight rushed back upon me. I was in my own rooms again and my two visitors were before me. They did not appear to notice that anything unusual had happened to me, though, for the rest of that conversation, they might well have supposed I was drunk. I was so happy. Indeed, in a way I was drunk; drunk with the sheer delight of being back in the real world, free, outside the horrible little prison of that land. There were birds singing close to a window; there was real sunlight falling on a panel. That panel needed repainting; but I could have gone down on my knees and kissed its very shabbiness—the precious real, solid thing it was. I noticed a tiny cut on Durward's cheek where he must have cut himself shaving that morning; and I felt the same about it.

Indeed anything was enough to make me happy; I mean, any Thing, as long as it really was a Thing.

Well, those are the facts; everyone may make what he pleases of them. My own hypothesis is the obvious one which will have occurred to most readers. It may be too obvious; I am quite ready to consider rival theories. My view is that by the operation of some unknown psychological—or pathological—law, I was, for a second or so, let into Peggy's mind; at least to the extent of seeing her world, the world as it exists for her. At the centre of that world is a swollen image of herself, remodelled to be as like the girls in the advertisements as possible. Round this are grouped clear and distinct images of the things she really cares about. Beyond that, the whole earth and sky are a vague blur. The daffodils and roses are especially instructive. Flowers only exist for her if they are the sort that can be cut and put in vases or sent as bouquets; flowers in themselves, flowers as you see them in the woods, are negligible.

As I say, this is probably not the only hypothesis which will fit the facts. But it has been a most disquieting experience. Not only because I am sorry for poor Durward. Suppose this sort of thing were to become common? And how if, some other time, I were not the explorer but the explored?

MINISTERING ANGELS

The Monk, as they called him, settled himself on the camp chair beside his bunk and stared through the window at the harsh sand and black-blue sky of Mars. He did not mean to begin his 'work' for ten minutes yet. Not, of course, the work he had been brought there to do. He was the meteorologist of the party, and his work in that capacity was largely done; he had found out whatever could be found out. There was nothing more, within the limited radius he could investigate, to be observed for at least twenty-five days. And meteorology had not been his real motive. He had chosen three years on Mars as the nearest modern equivalent to a hermitage in the desert. He had come there to meditate: to continue the slow, perpetual rebuilding of that inner structure which, in his view, it was the main purpose of life to rebuild. And now his ten minutes' rest was over. He began with his well-used formula. 'Gentle and patient Master, teach me to need men less and to love thee more.' Then to it. There was no time to waste. There were barely six months of this lifeless, sinless, unsuffering wilderness ahead of him. Three years were short . . . but when the shout came he rose out of his chair with the practised alertness of a sailor.

The Botanist in the next cabin responded to the same shout with a curse. His eye had been at the microscope when it came. It was maddening. Constant interruption. A man might as well try to work in the middle of Piccadilly as in this infernal camp. And his work was already a race against time. Six months more . . . and he had hardly begun. The flora of Mars, these tiny, miraculously hardy organisms, the ingenuity of their contrivances to live under all but impossible conditions—it was a feast for a lifetime. He would ignore the shout. But then came the bell. All hands to the main room.

Of Other Worlds

The only person who was doing, so to speak, nothing when the shout came was the Captain. To be more exact, he was (as usual) trying to stop thinking about Clare, and get on with his official journal. Clare kept on interrupting from forty million miles away. It was preposterous. *'Would have needed all hands,'* he wrote ... hands ... his own hands ... his own hands, hands, he felt, with eyes in them, travelling over all the warm-cool, soft-firm, smooth, yielding, resisting aliveness of her. 'Shut up, there's a dear,' he said to the photo on his desk. And so back to the journal, until the fatal words *'had been causing me some anxiety'*. Anxiety—oh God, what might be happening to Clare now? How did he know there was a Clare by this time? Anything could happen. He'd been a fool ever to accept this job. What other newly married man in the world would have done it? But it had seemed so sensible. Three years of horrid separation but then ... oh, they were made for life. He had been promised the post that, only a few months before, he would not have dared to dream of. He'd never need to go to Space again. And all the by-products; the lectures, the book, probably a title. Plenty of children. He knew she wanted that, and so in a queer way (as he began to find) did he. But damn it, the journal. Begin a new paragraph ... And then the shout came.

It was one of the two youngsters, technicians both, who had given it. They had been together since dinner. At least Paterson had been standing at the open door of Dickson's cabin, shifting from foot to foot and swinging the door, and Dickson had been sitting on his berth and waiting for Paterson to go away.

'What are you talking about, Paterson?' he said. 'Who ever said anything about a quarrel?'

'That's all very well, Bobby,' said the other, 'but we're not friends like we used to be. You know we're not. Oh, *I'm* not blind. I *did* ask you to call me Clifford. And you're always so stand-offish.'

'Oh, get to Hell out of this!' cried Dickson. 'I'm perfectly ready to be good friends with you and everyone else in an ordinary way, but all this gas—like a pair of school girls—I will not stand. Once and for all——'

'Oh look, look, look,' said Paterson. And it was then that Dickson shouted and the Captain came and rang the bell and within twenty seconds they were all crowded behind the biggest of the windows. A spaceship had just made a beautiful landing about a hundred and fifty yards from camp.

'Oh boy!' exclaimed Dickson. 'They're relieving us before our time.'

'Damn their eyes. Just what they would do,' said the Botanist.

Five figures were descending from the ship. Even in space suits it was clear that one of them was enormously fat; they were in no other way remarkable.

'Man the air lock,' said the Captain.

Drinks from their limited store were going round. The Captain had recognized in the leader of the strangers an old acquaintance, Ferguson. Two were ordinary young men, not unpleasant. But the remaining two?

'I don't understand,' said the Captain, 'who exactly—I mean we're delighted to see you all of course—but what exactly . . .?'

'Where are the rest of your party?' said Ferguson.

'We've had two casualties, I'm afraid,' said the Captain. 'Sackville and Dr Burton. It was a most wretched business. Sackville tried eating the stuff we call Martian cress. It drove him fighting mad in a matter of minutes. He knocked Burton down and by sheer bad luck Burton fell in just the wrong position: across that table there. Broke his neck. We got Sackville tied down on a bunk but he was dead before the evening.'

'Hadna he even the gumption to try it on the guinea pig first?' said Ferguson.

'Yes,' said the Botanist. 'That was the whole trouble. The funny thing is that the guinea pig lived. But its behaviour was remarkable. Sackville wrongly concluded that the stuff was alcoholic. Thought he'd invent a new drink. The nuisance is that once Burton was dead, none of us could do a reliable post-mortem on Sackville. Under analysis this vegetable shows——'

'A-a-a-h,' interrupted one of those who had not yet spoken. 'We must beware of oversimplifications. I doubt if the vegetable substance is the real explanation. There are stresses and strains. You are all, without knowing it, in a highly unstable condition, for reasons which are no mystery to a trained psychologist.'

Some of those present had doubted the sex of this creature. Its hair was very short, its nose very long, its mouth very prim, its chin sharp, and its manner authoritative. The voice revealed it as, scientifically speaking, a woman. But no one had had any doubt about the sex of her nearest neighbour, the fat person.

'Oh, dearie,' she wheezed. 'Not now. I tell you straight I'm that flustered and faint, I'll scream if you go on so. Suppose there ain't such a thing as a port and lemon handy? No? Well, a little drop more gin would settle me. It's me stomach reelly.'

The speaker was infinitely female and perhaps in her seventies. Her hair had been not very successfully dyed to a colour not unlike that of mustard. The powder (scented strongly enough to throw a train off the rails) lay like snow drifts in the complex valleys of her creased, many-chinned face.

'Stop,' roared Ferguson. 'Whatever ye do, dinna give her a drap mair to drink.'

' 'E's no 'art, ye see,' said the old woman with a whimper and an affectionate leer directed at Dickson.

'Excuse me,' said the Captain. 'Who are these—ah—ladies and what is this all about?'

'I have been waiting to explain,' said the Thin Woman, and cleared her throat. 'Anyone who has been following World-Opinion-Trends on the problems arising out of the psychological welfare aspect of interplanetary communication will be conscious of the growing agreement that such a remarkable advance inevitably demands of us far-reaching ideological adjustments. Psychologists are now well aware that a forcible inhibition of powerful biological urges over a protracted period is likely to have unforeseeable results. The pioneers of space travel are exposed to this danger. It would be unenlightened if a supposed ethicality were allowed to stand in the way of their protection. We must therefore nerve ourselves to face the view that immorality, as it has hitherto been called, must no longer be regarded as unethical——'

'I don't understand that,' said the Monk.

'She means,' said the Captain, who was a good linguist, 'that what you call fornication must no longer be regarded as immoral.'

'That's right, dearie,' said the Fat Woman to Dickson, 'she only means a poor boy needs a woman now and then. It's only natural.'

'What was required, therefore,' continued the Thin Woman, 'was a band of devoted females who would take the first step. This would expose them, no doubt, to obloquy from many ignorant persons. They would be sustained by the consciousness that they were performing an indispensable function in the history of human progress.'

'She means you're to have tarts, duckie,' said the Fat Woman to Dickson.

'Now you're talking,' said he with enthusiasm. 'Bit late in the day, but better late than never. But you can't have brought many girls in that ship. And why didn't you bring them in? Or are they following?'

'We cannot indeed claim,' continued the Thin Woman, who had apparently not noticed the interruption, 'that the response to our appeal was such as we had hoped. The personnel of the first unit of the Woman's Higher Aphrodiso-Therapeutic Humane Organisation (abbreviated WHAT-HO) is not perhaps . . . well. Many excellent women, university colleagues of my own, even senior colleagues, to whom I applied, showed themselves curiously conventional. But at least a start has been made. And here,' she concluded brightly, 'we are.'

And there, for forty seconds of appalling silence, they were. Then Dickson's face, which had already undergone certain contortions, became very red; he applied his handkerchief and spluttered like a man trying to stifle a sneeze, rose abruptly, turned his back on the company, and hid his face. He stood slightly stooped and you could see his shoulders shaking.

Paterson jumped up and ran towards him; but the Fat Woman, though with infinite gruntings and upheavals, had risen too.

'Get art of it, Pansy,' she snarled at Paterson. 'Lot o' good your sort ever did.' A moment later her vast arms were round Dickson; all the warm, wobbling maternalism of her engulfed him.

'There, sonny,' she said, 'it's goin' to be O.K. Don't cry, honey. Don't cry. Poor boy, then. Poor boy. I'll give you a good time.'

'I think,' said the Captain, 'the young man is laughing, not crying.'

It was the Monk who at this point mildly suggested a meal.

Some hours later the party had temporarily broken up.

Dickson (despite all his efforts the Fat Woman had contrived to sit next to him; she had more than once mistaken his glass for hers) hardly finished his last mouthful when he said to the newly arrived technicians:

'I'd love to see over your ship, if I could.'

You might expect that two men who had been cooped up in that ship so long, and had only taken off their space suits a few minutes ago, would have been reluctant to re-assume the one and return to the other. That was certainly the Fat Woman's view. 'Nar, nar,' she said. 'Don't you go fidgeting, sonny. They seen enough of that ruddy ship for a bit, same as me. 'Tain't good for you to go rushing about, not on a full stomach, like.' But the two young men were marvellously obliging.

'Certainly. Just what I was going to suggest,' said the first. 'O.K. by me, chum,' said the second. They were all three of them out of the air lock in record time.

Across the sand, up the ladder, helmets off, and then:

'What in the name of thunder have you dumped those two bitches on us for?' said Dickson.

'Don't fancy 'em?' said the Cockney stranger. 'The people at 'ome thought as 'ow you'd be a bit sharp set by now. Ungrateful of you, I call it.'

'Very funny to be sure,' said Dickson. 'But it's no laughing matter for us.'

'It hasn't been for us either, you know,' said the Oxford stranger. 'Cheek by jowl with them for eighty-five days. They palled a bit after the first month.'

'You're telling me,' said the Cockney.

There was a disgusted pause.

'Can anyone tell me,' said Dickson at last, 'who in the world, and why in the world, out of all possible women, selected those two horrors to send to Mars?'

'Can't expect a star London show at the back of beyond,' said the Cockney.

'My dear fellow,' said his colleague, 'isn't the thing perfectly obvious? What kind of woman, without force, is going to come and live in this ghastly place—on rations—and play doxy to half a dozen men she's never seen? The Good Time Girls won't come because they know you can't have a good time on Mars. An ordinary professional prostitute won't come as long as she has the slightest chance of being picked up in the cheapest quarter of Liverpool or Los Angeles. And you've got one who hasn't. The only other who'd come would be a crank who believes all that blah about the new ethicality. And you've got one of that too.'

'Simple, ain't it?' said the Cockney.

'Anyone,' said the other, 'except the Fools at the Top could of course have foreseen it from the word go.'

'The only hope now is the Captain,' said Dickson.

'Look, mate,' said the Cockney, 'if you think there's any question of our taking back returned goods, you've 'ad it. Nothing doin'. Our Captain'll 'ave a mutiny to settle if he tries that. Also 'e won't. 'E's 'ad 'is turn. So've we. It's up to you now.'

'Fair's fair, you know,' said the other. 'We've stood all we can.'

'Well,' said Dickson. 'We must leave the two chiefs to fight it out. But discipline or not, there are some things a man can't stand. That bloody schoolmarm——'

'She's a lecturer at a Redbrick university, actually.'

'Well,' said Dickson after a long pause, 'you were going to show me over the ship. It might take my mind off it a bit.'

The Fat Woman was talking to the Monk. '. . . and oh, Father dear, I know you'll think that's the worst of all. I didn't give it up when I could. After me brother's wife died . . . 'e'd 'av 'ad me 'ome with 'im, and money wasn't that short. But I went on, Gawd 'elp me, I went on.'

'Why did you do that, daughter?' said the Monk. 'Did you *like* it?'

'Well not all that, Father. I was never partikler. But you see—oh, Father, I was the goods in those days, though you wouldn't think it now . . . and the poor gentlemen, they did so enjoy it.'

'Daughter,' he said, 'you are not far from the Kingdom. But you were wrong. The desire to give is blessed. But you can't turn bad bank notes into good ones just by giving them away.'

The Captain had also left the table pretty quickly, asking Ferguson to accompany him to his cabin. The Botanist had leaped after them.

'One moment, sir, one moment,' he said excitedly. 'I am a scientist. I'm working at very high pressure already. I hope there is no complaint to be made about my discharge of all those other duties which so incessantly interrupt my work. But if I am going to be expected to waste any more time entertaining those abominable females——'

'When I give you any orders which can be considered *ultra vires*,' said the Captain, 'it will be time to make your protest.'

Paterson stayed with the Thin Woman. The only part of any woman that interested him was her ears. He liked telling women about his troubles; especially about the unfairness and unkindness of other men. Unfortunately the lady's idea was that the interview should be devoted either to Aphrodisio-Therapy or to instruction in psychology. She saw, indeed, no reason why the two operations should not be carried out simultaneously; it is only untrained minds that cannot hold more than one idea. The difference between these two conceptions of the conversation was well on its way to impairing its success. Paterson was becoming ill-tempered; the lady remained bright and patient as an iceberg.

'But as I was saying,' grumbled Paterson, 'what I do think so rotten is a fellow being quite fairly decent one day and then——'

'Which just illustrates my point. These tensions and maladjustments are bound, under the unnatural conditions, to arise. And provided we disinfect the obvious remedy of all those sentimental or—which is quite as bad—prurient associations which the Victorian Age attached to it——'

'But I haven't yet told you. Listen. Only two days ago——'

'One moment. This ought to be regarded like any other injection. If once we can persuade——'

'How any fellow can take a pleasure——'

'I agree. The association of it with pleasure (that is purely an adolescent fixation) may have done incalculable harm. Rationally viewed——'

'I say, you're getting off the point.'

'One moment——'

The dialogue continued.

They had finished looking over the spaceship. It was certainly a beauty. No one afterwards remembered who had first said, 'Anyone could manage a ship like this.'

Ferguson sat quietly smoking while the Captain read the letter he had brought him. He didn't even look in the Captain's direction. When at last conversation began there was so much circumambient happiness in the cabin that they took a long time to get down to the difficult part of their business. The Captain seemed at first wholly occupied with its comic side.

'Still,' he said at last, 'it has its serious side too. The impertinence of it, for one thing! Do they think——'

'Ye maun recall,' said Ferguson, 'they're dealing with an absolutely new situation.'

'Oh, *new* be damned! How does it differ from men on whalers, or even on windjammers in the old days? Or on the North West Frontier? It's about as new as people being hungry when food was short.'

'Eh mon, but ye're forgettin' the new light of modern psychology.'

'I think those two ghastly women have already learned some newer psychology since they arrived. Do they really suppose every man in the world is so combustible that he'll jump into the arms of any woman whatever?'

'Aye, they do. They'll be sayin' you and your party are verra abnormal. I wadna put it past them to be sending you out wee packets of hormones next.'

'Well, if it comes to that, do they suppose men would volunteer for a job like this unless they could, or thought they could, or wanted to try if they could, do without women?'

'Then there's the new ethics, forbye.'

'Oh stow it, you old rascal. What is new there either? Who ever tried to live clean except a minority who had a religion or were in love? They'll try it still on Mars, as they did on Earth. As for the majority, did they ever hesitate to take their pleasures wherever they could get them? The ladies of the profession know better. Did you ever see a port or a garrison town without plenty of brothels? Who are the idiots on the Advisory Council who started all this nonsense?'

'Och, a pack o' daft auld women (in trousers for the maist part) who like onything sexy, and onything scientific, and onything that makes them feel important. And this gives them all three pleasures at once, ye ken.'

'Well, there's only one thing for it, Ferguson. I'm not going to have either your Mistress Overdone or your Extension lecturer here. You can just——'

'Now there's no manner of use talkin' that way. I did my job. Another voyage with sic a cargo o' livestock I will not face. And my two lads the same. There'd be mutiny and murder.'

'But you must, I'm——'

At that moment a blinding flash came from without and the earth shook.

'Ma ship! Ma ship!' cried Ferguson. Both men peered out on empty sand. The spaceship had obviously made an excellent take-off.

'But what's happened?' said the Captain. 'They haven't——'

'Mutiny, desertion, and theft of a government ship, that's what's happened,' said Ferguson. 'Ma twa lads and your Dickson are awa' hame.'

'But good Lord, they'll get Hell for this. They've ruined their careers. They'll be——'

'Aye. Nae dout. And they think it cheap at the price. Ye'll be seeing why, maybe, before ye are a fortnight older.'

A gleam of hope came into the Captain's eyes. 'They couldn't have taken the women with them?'

'Talk sense, mon, talk sense. Or if ye hanna ony sense, use your ears.'

In the buzz of excited conversation which became every moment more audible from the main room, female voices could be intolerably distinguished.

As he composed himself for his evening meditation the Monk thought that perhaps he had been concentrating too much on 'needing less' and that must be why he was going to have a course (advanced) in 'loving more'. Then his face twitched into a smile that was not all mirth. He was thinking of the Fat Woman. Four things made an exquisite chord. First the horror of all she had done and suffered. Secondly, the pity—thirdly, the comicality—of her belief that she could still excite desire; fourthly, her bless'd ignorance of that utterly different loveliness which already existed within her and which, under grace, and with such poor direction as even he could supply, might one day set her, bright in the land of brightness, beside the Magdalene.

But wait! There was yet a fifth note in the chord. 'Oh, Master,' he murmured, 'forgive—or can you enjoy?—my absurdity also. I had been supposing you sent me on a voyage of forty million miles merely for my own spiritual convenience.'

FORMS OF THINGS UNKNOWN

['. . . *that what was myth in one world might always be fact in some other.*' PERELANDRA]

'Before the class breaks up, gentlemen,' said the instructor, 'I should like to make some reference to a fact which is known to some of you, but probably not yet to all. High Command, I need not remind you, has asked for a volunteer for yet one more attempt on the Moon. It will be the fourth. You know the history of the previous three. In each case the explorers landed unhurt; or at any rate alive. We got their messages. Every message short, some apparently interrupted. And after that never a word, gentlemen. I think the man who offers to make the fourth voyage has about as much courage as anyone I've heard of. And I can't tell you how proud it makes me that he is one of my own pupils. He is in this room at this moment. We wish him every possible good fortune. Gentlemen, I ask you to give three cheers for Lieutenant John Jenkin.'

Then the class became a cheering crowd for two minutes; after that a hurrying, talkative crowd in the corridor. The two biggest cowards exchanged the various family reasons which had deterred them from volunteering themselves. The knowing man said, 'There's something behind all this.' The vermin said, 'He always was a chap who'd do anything to get himself into the limelight.' But most just shouted out 'Jolly good show, Jenkin,' and wished him luck.

Ward and Jenkin got away together into a pub.

'You kept this pretty dark,' said Ward. 'What's yours?'

'A pint of draught Bass,' said Jenkin.

'Do you want to talk about it?' said Ward rather awkwardly

when the drinks had come. 'I mean—if you won't think I'm butting in—it's not just because of that girl, is it?'

That girl was a young woman who was thought to have treated Jenkin rather badly.

'Well,' said Jenkin. 'I don't suppose I'd be going if she had married me. But it's not a spectacular attempt at suicide or any rot of that sort. I'm not depressed. I don't feel anything particular about her. Not much interested in women at all, to tell you the truth. Not now. A bit petrified.'

'What is it then?'

'Sheer unbearable curiosity. I've read those three little messages over and over till I know them by heart. I've heard every theory there is about what interrupted them. I've——'

'Is it certain they were all interrupted? I thought one of them was supposed to be complete.'

'You mean Traill and Henderson? I think it was as incomplete as the others. First there was Stafford. He went alone, like me.'

'Must you? I'll come, if you'll have me.'

Jenkin shook his head. 'I knew you would,' he said. 'But you'll see in a moment why I don't want you to. But to go back to the messages. Stafford's was obviously cut short by something. It went: *Stafford from within 50 miles of Point XO308 on the Moon. My landing was excellent. I have*—then silence. Then come Traill and Henderson. *We have landed. We are perfectly well. The ridge M392 is straight ahead of me as I speak. Over.*'

'What do you make of *Over?*'

'Not what you do. You think it means *finis*—the message is over. But who in the world, speaking to Earth from the Moon for the first time in all history, would have so little to say—if he *could* say any more? As if he'd crossed to Calais and sent his grandmother a card to say "Arrived safely". The thing's ludicrous.'

'Well, what do *you* make of *Over?*'

'Wait a moment. The last lot were Trevor, Woodford, and Fox. It was Fox who sent the message. Remember it?'

'Probably not so accurately as you.'

Forms of Things Unknown

'Well, it was this. *This is Fox speaking. All has gone wonderfully well. A perfect landing. You shot pretty well for I'm on Point XO308 at this moment. Ridge M392 straight ahead. On my left, far away across the crater I see the big peaks. On my right I see the Yerkes cleft. Behind me.* Got it?'

'I don't see the point.'

'Well Fox was cut off the moment he said *behind me.* Supposing Traill was cut off in the middle of saying "Over my shoulder I can see" or "Over behind me" or something like that?'

'You mean?——'

'All the evidence is consistent with the view that everything went well till the speaker looked behind him. Then something got him.'

'What sort of a something?'

'That's what I want to find out. One idea in my head is this. Might there be something on the Moon—or something psychological about the experience of landing on the Moon—which drives men fighting mad?'

'I see. You mean Fox looked round just in time to see Trevor and Woodford preparing to knock him on the head?'

'Exactly. And Traill—for it was Traill—just in time to see Henderson a split second before Henderson murdered him. And that's why I'm not going to risk having a companion; least of all my best friend.'

'This doesn't explain Stafford.'

'No. That's why one can't rule out the other hypothesis.'

'What's it?'

'Oh, that whatever killed them all was something they found there. Something lunar.'

'You're surely not going to suggest life on the Moon at this time of day?'

'The word *life* always begs the question. Because, of course, it suggests organization as we know it on Earth—with all the chemistry which organization involves. Of course there could hardly be anything of that sort. But there might—I at any rate can't say there couldn't—be masses of matter capable of movements determined from within, determined, in fact, by intentions.'

'Oh Lord, Jenkin, that's nonsense. Animated stones, no doubt! That's mere science fiction or mythology.'

'Going to the Moon at all was once science fiction. And as for mythology, haven't they found the Cretan labyrinth?'

'And all it really comes down to,' said Ward, 'is that no one has ever come back from the Moon, and no one, so far as we know, ever survived there for more than a few minutes. Damn the whole thing.' He stared gloomily into his tankard.

'Well,' said Jenkin cheerily, 'somebody's got to go. The whole human race isn't going to be licked by any blasted satellite.'

'I might have known that was your real reason,' said Ward.

'Have another pint and don't look so glum,' said Jenkin. 'Anyway, there's loads of time. I don't suppose they'll get me off for another six months at the earliest.'

But there was hardly any time. Like any man in the modern world on whom tragedy has descended or who has undertaken a high enterprise, he lived for the next few months a life not unlike that of a hunted animal. The Press, with all their cameras and notebooks were after him. They did not care in the least whether he was allowed to eat or sleep or whether they made a nervous wreck of him before he took off. 'Flesh-flies,' he called them. When forced to address them, he always said, 'I wish I could take you all with me.' But he reflected also that a Saturn's ring of dead (and burnt) reporters circling round his space-ship might get on his nerves. They would hardly make 'the silence of those eternal spaces' any more homelike.

The take-off when it came was a relief. But the voyage was worse than he had ever anticipated. Not physically—on that side it was nothing worse than uncomfortable—but in the emotional experience. He had dreamed all his life, with mingled terror and longing, of those eternal spaces; of being utterly 'outside', in the sky. He had wondered if the agoraphobia of that roofless and bottomless vacuity would overthrow his reason. But the moment he had been shut into his ship there descended upon him the suffocating knowledge that the real danger of space-travel is claustrophobia. You have been put in a little metal container; somewhat like a cupboard, very like a coffin. You can't see out; you can see things only on the screen. Space and the stars are just as remote as they were on the earth. Where you are is always your world. The sky is never where you are. All you have done is to exchange a large world of earth and rock and water and clouds for a tiny world of metal.

This frustration of a life-long desire bit deeply into his mind as the cramped hours passed. It was not, apparently, so easy to jump out of one's destiny. Then he became conscious of another motive which, unnoticed, had been at work on him when he volunteered. That affair with the girl had indeed frozen him stiff; petrified him, you might say. He wanted to feel again, to be flesh, not stone. To feel anything, even terror. Well, on this trip there would be terrors enough before all was done. He'd be wakened, never fear. That part of his destiny at least he felt he could shake off.

The landing was not without terror, but there were so many gimmicks to look after, so much skill to be exercised, that it did not amount to very much. But his heart was beating a little more noticeably than usual as he put the finishing touches to his space-suit and climbed out. He was carrying the transmission apparatus with him. It felt, as he had expected, as light as a loaf. But he was not going to send any message in a hurry. That might be where all the others had gone wrong. Anyway, the longer he waited the longer those press-men would be kept out of their beds waiting for their story. Do 'em good.

The first thing that struck him was that his helmet had been too lightly tinted. It was painful to look at all in the direction of the sun. Even the rock—it was, after all, rock not dust (which disposed of one hypothesis)—was dazzling. He put down the apparatus; tried to take in the scene.

The surprising thing was how small it looked. He thought he could account for this. The lack of atmosphere forbade nearly all the effect that distance has on earth. The serrated boundary of the crater was, he knew, about twenty-five miles away. It looked as if you could have touched it. The peaks looked as if they were a few feet high. The black sky, with its inconceivable multitude and ferocity of stars, was like a cap forced down upon the crater; the stars only just out of his reach. The impression of a stage-set in a toy theatre, therefore of something arranged, therefore of something waiting for him, was at once disappointing and oppressive. Whatever terrors there might be, here too agoraphobia would not be one of them.

He took his bearings and the result was easy enough. He was, like Fox and his friends, almost exactly on Point XO308. But there was no trace of human remains.

If he could find any, he might have some clue as to how they died. He began to hunt. He went in each circle further from the ship. There was no danger of losing it in a place like this.

Then he got his first real shock of fear. Worse still, he could not tell what was frightening him. He only knew that he was engulfed in sickening unreality; seemed neither to be where he was nor to be doing what he did. It was also somehow connected with an experience long ago. It was something that had happened in a cave. Yes; he remembered now. He had been walking along supposing himself alone and then noticed that there was always a sound of other feet following him. Then in a flash he realised what was wrong. This was the exact reverse of the experience in the cave. Then there had been too many footfalls. Now there were too few. He walked on hard rock as silently as a ghost. He swore at himself for a fool—as if every child didn't know that a world without air would be a world without noise. But the silence, though explained, became none the less terrifying.

He had now been alone on the Moon for perhaps thirty-five minutes. It was then that he noticed the three strange things.

The sun's rays were roughly at right angles to his line of sight, so that each of the things had a bright side and a dark side; for each dark side a shadow like Indian ink lay out on the rock. He thought they looked like Belisha beacons. Then he thought they looked like huge apes. They were about the height of a man. They were indeed like clumsily shaped men. Except—he resisted an impulse to vomit—that they had no heads.

They had something instead. They were (roughly) human up to their shoulders. Then, where the head should have been, there was utter monstrosity—a huge spherical block; opaque, featureless. And every one of them looked as if it had that moment stopped moving or were at that moment about to move.

Ward's phrase about 'animated stones' darted up hideously from his memory. And hadn't he himself talked of something that we couldn't call life, not in our sense, something that could nevertheless produce locomotion and have intentions? Something which, at any rate, shared with life life's tendency to kill? If there were such creatures—mineral equivalents to organisms —they could probably stand perfectly still for a hundred years without feeling any strain.

Were they aware of him? What had they for senses? The opaque globes on their shoulders gave no hint.

There comes a moment in nightmare, or sometimes in real battle, when fear and courage both dictate the same course: to rush, planless, upon the thing you are afraid of. Jenkin sprang upon the nearest of the three abominations and rapped his gloved knuckles against its globular top.

Ach!—he'd forgotten. No noise. All the bombs in the world might burst here and make no noise. Ears are useless on the Moon.

He recoiled a step and next moment found himself sprawling on the ground. 'This is how they all died,' he thought.

But he was wrong. The figure above him had not stirred. He was quite undamaged. He got up again and saw what he had tripped over.

It was a purely terrestrial object. It was, in fact, a transmission set. Not exactly like his own, but an earlier and supposedly inferior model—the sort Fox would have had.

As the truth dawned on him an excitement very different

from that of terror seized him. He looked at their mis-shaped bodies; then down at his own limbs. Of course; that was what one looked like in a space suit. On his own head there was a similar monstrous globe, but fortunately not an opaque one. He was looking at three statues of spacemen: at statues of Trevor, Woodford, and Fox.

But then the Moon must have inhabitants; and rational inhabitants; more than that, artists.

And what artists! You might quarrel with their taste, for no line anywhere in any of the three statues had any beauty. You could not say a word against their skill. Except for the head and face inside each headpiece, which obviously could not be attempted in such a medium, they were perfect. Photographic accuracy had never reached such a point on earth. And though they were faceless you could see from the set of their shoulders and indeed of their whole bodies, that a momentary pose had been exactly seized. Each was the statue of a man turning to look behind him. Months of work had doubtless gone to the carving of each; it caught that instantaneous gesture like a stone snapshot.

Jenkin's idea was now to send his message at once. Before anything happened to himself, Earth must hear this amazing news. He set off in great strides, and presently in leaps—now first enjoying lunar gravitation—for his ship and his own set. He was happy now. He *had* escaped his destiny. Petrified, eh? No more feelings? Feelings enough to last him forever.

He fixed the set so that he could stand with his back to the sun. He worked the gimmicks. 'Jenkin, speaking from the Moon,' he began.

His own huge black shadow lay out before him. There is no noise on the Moon. Up from behind the shoulders of his own shadow another shadow pushed its way along the dazzling rock. It was that of a human head. And what a head of hair. It was all rising, writhing—swaying in the wind perhaps. Very thick the hairs looked. Then, as he turned in terror, there flashed through his mind the thought, 'But there's no wind. No air. It can't be *blowing* about.' His eyes met hers.

AFTER TEN YEARS

For several minutes now Yellowhead had thought seriously of moving his right leg. Though the discomfort of his present position was almost unbearable, the move was not lightly to be undertaken. Not in this darkness, packed so close as they were. The man next to him (he could not remember who it was) might be asleep or might at least be tolerably comfortable, so that he would growl or even curse if you pressed or pushed him. A quarrel would be fatal; and some of the company were hot-tempered and loud-voiced enough. There were other things to avoid too. The place stank vilely; they had been shut up for hours with all their natural necessities (fears included) upon them. Some of them—skeery young fools—had vomited. But that had been when the whole thing moved, so there was some excuse; they had been rolled to and fro in their prison, left, right, up and (endlessly, sickeningly) down; worse than a storm at sea.

That had been hours ago. He wondered how many hours. It must be evening by now. The light which, at first, had come down to them through the sloping shaft at one end of the accursed contraption, had long ago disappeared. They were in perfect blackness. The humming of insects had stopped. The stale air was beginning to be chilly. It must be well after sunset.

Cautiously he tried to extend his leg. It met at once hard muscle; defiantly hard muscle in the leg of someone who was wide awake and wouldn't budge. So that line was no good. Yellowhead drew back his foot further and brought his knee up under his chin. It was not a position you could hold for long, but for a moment it was relief. Oh, if once they were out of this thing . . .

And when they were, what next? Plenty of chance to get the

127

fidgets out of one's limbs then. There might be two hours of pretty hard work; not more, he thought. That is, if everything went well? And after that? After that, he would find the Wicked Woman. He was sure he would find her. It was known that she had been still alive within the last month. He'd get her all right. And he would do such things to her. . . . Perhaps he would torture her. He told himself, but all in words, about the tortures. He had to do it in words because no pictures of it would come into his mind. Perhaps he'd have her first; brutally, insolently, like an enemy and a conqueror; show her she was no more than any other captured girl. And she was no more than any girl. The pretence that she was somehow different, the endless flattery, was most likely what had sent her wrong to begin with. People were such fools.

Perhaps, when he had had her himself, he'd give her to the other prisoners to make sport for them. Excellent. But he'd pay the slaves out for touching her too. The picture of what he'd do to the slaves formed itself quite easily.

He had to extend his leg again, but now he found that the place where it had lain had somehow filled itself up. That other man had overflowed into it and Yellowhead was the worse off for his move. He twisted himself round a little so as to rest partly on his left hip. This too was something he had to thank the Wicked Woman for; it was on her account that they were all smothering in this den.

But he wouldn't torture her. He saw that was nonsense. Torture was all very well for getting information; it was no real use for revenge. All people under torture have the same face and make the same noise. You lose the person you hated. And it never makes them feel wicked. And she was young; only a girl. He could pity her. There were tears in his eyes. Perhaps it would be better just to kill her. No rape, no punishments; just a solemn, stately, mournful, almost regretful killing, like a sacrifice.

But they had to get out first. The signal from outside ought to have come hours ago. Perhaps all the others, all round him in the dark, were quite certain that something had gone wrong, and each was waiting for someone else to say it. There was no difficulty in thinking of things that might have gone wrong. He saw now that the whole plan had been crazy from the beginning. What was there to prevent their all being roasted alive where they sat? Why should their own friends from outside ever find them? Or find them alone and unguarded? How if no signal ever came and they never got out at all? They were in a death-trap.

He dug his nails into his palms and shut off these thoughts by mere force. For everyone knew, and everyone had said before they got in, that these were the very thoughts that would come during the long wait, and that at all costs you must not think them; whatever else you pleased, but not those.

He started thinking about the Woman again. He let pictures rise in the dark, all kinds; clothed, naked, asleep, awake, drinking, dancing, nursing the child, laughing. A little spark of desire began to glow; the old, ever-renewed astonishment. He blew on it most deliberately. Nothing like lust for keeping fear at a distance and making time pass.

But nothing would make the time pass.

Hours later cramp woke him with a scream on his mouth. Instantly a hand was thrust beneath his chin forcing his teeth shut. 'Quiet. Listen,' said several voices. For now at last there was a noise from outside; a tapping from beneath the floor. Oh Zeus, Zeus make it to be real; don't let it be a dream. There it came again, five taps and then five and then two, just as they had arranged. The darkness around him was full of elbows and knuckles. Everyone seemed to be moving. 'Get back there,' said someone. 'Give us room.' With a great wrenching sound the trap door came up. A square of lesser darkness—almost, by comparison, of light—appeared at Yellowhead's feet. The joy of mere seeing, of seeing anything at all, and the deep draughts he took of the clean, cold air, put everything else out of his mind for the moment. Someone beside him was paying a rope out through the opening.

'Get on then,' said a voice in his ear.

He tried to, then gave it up. 'I must unstiffen first,' he said. 'Then out of my way,' said the voice. A burly figure thrust itself forward and went hand over hand down the rope and out of sight. Another and another followed. Yellowhead was almost the last.

And so, breathing deep and stretching their limbs, they all stood by the feet of the great wooden horse with the stars above them, and shivered a little in the cold night wind that blew up the narrow streets of Troy.

II

'Steady, men,' said Yellowhead Menelaus. 'Don't go inside yet. Get your breath.' Then in a lower voice, 'Get in the doorway, Eteoneus, and don't let them in. We don't want them to start looting yet.'

It was less than two hours since they had left the horse, and all had gone extremely well. They had had no difficulty in finding the Scaean gate. Once you are inside a city's wall every unarmed enemy is either a guide or a dead man, and most choose to be the first. There was a guard at the gate, of course, but they had disposed of it quickly and, what was best of all, with very little noise. In twenty minutes they had got the gate open and the main army was pouring in. There had been no serious fighting till they reached the citadel. It had been lively enough there for a bit, but Yellowhead and his Spartans had suffered little, because Agamemnon had insisted on leading the van. Yellowhead had thought, all things considered, that this place should have been his own, for the whole war was in a sense his war, even if Agamemnon were the King of Kings and his elder brother. Once they were inside the outer circling wall of the citadel, the main body had set about the inner gate which was very strong, while Yellowhead and his party had been sent round to find a back way in. They had overpowered what defence they found there and now they stopped to pant and mop their faces and clean their swords and spear-blades.

After Ten Years

This little porch opened on a stone platform circled by a wall that was only breast-high. Yellowhead leaned his elbow on it and looked down. He could not see the stars now. Troy was burning. The glorious fires, the loud manes and beards of flame and the billows of smoke, blotted out the sky. Beyond the city the whole countryside was lit up with the glare; you could see even the familiar and hated beach itself and the endless line of ships. Thank the gods, they would soon bid good-bye to that!

While they had been fighting he had never given Helen a thought and had been happy; he had felt himself once more a king and a soldier, and every decision he made had proved right. As the sweat dried, though he was thirsty as an oven and had a smarting little gash above his knee, some of the sweetness of victory began to come into his mind. Agamemnon no doubt would be called the City-Sacker. But Yellowhead had a notion that when the story reached the minstrels he himself would be the centre of it. The pith of the song would be how Menelaus King of Sparta had won back from the barbarians the most beautiful woman in the world. He did not yet know whether he would take her back to his bed or not, but he would certainly not kill her. Destroy a trophy like that?

A shiver reminded him that the men would be getting cold and that some might be losing their nerve. He thrust through the mass and went up the shallow steps to where Eteoneus was standing. 'I'll come here,' he said. 'You bring up the rear and chivvy them on.' Then he raised his voice. 'Now, friends,' he said, 'we're going in. Keep together and keep your eyes open. There may be mopping up to do. And they're probably holding some passage further in.'

He led them for a few paces under darkness past fat pillars and then out into a small court open to the sky; brilliantly lit at one moment as the flames shot up from some house collapsing in the outer city and then again almost totally dark. It was clearly slaves' quarters. A chained dog, standing on its hind legs, barked at them with passionate hatred from one corner and there were piles of garbage. And then—'Ah! Would you?' he cried. Armed men were pouring out of a doorway straight ahead. They were princes of the blood by the look of their armour, one of them little more than a child, and they had the look—Yellowhead had seen it before in conquered towns—of men who are fighting to die rather than to kill. They are the most dangerous sort while they last. He lost three men there, but they got all the Trojans. Yellowhead bent down and finished off the boy who was still writhing like a damaged insect. Agamemnon had often told him that this was a waste of time, but he hated to see them wriggle.

The next court was different. There seemed to be much carved work on the walls, the pavement was of blue and white flagstones, and there was a pool in the middle. Female shapes, hard to see accurately in the dancing firelight, scattered away from them to left and right into the shadows, like rats when you come suddenly into a cellar. The old ones wailed in high, senseless voices as they hobbled. The girls screamed. His men were after them; as if terriers had been sent in among the rats. Here and there a scream ended in a titter.

'None of that,' shouted Yellowhead. 'You can have all the women you want tomorrow. Not now.'

A man close beside him had actually dropped his spear to have both hands free for the exploration of a little, dark sixteen-year-old who looked like an Egyptian. His fat lips were feeding on her face. Yellowhead fetched him one across the buttocks with the flat of his sword.

'Let her go, with a curse on you,' he said, 'or I'll cut your throat.'

'Get on. Get on,' shouted Eteoneus from behind. 'Follow the King.'

Through an archway a new and steadier light appeared; lamplight. They came into a roofed place. It was extraordinarily still and they themselves became still as they entered it. The noise of the assault and the battering ram at the main gate on the other side of the castle seemed to be coming from a great distance. The lamp flames were unshaken. The room was full of a sweet smell, you could smell the costliness of it. The floor was covered with soft stuff, dyed in crimson. There were cushions of silk piled upon couches of ivory; panels of ivory also on the walls and squares of jade brought from the end of the world. The room was of cedar and gilded beams. They were humiliated by the richness. There was nothing like this at Mycenae, let alone at Sparta; hardly perhaps at Cnossus. And each man thought, 'And thus the barbarians have lived these ten years, while we sweated and shivered in huts on the beach.'

'It was time it ended,' said Yellowhead to himself. He saw a great vase so perfect in shape that you would think it had grown like a flower, made of some translucent stuff he had never seen before. It stupefied him for a second. Then, in retaliation, he drove at it as hard as he could with the butt-end of his spear and shattered it into a hundred tinkling and shining fragments. His men laughed. They began following his example—breaking, tearing. But it disgusted him when they did it.

'Try what's behind the doors,' he said. There were many doors. From behind some of them they dragged or led the women out; not slaves but kings' wives or daughters. The men attempted no foolery; they knew well enough these were reserved for their betters. And their faces showed ghastly. There was a curtained doorway ahead. He swept the heavy, intricately embroidered, stuff aside and went in. Here was an inner, smaller, more exquisite room.

It was many-sided. Four very slender pillars held up the painted roof and between them hung a lamp that was a marvel of goldsmith's work. Beneath it, seated with her back against one of the pillars, a woman, no longer young, sat with her distaff, spinning; as a great lady might sit in her own house a thousand miles away from the war.

Yellowhead had been in ambushes. He knew what it costs even a trained man to be still on the brink of deadly danger. He thought, 'That woman must have the blood of gods in her.' He resolved he would ask her where Helen was to be found. He would ask her courteously.

She looked up and stopped her spinning but still she did not move.

'The child,' she said in a low voice. 'Is she still alive? Is she well?' Then, helped by the voice, he recognized her. And with the first second of his recognition all that had made the very shape of his mind for eleven years came tumbling down in irretrievable ruin. Neither that jealousy nor that lust, that rage nor that tenderness, could ever be revived. There was nothing inside him appropriate to what he saw. For a moment there was nothing inside him at all.

For he had never dreamed she would be like this; never dreamed that the flesh would have gathered under her chin, that the face could be so plump and yet so drawn, that there would be grey hair at her temples and wrinkles at the corners of her eyes. Even her height was less than he remembered. The smooth glory of her skin which once made her seem to cast a light from her arms and shoulders was all gone. An ageing woman; a sad, patient, composed woman, asking for her daughter; for their daughter.

The astonishment of it jerked a reply out of him before he well knew what he was doing. 'I've not seen Hermione for ten years,' he said. Then he checked himself. How had she the effrontery to ask like that, just as an honest wife might? It would be monstrous for them to fall into an ordinary husbandly and wifely conversation as if nothing had come between. And yet what had come between was less disabling than what he now encountered.

About that he suffered a deadlock of conflicting emotions. It served her right. Where was her vaunted beauty now? Vengeance? Her mirror punished her worse than he could every day. But there was pity too. The story that she was the daughter of Zeus, the fame that had made her a legend on both sides of the Aegean, all dwindled to this, all destroyed like the vase he had shivered five minutes ago. But there was shame too. He had dreamed of living in stories as the man who won back the most beautiful woman in the world, had he? And what he had won back was this. For this Patroclus and Achilles had died. If he appeared before the army leading this as his prize, as their prize, what could follow but universal curses or universal laughter? Inextinguishable laughter to the world's end. Then it darted into his mind that the Trojans must have known it for years. They too must have roared with laughter every time a Greek fell. Not only the Trojans, the gods too. They had known all along. It had diverted them through him to stir up Agamemnon and through Agamemnon to stir up all Greece, and set two nations by the ears for ten winters, all for a woman whom no one would buy in any market except as a housekeeper or a nurse. The bitter wind of divine derision blew in his face. All for nothing, all a folly and himself the prime fool.

He could hear his own men clattering into the room behind him. Something would have to be decided. Helen did and said nothing. If she had fallen at his feet and begged for forgiveness; if she had risen up and cursed him; if she had stabbed herself. . . . But she only waited with her hands (they were knuckley hands now) on her lap. The room was filling with men. It would be terrible if they recognized Helen; perhaps worse if he had to tell them. The oldest of the soldiers was staring at her very hard and looking from her to Yellowhead.

'So!' said the man at last, almost with a chuckle. 'Well, by all the——'

Eteoneus nudged him into silence. 'What do you wish us to do, Menelaus?' he asked, looking at the floor.

'With the prisoners—the other prisoners?' said Yellowhead. 'You must detail a guard and get them all down to camp. The rest at Nestor's place, for the distribution. The Queen—this one—to our own tents.'

'Bound?' said Eteoneus in his ear.

'It's not necessary,' said Yellowhead. It was a loathsome question: either answer was an outrage.

There was no need to lead her. She went with Eteoneus. There was noise and trouble and tears enough about roping up the others and it felt long to Yellowhead before it was over. He kept his eyes off Helen. What should his eyes say to hers? Yet how could they say nothing? He busied himself picking out the men who were to be the prisoners' escort.

At last. The women and, for the moment, the problem, were gone.

'Come on, lads,' he said. 'We must be busy again. We must go right through the castle and meet the others. Don't fancy it's all over.'

He longed to be fighting again. He would fight as he'd never fought before. Perhaps he would be killed. Then the army could do what they pleased with her. For that dim and mostly comfortable picture of a future which hovers before most men's eyes had vanished.

III

The first thing Yellowhead knew next morning was the burning of the cut above his knee. Then he stretched and felt the after-battle ache in every muscle; swallowed once or twice and found he was very thirsty; sat up, and found his elbow was bruised. The door of the hut was open and he could tell by the light that it was hours after sunrise. Two thoughts hung in his mind— the war is over—Helen is here. Not much emotion about either.

He got up, grunting a little, rubbed his eyes, and went out into the open. Inland, he saw the smoke hanging in still air above the ruins of Troy, and, lower down, innumerable birds. Everything was shockingly quiet. The army must be sleeping late.

Eteoneus, limping a little and wearing a bandage on his right hand, came towards him.

'Have you any water left?' said Menelaus. 'My throat's as dry as that sand.'

'You'll have to have wine in it, Yellowhead Menelaus. We've wine enough to swim in, but we're nearly out of water.'

Menelaus made a face. 'Make it as weak as you can,' he said.

Eteoneus limped away and returned with the cup. Both went into the King's hut and Eteoneus pulled the door to.

'What did you do that for?' said Yellowhead.

'We have to talk, Menelaus.'

'Talk? I think I'll sleep again.'

'Look,' said Eteoneus, 'here's something you ought to know. When Agathocles brought all our share of the women down last night, he penned the rest of them in the big hut where we've been keeping the horses. He picketed the horses outside—safe enough now. But he put the Queen by herself in the hut beyond this.'

'*Queen*, you call her? How do you know she's going to be a queen much longer? I haven't given any orders. I haven't made up my mind.'

'No, but the men have.'

'What do you mean?'

'That's what they call her. And they call her Daughter of Zeus. And they saluted her hut when they went past it.'

'Well, of all the——'

'Listen, Menelaus. It's no use at all thinking about your anger. You *can't* treat her as anything but your Queen. The men won't stand it.'

'But, gates of Hades, I thought the whole army was longing for her blood! After all they've been through because of her.'

'The army in general, yes. But not our own Spartans. She's still the Queen to them.'

'That? That faded, fat, old trot? Paris's cast-off whore and the gods know whose besides? Are they mad? What's Helen to them? Has every one forgotten that it's I who am her husband and her king, and their king too, curse them?'

'If you want me to answer that, I must say something that's not to your liking.'

'Say what you please.'

'You said you were her husband and their king. They'd say you are their king only because you're her husband. You're not of the blood royal of Sparta. You became their king by marrying her. Your kingship hangs on her queenship.'

Yellowhead snatched up an empty scabbard and hit savagely

three or four times at a wasp that was hovering above a spilled wine-drop. 'Cursed, cursed creature!' he yelled. 'Can't I kill even you? Perhaps you're sacred too. Perhaps Eteoneus here will cut my throat if I swot you. There! There!'

He did not get the wasp. When he sat down again he was sweating.

'I knew it wouldn't please you,' said Eteoneus, 'but——'

'It was the wasp that put me out of patience,' said Yellow-head. 'Do you think I'm such a fool as not to know how I got my own throne? Do you think *that* galls me? I thought you knew me better. Of course they're right; in law. But no one ever takes notice of these things once a marriage has been made.'

Eteoneus said nothing.

'Do you mean,' said Yellowhead, 'that they've been thinking that way all the time?'

'It never came up before. How should it? But they never forgot about her being the daughter of the highest god.'

'Do you believe it?'

'Till I know what it pleases the gods to have said about it, I'll keep my tongue between my teeth.'

'And then,' said Yellowhead, jabbing once more at the wasp, 'there's this. If she was really the daughter of Zeus she wouldn't be the daughter of Tyndareus. She'd be no nearer the true line than I am.'

'I suppose they'd think Zeus a greater king than either you or Tyndareus.'

'And so would you,' said Yellowhead, grinning.

'Yes,' said Eteoneus. Then, 'I've had to speak out, Son of Atreus. It's a question of my own life as well as yours. If you set our men fighting-mad against you, you know very well I'll be with you back to back, and they won't slit your throat till they've slit mine.'

A loud, rich, happy voice, a voice like an uncle's, was heard singing outside. The door opened. There stood Agamemnon. He was in his best armour, all the bronze newly polished, and the cloak on his shoulders was scarlet, and his beard gleaming with sweet oil. The other two looked like beggars in his presence. Eteoneus rose and bowed to the King of Men. Yellowhead nodded to his brother.

'Well, Yellowhead,' said Agamemnon. 'How are you? Send your squire for some wine.' He strode into the hut and ruffled the curls on his brother's head as if they were a child's. 'What cheer? You don't look like a sacker of cities. Moping? Haven't we won a victory? And got your prize back, eh?' He gave a chuckle that shook the whole of his big chest.

'What are you laughing at?' said Yellowhead.

'Ah, the wine,' said Agamemnon, taking the cup from Eteoneus's hand. He drank at length, put the cup down, sucked his wet moustache, and said, 'No wonder you're glum, brother. I've seen our prize. Took a look into her hut. Gods!' He threw his head back and laughed his full.

'I don't know that you and I have any need to talk about my wife,' said Yellowhead.

'Indeed we have,' said Agamemnon. 'For the matter of that, it might have been better if we'd talked about her before you married. I might have given you some advice. You don't know how to handle women. When a man does know, there's never any trouble. Look at me now. Ever heard of Clytemnestra giving me any trouble? She knows better.'

'You said we had to talk now, not all those years ago.'

'I'm coming to that. The question is what's to be done about this woman. And, by the way, what do you *want* to do?'

'I haven't made up my mind. I suppose it's my own business.'

'Not entirely. The army has made up its mind, you see.'

'What's it to do with them?'

'Will you never grow up? Haven't they been told all these years that she's the cause of the whole thing—of their friends' deaths and their own wounds and the gods only know what troubles waiting for them when they get home? Didn't we keep on telling them we were fighting to get Helen back? Don't they want to make her pay for it?'

'It would be far truer to say they were fighting for me. Fighting to get me my wife. The gods know that's true. Don't rub that wound. I wouldn't blame the army if they killed me. I didn't want it this way. I'd rather have gone with a handful of my own men and taken my chance. Even when we got here I tried to settle it by a single combat. You know I did. But if it comes to——'

'There, there, there, Yellowhead. Don't start blaming yourself all over again. We've heard it before. And if it's any comfort to you, I see no harm in telling you (now the thing's over) that you weren't quite as important in starting the war as you seem to think. Can't you understand that Troy had to be crushed? We couldn't go on having her sitting there at the gate to the Euxine, levying tolls on Greek ships and sinking Greek ships and putting up the price of corn. The war had to come.'

'Do you mean I—and Helen—were just pretexts? If I'd thought——'

'Brother, you make everything so childishly simple. Of course I wanted to avenge your honour, and the honour of Greece. I was bound to by my oaths. And I also knew—all the Greek kings who had any sense knew—that we had to make an end of Troy. But it was a windfall—a gift from the gods—that Paris ran off with your wife at exactly the right moment.'

'Then I'd thank you to have told the army the truth at the very outset.'

'My boy, we told them the part of the truth that they would care about. Avenging a rape and recovering the most beautiful woman in the world—that's the sort of thing the troops can understand and will fight for. What would be the use of talking to them about the corn-trade? You'll never make a general.'

'I'll have some wine too, Eteoneus,' said Yellowhead. He drank it fiercely when it was brought and said nothing.

'And now,' continued Agamemnon, 'now they've got her, they'll want to see her killed. Probably want to cut her throat on Achilles' tomb.'

'Agamemnon,' said Eteoneus, 'I don't know what Menelaus

means to do. But the rest of us Spartans will fight if there's any attempt to kill the Queen.'

'And you think I'd sit by and watch?' said Menelaus, looking angrily at him. 'If it comes to fighting, I'll be your leader still.'

'This is very pretty,' said Agamemnon. 'But you are both so hasty. I came, Yellowhead, to tell you that the army will almost certainly demand Helen for the priest's knife. I half expected you'd say "Good riddance" and hand her over. But then I'd have had to tell you something else. When they see her, as she now is, I don't think they'll believe it is Helen at all. That's the real danger. They'll think you have a beautiful Helen—the Helen of their dreams—safely hidden away. There'll be a meeting. And you'll be the man they'll go for.'

'Do they expect a girl to look the same after ten years?' said Yellowhead.

'Well, I was a bit surprised when I saw her myself,' said Agamemnon. 'And I've a notion that you were too.' (He repeated his detestable chuckle.) 'Of course we may pass some other prisoner off as Helen. There are some remarkably pretty girls. Or even if they weren't quite convinced, it might keep them quiet; provided they thought the real Helen was unobtainable. So it all comes to this. If you want you and your Spartans and the woman to be safe, there's only one way. You must all embark quietly tonight and leave me to play my hand alone. I'll do better without you.'

'You'll have done better without me all your life.'

'Not a bit, not a bit. I go home as the Sacker of Troy. Think of Orestes growing up with that to back him! Think of the husbands I'll be able to get for my girls! Poor Clytemnestra will like it too. I shall be a happy man.'

IV

I only want justice. And to be let alone. From the very beginning, from the day I married Helen down to this moment, who can say I've done him a wrong? I had a right to marry her.

Tyndareus gave her to me. He even asked the girl herself and she made no objection. What fault could she find in me after I was her husband? I never struck her. I never rated her. I very seldom even had one of the housegirls to my bed, and no sensible woman makes a fuss about that. Did I ever take her child from her and sacrifice it to the Storm-gods? Yet Agamemnon does that, and has a faithful, obedient wife.

Did I ever work my way into another man's house and steal his woman? Paris does that to me. I try to have my revenge in the right way, single combat before both armies. Then there's some divine interference—a kind of black-out—I don't know what happened to me—and he has escaped. I was winning. He was as good as dead man if I'd had two minutes more. Why do the gods never interfere on the side of the man who was wronged?

I never fought against gods as Diomede did, or says he did. I never turned against our own side and worked for the defeat of the Greeks, like Achilles. And now he's a god and they make his tomb an altar. I never shirked like Odysseus, I never committed sacrilege like Odysseus. And now he's the real captain of them all—Agamemnon for all his winks and knowingness couldn't rule the army for a day without him—and I'm nothing.

Nothing and nobody. I thought I was the King of Sparta. Apparently I'm the only one who ever thought so. I am simply that woman's head servant. I'm to fight her wars and collect her tribute and do all her work, but she's the Queen. She can turn whore, turn traitress, turn Trojan. That makes no difference. The moment she's in our camp she is Queen just as before. All the archers and horseboys can tell me to mend my manners and take care I treat her majesty with proper respect. Even Eteoneus—my own sworn brother—taunts me with being no true king. Then next moment he says he'll die with me if the Spartans decide I'd better be murdered. I wonder. Probably he's a traitor too. Perhaps he's this raddled Queen's next lover.

Not a king. It's worse than that. I'm not even a freeman. Any hired man, any peddlar, any beggar, would be allowed to teach his own wife a lesson, if she'd been false to him, in the way he thought best. For me it's Hands Off. She's the Queen, the Daughter of Zeus.

And then comes Agamemnon sneering—just as he always did ever since we were boys—and making jokes because she's lost her beauty. What right has he to talk me about her like that? I wonder what his own Clytemnestra looks like now. Ten years, ten years. And they must have had short commons in Troy for some time. Unhealthy too, cooped up inside the walls. Lucky there seems to have been no plague. And who knows how those barbarians treated her once the war began to turn against them? By Hera, I must find out about that. When I can talk to her. Can I talk to her? How would I begin?

Eteoneus worships her, and Agamemnon jeers at her, and the army wants to cut her throat. Whose woman is she? Whose business is she? Everyone's except mine, it seems. I count for nothing. I'm a bit of her property and she's a bit of everyone else's.

I've been a puppet in a war about corn-ships.

I wonder what she's thinking herself. Alone all those hours in that hut. Wondering and wondering, no doubt. Unless she's giving an audience to Eteoneus.

Shall we get away safely tonight? We've done all we can do by daylight. Nothing to do but wait.

Perhaps it would be best if the army got wind of it and we were all killed, fighting, on the beach. She and Eteoneus would see there's one thing I can still do. I'd kill her before they took her. Punish her and save her with one stroke.

Curse these flies.

V

(Later. Landed in Egypt and entertained by an Egyptian.)

'I'm sorry you've asked for that, Father,' said Menelaus. 'But you said it to spare me. Indeed, indeed, the woman's not worth your having.'

'The cold water a man wants is better than the wine he's no taste for,' said the old man.

'I'd give something better than such cold water. I beseech you to accept this cup. The Trojan King drank from it himself.'

'Will you deny me the woman, Guest?' said the old man, still smiling.

'You must pardon me, Father,' said Menelaus. 'I'd be ashamed——'

'She's the thing I ask for.'

'Curse these barbarians and their ways,' thought Menelaus to himself. 'Is this a courtesy of theirs? Is it the rule always to ask for something of no value?'

'You will not deny me surely?' said his host, still not looking at Helen, but looking sidelong at Menelaus.

'He really wants her,' Menelaus thought. It began to make him angry.

'If you won't give her,' said the Egyptian, a little scornfully, 'perhaps you'll sell.'

Menelaus felt his face reddening. He had found a reason for his anger now: it accordingly grew hotter. The man was insulting him.

'I tell you the woman's not for giving,' he said. 'And a thousand times not for selling.'

The old man showed no anger—could that smooth, brown face ever show it?—and kept on smiling.

'Ah,' he said at last, drawing it out very long. 'You should have told me. She is perhaps your old nurse or——'

'She's my wife,' Menelaus shouted. The words came out of his mouth, loud, boyish, and ridiculous; he hadn't meant to say them at all. He darted his eyes round the room. If anyone laughed he'd kill them. But all the Egyptian faces were grave, though anyone could see that the minds within them were mocking him. His own men sat with their eyes on the floor. They were ashamed of him.

'Stranger,' said the old man. 'Are you sure that woman is your wife?'

After Ten Years

Menelaus glanced sharply towards Helen, half believing for the moment that these foreign wizards might have played some trick. The glance was so quick that it caught hers and for the first time their eyes met. And indeed she was changed. He surprised a look of what seemed to be, of all things, joy. In the name of the House of Hades, why? It passed in an instant; the set desolation returned. But now his host was speaking again.

'I know very well who your wife is, Menelaus son of Atreus. You married Helen Tyndaris. And that woman is not she.'

'But this is madness,' said Menelaus. 'Do you think I don't know?'

'That is indeed what I think,' replied the old man, now wholly grave. 'Your wife never went to Troy. The gods have played a trick with you. That woman was in Troy. That woman lay in Paris's bed. Helen was caught away.'

'Who is that, then?' said Menelaus.

'Ah, who could answer? It is a thing—it will soon go away—such things sometimes go about the earth for a while. No one knows what they are.'

'You are making fun of me,' said Menelaus. He did not think so; still less did he believe what he was told. He thought he was out of his right mind; drunk perhaps, or else the wine had been drugged.

'It is no wonder if you say that,' replied the host. 'But you will not say it when I have shown you the real Helen.'

Menelaus sat still. He had the sense that some outrage was being done to him. One could not argue with these foreign devils. He had never been clever. If Odysseus had been here he would have known what to say. Meanwhile the musicians resumed their playing. The slaves, cat-footed, were moving about. They were moving the lights all into one place, over on the far side near a doorway, so that the rest of the large hall grew darker and darker and one looked painfully at the glare of the clustered candles. The music went on.

'Daughter of Leda, come forth,' said the old man.

And at once it came. Out of the darkness of the doorway

NOTES TO *AFTER TEN YEARS*

I

ROGER LANCELYN GREEN

This story of Helen and Menelaus after the fall of Troy was started, and the first chapter written in, I think, 1959—before Lewis's visit to Greece. It began, as Lewis wrote that the Narnian stories began and grew, from 'seeing pictures' in his mind—the picture of Yellow-head *in* the Wooden Horse and the realization of what he and the rest must have experienced during almost twenty-four hours of claustrophobia, discomfort, and danger. I remember him reading to me the first chapter, and the thrill of the growing knowledge of where we were and who Yellowhead was.

But Lewis had not worked out any plot for the rest of the story. We discussed all the legends of Helen and Menelaus that either of us knew—and I was rather 'up' in Trojan matters at the time, as I was writing my own story *The Luck of Troy* which ends where Lewis's begins. I remember pointing out that Menelaus was only King of Sparta on account of his marriage with Helen, who was the heiress of Tyndareus (after the death of Castor and Polydeuces)—a point which Lewis did not know, but seized upon eagerly and used in the next chapters.

He read the rest of the fragment to me in August 1960, after our visit to Greece—and after Joy's (his wife) death. The Egyptian scrap came later still, I think: but after that year Lewis found that he could no longer make up stories—nor go on with this one. It was because of this drying up of the imaginative spring (perhaps the inability to 'see pictures' any longer) that he planned to collaborate with me in a new version of my story *The Wood that Time Forgot* which I had written about 1950 and which Lewis always said was my best—though no publisher would risk it. But this was late 1962 and early 1963—and nothing came of it.

Naturally it is not possible to be certain what Lewis would have done in *After Ten Years* if he had gone on with it: he did not know

146

Notes to After Ten Years

himself—and we discussed so many possibilities that I cannot even be certain which he preferred.

The next 'picture' after the scene in the Horse was the idea of what Helen must really have looked like after ten years as a captive in besieged Troy. Of course the Classical authors—Quintus Smyrnaeus, Tryphiodorus, Apollodorus, etc.—insist on her divine beauty remaining unimpaired. Some authors say that Menelaus drew his sword to kill her after Troy had fallen, then saw her beauty, and the sword fell from his hand; others say that the soldiers were preparing to stone her—but she let fall her veil, and they dropped the stones and worshipped instead of slaying. Her beauty excused all: 'To Heracles Zeus gave strength, to Helen beauty, which naturally rules over even strength itself,' wrote Isocrates—and as I pointed out to Lewis, Helen returned to Sparta with Menelaus and was not only the beautiful Queen who welcomes Telemachus in the *Odyssey*, but was worshipped as a goddess, whose shrine may still be seen at Theraphai near Sparta.

However the scrap of the story set in Egypt is based on the legend begun by Stesichorus and developed by Euripides in his play *Helena* that Helen never went to Troy at all. On the way, she and Paris stopped in Egypt, and the gods fashioned an imitation Helen, an 'Eidolon', a thing of air, which Paris took to Troy, thinking it was the real Helen. For this phantom the Greeks fought and Troy fell. On his return (and he took nearly as long to get home as Odysseus) Menelaus visited Egypt: and there the Eidolon vanished and he found the true Helen, lovely and unsullied, and took *her* back to Sparta with him. (This legend gave Rider Haggard and Andrew Lang the idea for their romance of Helen in Egypt, *The World's Desire*—though it was set some years after the end of the *Odyssey*— a book which Lewis read and admired, even if he did not value it quite as highly as I do.)

The idea which Lewis was following—or with which he was experimenting—was a 'twist' of the Eidolon legend. 'Out of the darkness of the doorway' came the beautiful Helen whom Menelaus had originally married—Helen so beautiful that she must have been the daughter of Zeus—the dream beauty whose image Menelaus had built up during the ten years of the siege of Troy, and which had been so cruelly shattered when he found Helen in Chapter II. *But* this was the Eidolon: the story was to turn on the conflict between dream and reality. It was to be a development of the *Mary Rose* theme, again with a twist: Mary Rose comes back after many years in Fairyland, but exactly as on the moment of her disappearance— her husband and parents have thought of her, longed for her, like this—but when she does return, she just doesn't fit.

Menelaus had dreamed of Helen, longed for Helen, built up his image of Helen and worshipped it as a false idol: in Egypt he is offered that idol, the Eidolon. I don't think he was to know which was the true Helen, but of this I am not certain. But I think he was to discover in the end that the middle-aged, faded Helen he had brought from Troy was the real woman, and between them was the real love or its possibility: the Eidolon would have been a *Belle Dame sans merci* . . .

But I repeat that I do not know—and Lewis did not know—what exactly would have happened if he had gone on with the story.

II

ALASTAIR FOWLER

Lewis spoke more than once about the difficulties he was having with this story. He had a clear idea of the kind of narrative he wanted to write, of the theme, and of the characters; but he was unable to get beyond the first few chapters. As his habit was in such cases, he put the piece aside and went on with something else. From the fragment written, one might expect that the continuation would have been a myth of very general import. For the dark belly of the horse could be taken as a womb, the escape from it as a birth and entry on life. Lewis was well aware of this aspect. But he said that the idea for the book was provoked by Homer's tantalizingly brief account of the relationship between Menelaus and Helen after the return from Troy (*Od.* iv 1–305). It was, I suppose, a moral as much as a literary idea. Lewis wanted to tell the story of a cuckold in such a way as to bring out the meaningfulness of his life. In the eyes of others Menelaus might seem to have lost almost all that was honourable and heroic; but in his own he had all that mattered: love. Naturally, the treatment of such a theme entailed a narrative stand-point very different from Homer's. And this is already apparent in the present fragment: instead of looking on the horse from without as we do when Demodocus sings (*Od.* viii 499–520), here we feel something of the difficult life inside.

148

CPSIA information can be obtained at www.ICGtesting.com
Printed in the USA
BVOW02s1830190813

328903BV00001B/48/P

THE
ARAB WORLD
HANDBOOK

Arabian Peninsula Edition

THE
ARAB WORLD
HANDBOOK

STACEY INTERNATIONAL

THE
ARAB WORLD HANDBOOK
Arabian Peninsula Edition

Published by Stacey International
128 Kensington Church Street
London W8 4BH

ISBN: 1 900988 16X

Editor Max Scott
Designer Kitty Carruthers
Cover design by Nimbus Design & Communications
Films by Aurora Printing Co Ltd, Croydon
Printed & bound by Oriental Press, Dubai

British Library Cataloguing-in-Publication Data
A catalogue record for this book is available from
the British Library

1 3 5 7 9 8 6 4 2

4

ACKNOWLEDGEMENTS

I am especially indebted to Sir John Wilton, KCMG, KCVO, MC, the Hon Ivor Lucas, CMG, Patrick de Courcy-Ireland, CVO, Miles Reinhold, the late Patrick Bannerman, Christopher Wilton, Hugh Tunnell and Lawrie Walker for their kind advice and assistance with the manuscript of this book. However, the responsibility for the content and any errors is mine alone. I am indebted also to AJMC, PRMH and YIY.

Finally, I would like to express my sincere thanks to Max Scott, Kitty Carruthers and Tom Stacey of Stacey International for their invaluable contributions.

JP

Readers' Comments

Every effort has been made to ensure that *The Arab World Handbook* is as complete and up-to-date as possible. In the interests of ensuring that the standard is maintained, we welcome any comments from our readers for the sake of future editions.

Comments should be addressed to the publishers at

Stacey International
128 Kensington Church Street
London W8 4BH
Telephone: 020 7221 7166   Fax: 020 7792 9288
E-mail: stacey.international@virgin.net

CONTENTS

CONTENTS

CONTENTS

INTRODUCTION

Foreign visitors entering the region of Arabia and the Gulf for the first time will find themselves in a world that in certain aspects is profoundly unfamiliar. The mindset is different, at first inexplicably so. The most sympathetic person will find the scene confusing. The language is complicated, the social etiquette by which the Arabs set so much store takes time to pick up and the Muslim religion is in evidence everywhere as the major influence on daily life. Even the conduct of business has its own special rules. Finally, the whole often seems clouded by that indefinable element, the mystique of the Orient.

Few books succeed in presenting the subject in an easily understandable form, but **The Arab World Handbook**, building on the success of my two previous works *Simple Etiquette in Arabia* and *Very Simple Arabic*, aims to do just that. Cutting through the mystique, it sets out the essential information needed by the short–term visitor, the expatriate and the business traveller. It outlines the basic elements of the culture, language and religion. The chapter on etiquette tells a foreigner how to behave in the most commonly experienced situations, and subsequent chapters give advice on the planning and conduct of a visit to the region and on living there.

The final chapter outlines the basis for commercial success, helping the business traveller to operate effectively from the outset. Competition in the region is now so keen that business travellers cannot afford to jeopardise their chances through ignorance of the basic rules. This book tells them the steps they will need to take to achieve success.

Do not be too concerned by the amount of information you have to absorb. Read up on your immediate needs then refer back as the situation develops. Experience shows that information is much easier to assimilate once you are involved in a real-life situation.

James Peters

CHAPTER ONE
Background

GEOGRAPHY AND CLIMATE

The Arabian Peninsula, or Arabia as it was also traditionally known, is that major part of the Arab world resembling the head of an axe, with its butt bordering on Jordan and Iraq and its cutting edge lying on the Arabian Sea and the Gulf of Aden. In the west, the Red Sea separates it from Africa and in the east, the Gulf divides it from Iran.

Geography

The Peninsula divides into two main types of terrain. One consists of rugged hills and mountains of volcanic and igneous origin. The western third of the Peninsula, inland from the Red Sea, and incorporating all of the Hejaz, the Asir and most of Yemen, is of this type. The Hajar mountains of Oman, including the Jebel Akhdar, is a geologically distinct but superficially similar area of rough mountains covering most of northern Oman.

The rest of the Peninsula consists of very flat and featureless expanses of sand, gravel and sedimentary rock, relieved in some places by low escarpments and dry wadi beds. The main sand deserts are the famous Empty Quarter, or Rub' al-Khali, in the southeast and the Great Nefud in the north.

Overall, the Peninsula tilts gradually from the heights of Yemen which rise in places to over 3,000 metres, down to sea level in the east and northeast. A few small areas of southwest Arabia receive enough rainfall to support extensive areas of low forest; the rest of the land surface is arid or semi-arid desert, which nonetheless is sufficiently vegetated to support extensive seasonal grazing and to sustain an interesting population of bird and animal life. Much of the scenery possesses a bleak but dramatic beauty.

The Peninsula has a reputation as a hot and dusty place, and indeed the temperature in the dry summer months of May to September can be very high, reaching 40°C on the coasts and up to 50°C in inland areas. The effects of the high temperatures are made worse by the high humidity around the coasts of the Gulf and the Red Sea in summer and early autumn. In spring and

Climate

autumn the weather is pleasant with comfortable temperatures, clear skies and cool breezes. Most of the scanty annual rains fall in winter when it can also be cold, especially in the heart of the Peninsula. A visitor to the region need take very little precaution against the weather, other than a sweater and an umbrella during the winter months.

More detailed information on both the geography and the weather are given in the country sections in the annexes of the book.

HISTORICAL SUMMARY

Recent archaeological work in all parts of Arabia has demonstrated the antiquity of human settlement there. Shuwaiyhitiyah in northern Nejd is one of the world's most ancient settlement sites; thousands of other Stone Age sites across the Peninsula testify to the expansion and cultural development of the earliest Arabian.

Later, beginning about 5000 BC, we find evidence (on the Gulf coasts) of a succession of cultures - Ubaid, Dilmun, Umm al-Nar and others - which emerged under the twin stimuli of seafaring contacts between Mesopotamia and the Indus Valley, and the discovery and production of valuable resources of copper in Oman and pearls in Bahrain. On the Red Sea, copper, gold and incense were the commodities which encouraged the development of trading links and settlement along the coast.

From the earliest historical times until the 20th century, Arabia has been isolated. The harshness of the terrain has been a complete deterrent to invaders and colonisers, which has guaranteed a remarkable continuity of the ancient ways in most parts of the Peninsula. Contacts with the outside world were limited to coastal trade. Very occasional foreign military expeditions such as that of the Roman legion under Aelius Gallus, or the Ethiopian king Abraha in the 6th century AD, were rare events which left no lasting effect.

Even after the emergence of Islam, the fact that the

centres of political power of the Umayyad and Abbasid empires were in Syria and Iraq meant that Arabia remained a backwater, except for the pilgrimage route to Makkah and Madinah.

THE ANCIENT ARAB CIVILISATION

Scientifically and culturally the Arabs were at the forefront of learning during early mediaeval times, keeping alive Greek learning and eventually passing it on to Western Europe; and in the process adding much that was new in medicine, physics, astronomy and many other branches of science. As Professor Philip Hitti puts it in his *Short History of the Arabs,* "No people in the Middle Ages contributed to human progress so much as did the Arabs...Arab scholars were studying Aristotle when Charlemagne and his lords were reportedly learning to write their names. Scientists in Cordova, with their seventeen great libraries, each alone of which included more than 400,000 volumes, enjoyed luxurious baths at a time when washing the body was considered a dangerous custom at the University of Oxford." The Arab contribution to science is amply evidenced by the numerous Arabic words in the English language such as alchemy, alcohol, algebra, calibre, arsenal and admiral. Our star names are also largely Arabic - Rigel, Betelgeuse, Fomelhaut and many others.

1

Makkah, the principal destination of the pilgrim, is the city where the Prophet Muhammad was born in 571 AD and where he lived until 622 AD, when he fled to Madinah. The gradual revelation to him of the Holy Quran was met by the initial scepticism and opposition of many of his fellow citizens, but by the time of his death in 632 AD, the newly revealed faith of Islam was spread widely throughout Arabia. His successors, the four orthodox caliphs, continued the expansion of the faith through what

The birth of the Prophet Muhammad

15

is now known as the Arab world and Iran. Thereafter, when the caliphate moved to Damascus, Arabia's role became politically and militarily less significant, but the pilgrimage has continued uninterrupted every year for 1300 years, to act as an enormously important factor in welding Islamic society together. The opportunity to exchange information, to travel, to meet and talk with fellow-Muslims from distant parts of the Islamic world has always acted as a leaven in broadening the Muslim's mind and a brake on the centrifugal forces which act on any such widespread society.

The isolation of Arabia from foreign influence and interference was challenged in the 16th century by the Portuguese and the Ottoman Turks. The Portuguese wanted to consolidate their grip on the sea routes to Asia and as part of this strategy built a series of forts, most of which still exist, to control various ports around the coast, at Muscat, Bahrain and Tarut, where they remained until late in the 17th century. Their interest was maritime, and so they affected the land and the people very little.

The Ottoman Turks

The Ottoman Turks had a more profound influence. After their capture of Constantinople in 1453, they rapidly took the Levant and North Africa under their control, and by 1568 had conquered Yemen and brought the holy cities of Makkah and Madinah under their control. They continued to exercise this control off and on until the collapse of the Ottoman Empire during the First World War, and have left numerous traces of their occupation through the Hejaz, most famously the Hejaz railway. In the northern Gulf, too, they extended their influence from their province of Iraq as far as Bahrain and al Hasa; but they never controlled the centre of Arabia. The famous military expedition of Muhammad Ali which razed the town of Dir'iyyah near Riyadh in 1818 was purely a punitive raid.

Britain was the last outside power to wield influence in Arabia, primarily - like the Portuguese before them - as an adjunct to their interests further east. The colonisation of Aden, and the various treaties of protection and exclusivity signed with the rulers of the Gulf states and the Aden Protectorate, lasted until the middle years of the 20th century, by which time all of the present states of the Peninsula were independent and self-governing.

Following the Second World War the politics and economics of the region were transformed by the exploitation of the region's vast oil resources. The transformation wrought to the infrastructure of many of the Arab countries since the assertion of direct control of their oil wealth after 1973 has been remarkable by any standards. It has also meant that most countries in the Arabian Peninsula have made a lightning transition into the technological age. Lower oil prices in recent years have resulted in more measured progress and a consolidation of past achievements, together with a diversification of their economies wherever possible. Saudi Arabia, Kuwait, Qatar, Bahrain, the United Arab Emirates and Oman form a political, economic and military grouping known as the Gulf Co-operation Council (GCC) and, with the exception of Oman, are also members of the Organisation of Arab Petroleum Exporting Countries (OAPEC). All the countries of the Peninsula are members of the Arab League. (*See* the Annexes for Regional Organisations and information on individual countries of the Peninsula.)

The discovery of oil

1

Various terms are used to describe the region and it is as well to be aware of some possible local sensitivities in this regard. The term 'Middle East' is finding less favour in the Peninsula region because it was conceived in the West and lumps various cultures and peoples of the Arab world together as one, whereas the Gulf Arabs feel that their culture is distinctively different. It is better to talk of the Arab world, the Arabian Peninsula and the Gulf Arabs. Secondly, although the Gulf itself has often been described as the Persian Gulf, and some may refer to it as the Arabian Gulf, it is simpler to refer to it as the Gulf. Finally, when Arabs talk of the Gulf States they generally mean Bahrain, Kuwait, Qatar, the UAE, Saudi Arabia and Oman – i.e. the GCC states. If in doubt, it is best to specify which countries you are referring to by name.

Terminololgy

CULTURE AND SOCIETY

Despite the introduction of Western technology and consumer products, all of which have had a marked modernising influence on Arab life, the culture of the Peninsula countries retains its own distinctively Arab character.

The Desert Tradition

The Bedu

Although it is fast disappearing, the way of life of the nomadic Bedu (*sing.* Bedouin), the inhabitants of the desert hinterland, remains the basis of today's Arab culture, and has remained unchanged for centuries. The Bedu are superbly adapted to the harsh desert conditions in which they tend their flocks of sheep and goats, supported by their other lifeline, the camel. The camel provides them with milk, meat, material for their clothing, tents, and transport. The staple diet of the Bedu is dates, flour, camel's or goat's milk and meat from their flocks. Their clothing, ideally suited to the heat, is a long loose shirt and headcloth. They are hardy, self-reliant and fiercely independent. In the past, armed with rifle and sword and mounted on horseback, they raided other Bedu tribes and camel caravans, capturing their livestock and possessions. Although interdependent with the settled folk in the towns and village, the Bedu have always considered themselves superior.

The Bedu way of life

At the core of Bedu society lies the concept of the tribe, which has its own strict hierarchy. Some of the tribes were renowned for a particular expertise – such as camel-breeding, fighting or tracking. The tribes dominated a territorial area, usually designated by water wells which were jealously guarded against all comers. Each tribe was then subdivided into clans, consisting of a number of families and led by a Shaikh who was elected by consensus. Although the position of Shaikh was not always passed from father to son as of right, it tended to stay within the same family.

The daily life of the Bedu is governed by a time-honoured and strict code of conduct, with set procedures for the settlement of inter-tribal disputes and the punishment of crimes. Traditionally, each member of the tribe had a direct right of access to the Shaikh, with whom he could converse on equal terms. Deference is always shown to the elders in the community, and the poor are cared for. On an individual level, a Bedouin's word is his bond, the rule of hospitality inviolable, and his loyalty to family and tribe is of paramount importance. These values were equally shared by the settled foundations of Arabia.

This emphasis on family loyalty and the importance of the extended family continues today – grandparents, parents and children often living together in one house. Men and women have separate quarters. A male foreigner who is privileged to be invited to an Arab home would not normally meet the womenfolk but he might be surprised to learn of the enormous influence they exert behind the scenes. Although Islam permits four wives, most Arabs these days have only one. If a man has more than one wife, the Holy Quran rules that they must all be treated equally.

Values

Although the Arabs of the region are increasingly aware of Western culture through the media and through frequent travel to the West – and indeed many are educated in the West, own property and have business interests there as well – there is a strong desire to protect the Arab and Islamic culture. They accept the inevitability of change, but wish it to take place slowly and in a controlled manner, enabling them among other things to avoid the unacceptable elements.

The traditional Arab values of honourable behaviour, courtesy and unfailing hospitality survive. Honouring his word, loyalty to the family, respect for age, and the care of the poor continue to be a major influence on an Arab's way of life. He is by tradition a very proud and dignified person; status, influence and appearances matter. Although modest himself, he does not admire those who fail to exercise their authority or are self-deprecating. The Arab is none the less sensitive – personal remarks about

1

The Arab character

19

his honour, family or Faith, however light-hearted, could well cause offence. Conscious of recent history and the considerable influence wielded by the Western powers in the region, the Arab is not unnaturally sensitive to anything which could be interpreted as exploiting his position or is in any way patronising. He expects to be dealt with fairly and on equal terms.

Friendship

The people of the Gulf tend to be demonstrative, tactile and unafraid of emotion. The elaborate courtesies of Arab etiquette may seem exaggerated, but the reserve of Westerners often strikes the Arab as coldness. They do not have our shyness of physical contact and men often hold hands in public as a simple mark of friendship. They shake hands a great deal and may hold on to someone's hand long after shaking it. This is a demonstration of friendship and it would be unfriendly to withdraw it. It is commonplace for Arabs to embrace relatives, close friends, dignitaries and members of a ruling family when they meet them and kiss them symbolically on the cheeks, forehead or nose (depending on the relationship and local custom), but an Arab would have to know a Westerner extremely well before greeting him in this way.

The traditional recreations are as keenly pursued today as they ever were. The Shaikhly sport of falconry is still highly popular.

Camels are still widely owned and are bred for racing, which is a major public sporting event.

Personal Relationships

Arabs are distinguished by being friendly, courteous and hospitable. They set great store by personal relationships. The custom of greeting, shaking hands and asking after someone's health is more than mere formality. The enquiries are often searching and evidence a genuine desire to know of one's well-being and that of one's family.

The establishment of good personal relationships is crucial to success in any dealings in the Peninsula, something which many foreign organisations are even

1

THE ARAB HORSE

The Arab passion for horses is well known. The Bedu were first attracted to the horse by its speed and agility which made it particularly suitable for raiding and warfare. The famous Arab horse originated in the Nejd region of Saudi Arabia and by the 6th century AD they had succeeded in breeding strains which were subsequently used to improve stock throughout Europe and elsewhere. The Arab horse of today is still characterised by its beauty, agility, speed and stamina. Michael Clayton, editor of Horse and Hound, writes: "The origins of the [British] Thoroughbred were in Arabia... Three stallions are credited with the creation of the Thoroughbred in the late seventeenth and early eighteenth centuries: the Godolphin Arabian, the Darley Arabian and the Byerley Turk. None ran a race, but they sired stock and all modern Thoroughbreds descend from them in the male line."

1

now slow to recognise. Whereas in the West a friendship may develop from a successful business deal, in the Arab world the reverse is true. The degree of success in establishing a rapport depends on one's character, but someone who is polite and sensitive, staightforward and open, is likely to succeed. Perhaps the single most important additional quality that an Arab will look for is integrity.

Establishing a rapport

A meaningful relationship in the Peninsula takes time to establish. It may take months or even years. The process may be shortened slightly if the newcomer is personally recommended to an Arab or if their standing and reputation are well known, but an Arab will still wish to make his own independent judgement.

If you think you get on well with Arabs be careful not to overdo it. Some foreigners become over familiar or attempt to imitate the Arab way of life. Experience shows that this can lead to contempt or may even offend. The

21

outsider who gets on best is the person who, while respecting the Arab way of life, maintains a respectful distance from it.

Arab Women

The special situation with regard to women in the region is one of the most difficult for a foreigner to understand. The apparent domination by men and the seclusion of women is sometimes criticised by Westerners, who judge what they see by their own standards. They would do well to remind themselves that they are dealing with a radically different culture and moral code.

Women in the Arab world are not judged inferior to men. That may have been the case before Islam but an important aspect of the Faith is that the rights of women are protected. In the Peninsula, Arab women, who have always been influential in private life, now play an increasingly important role in public life as well. The seclusion of women is, however, a long-standing tradition in Arabia and one that remains strong. The degree of seclusion varies from country to country. In most, it is still strictly followed. Arab women live in separate quarters and are not seen by male visitors. Throughout the Peninsula, when appearing in public, it is commonplace to see women wearing the traditional long black cloak (*abaya*) and head shawl either with all of the face except the eyes covered (*hijab*) or with a mask covering the lower part of the face (*burga*). Women pray separately from men. You will also see wives walking behind their husbands. Women may go shopping alone, but if they visit a friend or appear in public they will often be accompanied by their husband or chaperoned by a brother. In Saudi Arabia women are required to cover their arms and legs in public (*see General Comments* in the Saudi Arabia Annex) and are not at present permitted to drive motor cars. In other countries of the Peninsula you may find many women apparently behaving very much as they do in the West, wearing Western clothes (perhaps with a head shawl) and driving cars. Nevertheless, the fundamental custom

Seclusion of women

of seclusion still applies and in all other respects they would behave as described above.

Although you may hear that in Islam a man may divorce his wife simply by renouncing her, it is seldom practised and divorce is by no means as common as in the West. A divorced man must make full financial and other provision for his ex-wife. In addition, an Arab woman may own property, inherit goods and money and a wife's individual possessions are always protected – she does not have to share them with her husband.

Divorce

It is less well known that even in the most conservative of households women are often the power behind the throne, that although marriages are often arranged, the bride is still free to decline to marry someone if she wishes. Whatever happens, a woman can usually find out a lot about her prospective husband before a decision on marriage is taken and modern reforms have secured the eradication of any discriminatory practices in the marriage agreement.

Modern Arab women have travelled further afield and are better informed through newspapers, radio, television and films than were their forbears. The most significant advance in recent years, as with men, has been in education. Women are now able to play an increasingly wide role in society in a variety of occupations. These are currently in the teaching profession (girls' schools and universities), in medicine (as nurses and doctors), television and radio, light industry and, in rural communities, agriculture. There are also a number of highly successful Arab businesswomen, and lawyers, and others who have risen to the highest echelons of government.

The modern Arab woman

Male visitors to the Peninsula should, of course, always show great respect for the seclusion of women. And the same applies if they meet an Arab woman abroad. An Arab woman may be dressed in a Western style but one must not assume she may be treated as a Westerner. To take any liberty would have serious repercussions.

23

Dress

For the Arabs of the Peninsula the traditional male dress is a long loose garment called variously a *thobe* or *dishdasha*. Of fine white cotton in summer, it is ideally suited to the hot climate. In winter, it is of heavier weave and may be augmented by a brown or black cloak (a *bisht* or *mishla*) or sometimes with a jacket or overcoat. The *bisht* of a senior citizen or member of a ruling family might be trimmed with gold braid. In the Arab Gulf countries and Saudi Arabia a head cloth (a ***gh**ūtra* or *she**maag**)* is also worn and kept in place with a black rope (an *aqaal*). A white cotton head cloth is usual in summer and a thicker cloth in winter, patterned either in red-and-white or green-and-white. In one variation of style, fashionable with the younger generation, the head cloth is worn wrapped around the head without the rope and in another variant strict followers of Islam wear the red-and-white patterned head cloth loose over the head, again without the head rope. Such religious men may also cultivate a large untrimmed beard and shortened *thobe*. In Yemen and sometimes Oman the head cloth is wrapped tightly round the head or piled high like a turban. The most common headgear in Oman however, is a small round woven hat (*qūbba'a*) worn in a variety of colours and decorations.

Headdress

1

LANGUAGE, LITERATURE AND ART

Because the Holy Quran was revealed by the Archangel Gabriel to the Prophet Muhammad in Arabic, the language is esteemed by Muslims as the language of God. Arabic is the official language of the Peninsula although English is also widely used and understood.

Arab literature is dominated by the writings of the Holy Quran, by poetry and prose. The Holy Quran is neither prose nor poetry but is universally considered by Muslims to be a work of unsurpassable excellence. The true meaning and sound can only be appreciated in the original. Although at one time translation was forbidden as an irreverent act, the Holy Quran has now been translated into several languages, including English, for the benefit of the many non-Arab Muslims in the world.

In art, the Holy Quran has been interpreted as forbidding the portrayal of the human form, at least in decorating religious buildings. As a result, the art style in the Arab world developed from decorative floral and geometric forms and evolved into the unique interwoven recurrent motifs of abstract design known as Arabesque. This explains the almost total absence of naturalistic or representational art which is so much a part of art in other cultures. Another extremely popular form of Arab art is calligraphy and various forms of the Arabic script are used to decorate pottery, glass and metalwork with dense but highly organised and skilfully executed designs.

In the Peninsula the architectural style is distinct from the rest of the Arab world. Traditional buildings use local materials – clay, stone, gypsum are plain and undecorated, and rely on form and volume for their beauty. The Red Sea towns used more coral stone and timber in their construction and are generally more elegant than central and eastern Arabian towns. Weaving, pottery and other crafts also have a simple functional beauty far removed from their sophisticated urban equivalents in Cairo, Istanbul or Damascus.

Arab craftsmanship

1

GOVERNMENT AND BUSINESS

The States of the Arabian Peninsula, in their present form, came into existence in the last 70 years. In nearly all countries one finds that one or other tribe or family occupies the dominant political position and all, with the exception of Yemen, are monarchies. The political power-base generally lies in the hands of the senior members of the ruling family, other leading families (particularly the leading merchant families) and the armed forces. The rulers (or in the case of Yemen, the President) are assisted in government by a consultative

Political power

council, except in the case of Kuwait, which has an elected parliament. The routine of government is carried out by the tried and tested traditional system of consultation by the ruler and executed by the Cabinet and Government Ministers. Members of the ruling family usually hold the key ministerial appointments such as defence, foreign affairs and the interior.

Bureaucracy

Although the newcomer to the region will probably find the apparent bureaucracy of government similar to his own, the procedures may be new to him and may seem excessively ponderous. Expatriates and business travellers find it eminently sensible to enlist the aid of a local representative to help them deal with routine, but time-consuming, procedures. If you attempt to do things on your own and encounter difficulties, do not lose your cool, do not attempt to brow-beat anyone and do not even consider attempting to bribe a government official. It is considered a serious offence.

The decision-makers

The non-routine decision-making process in a Peninsula government or institution is usually tightly controlled by a surprisingly small number of high-ranking people. The decision-maker may have a large number of seemingly influential subordinates but even relatively minor decisions have to be referred to the top. This may be frustrating, but only patience and local advice will help you determine if you can short-cut the system. It is always in a Westerner's interest to get along with the subordinates in an organisation and such a tightly controlled system also has the advantage that major decisions can sometimes be made remarkably quickly, cutting through all obstacles and allowing swift implementation of a project. In recent years the bureaucratic system of boards and committees who investigate, consider and report has been increasingly introduced as an aid to decision-taking in the public sector, although the final decision still has to be made at the top level.

Finally, the pace of life in the Arab world is slower than in the West. This is not inefficiency but simply the result of a difference in outlook. It is not sensible to attempt to keep to a tight schedule on a visit to the region. (*See* Chapter 3 - *The Arab Perception of Time*).

LAW, ORDER AND DECORUM

Arabs are generally extremely law-abiding people and Arab countries very safe places to live in. Theoretical Islam and the Islamic law (*Shari'a*), based on the Holy Quran and the *Hadith* (authenticated teachings, sayings and actions of the Prophet Muhammad), provide the basis for every aspect of modern life. In practice, the administrative needs of the modern state result in an increasing amount of legislation and regulation in the fields of finance, commerce, defence, health, education, social security, etc. In religious, family and social affairs, however, the influence of Islam remains predominant and is the more jealously defended as society witnesses the increase in what are seen as Western influences and the demands of the contemporary state. The defence of traditional Islamic values against the social and economic values of the West is a prime factor in the reassertion of Islam. In particular, the orderly and law-abiding characteristics of Muslim society are contrasted with the violence and degeneration seen in contemporary Western society. Standards of dress, laws against blasphemy and the prohibition on alcohol are being strictly enforced and foreign visitors should take care in this regard. (*See* Chapter 4 - *Standards of Dress; Prohibited Goods*, and Chapter 5 - *Local Laws and Customs.*)

Some important aspects of the local law in individual countries are given in the Country Annexes.

Sharia law

ISLAM

Islam is all-pervasive in Arabia. A visitor who knows nothing of it will find it difficult to understand the society he has come across, since its teachings govern so much of the daily life of the people of Arabia.

Translated from the Arabic, the word Islam means

27

'submission to the will of God'. Thus a Muslim is one who submits. Islam consists of three essential elements. The first and most important is faith and belief in God and in the fact that Muhammad was his Prophet, the last in the line of prophets, through whom the definitive revelation was made. These central beliefs are repeated five times a day in the call to prayer. The second element is a respect for the rites of worship and the revealed law (known as *Shari'a*). The Holy Quran, the record of God's revelation through the Prophet Muhammad, is the primary source of these obligations, but is supplemented as a source of law by the *Hadith*, which are collections of reports of the deeds and sayings of the Prophet Muhammad. Thirdly, Islam imposes an obligation of virtue and excellence in the way the Muslim leads his life.

THE HOLY QURAN

The physical entity of the Holy Quran as a book carries a sanctity and reverence as the direct revelation of God to the Prophet Muhammad. In a Muslim home it often rests on a special stand. A non-Muslim visitor should not handle it without permission.

God's revelation to the Prophet Muhammad is set out in 114 Suras, or chapters. Included within its pages are detailed prescriptions of personal and social conduct covering such things as moral standards, divorce, food, drink and the treatment of prisoners.

The Arabic word for God is *Allah* and the Muslim's creed is expressed in the brief statement:

> *La Allaha il-la Allah. Muhammad Rasool Allah!*
> (There is) no God but one God (and) Muhammad
> (is the) Messenger of God!

The Holy Quran occupies a very different place in

Islam from that of the Bible in Christianity. For one thing, it reproduces the very word of God as spoken in Arabic through the Prophet Muhammad. It is agreed by Arabs to be the most powerful and most beautiful work in the Arabic language, affecting readers and listeners with the power of its language in a way which non-Arabic speakers find impossible to share. The language is in places plain and straightforward in meaning, in others elliptical and poetic.

Any copy of the Holy Quran is treated with great respect; non-Muslims should not handle one without permission, and will give offence if they show any disrespect to it.

The speech of an Arab Muslim is full of references to God. There are dozens - even hundreds - of expressions in everyday speech which invoke the name of Allah. Perhaps the best known is the expression *"In sha'Allah"* - if God wills - which is usually added to the expression of any future intention. This is not just a formulaic religious sentiment; the speaker believes that it is a necessary qualification of his intention. When you say to an Arab that you will see him at 9 a.m. the next day, and he replies *"In-sha'Allah"*, show him that you respect this belief by not commenting on it. The correct response is *"In-sha'Allah"*.

A feature of Islam which will be evident to a visitor to the Peninsula is the extent to which so many aspects of daily life are regulated by precise directions. These directions stem from the Quran and *Hadith*, and are therefore not changeable. Whereas Christianity sets out general moral principles against which actions may be judged, and the law in a Christian society may be amended as circumstances change, Islam and the *Shari'a* are indissolubly linked, and any prescriptions in them may not be altered. So the laws of the *Shari'a* tell a Muslim precisely how and when to worship; they cover eating and drinking; marriage, divorce and inheritance; they define honourable behaviour and stipulate how a person should act towards the poor, prisoners and orphans; they lay down penalties for crimes; they

The will of
Allah

1

29

govern tax, capital and the return on capital; and many things besides. To unfamiliar eyes, this may appear as an irksomely restrictive system, but to the Muslim their unchanging nature gives him a comfortable feeling that he knows where he stands.

The Five Pillars of Islam

There are five obligatory acts required of every Muslim:

- The Declaration of Faith *(Shahaada)*
- Prayer *(Salah)*
- Almsgiving *(Zakat)*
- Fasting *(Sawm)*
- The Pilgrimage to Makkah *(Hajj)*

(1) **The Declaration of Faith** *(Shahaada* - lit. 'bearing witness')
To testify to the unity of God and that Muhammad is His Prophet.

(2) **Prayer** *(Salah)*
To observe the five daily prayers at the following times: at dawn, at noon, in late afternoon, at sunset, and at night.

Worship is preceded by ablutions when the worshipper washes his head, arms and feet with water. If no water is available, for example in the desert, then a symbolic ablution is performed with sand. The prayer, which must be said facing in the direction of Makkah, consists of between two and four sections, with a prologue and an epilogue. It is performed in several attitudes - sitting, standing, bowing and with the forehead touching the ground. The direction of Makkah is usually indicated in hotel rooms in the Peninsula and even on aircraft of Peninsula airlines.

The mosque *(masjid* – 'a place of prostration') is the place of public prayer. Although worship may be performed anywhere it is preferably done in a mosque. The worshipper may also pray wherever he happens to be at the time of prayer provided the place is clean and relatively undisturbed. A prayer rug is often used to cover the ground. The visitor to the Arab world should not be surprised when he sees prayers being performed in offices, in the airport lounge, on aircraft or on the street. This is normal practice. Do not walk in front of someone in prayer or take special notice of them.

The call to prayer is chanted by the *muezzin* from the minaret (*manaara*) which is the tall tower of the mosque. You will hear the call to prayer chanted as follows:

1. *Allahu Akbar!*
God is most great!
2. *Ash-hadu an laa Allaha illa Allah!*
I testify that there is no God but God!
3. *Ash-hadu anna Muhammad Rasool Allah!*
I testify that Muhammad is the messenger of God!
4. *Hayy ala-as-salah!*
Come to prayer!
5. *Hayy ala-al-Falah!*
Come to salvation!
As-Salaa Khairun min An-Nawm!
Prayer is better than sleep! (said only at dawn prayer)
6. *Allahu Akbar!*
God is most great!
7. *Laa Allaha Illa Allah!*
There is no God but God!

(All lines are repeated twice except the first, which is called four times, and the last which is called once)

On entering a mosque, Muslims remove their shoes, keep their heads covered and perform a minor ablution (*wūdooh*) before prayer. Inside the mosque there is a niche (*mihraab*) in one wall which indicates the direction of the holy city of Makkah. There is

31

also a pulpit (*minbar*) from which the oration is given at the public prayers held at noon each Friday. The public prayer in the mosque is led by the *Imaam* (the local religious leader). Except within the principal Shia group, the Ithna-Asharis, there is no hierarchy of priests in Islam as in Christianity. The mosque is attended mainly by men. Women either pray at home or use the special place allotted to them in most large mosques.

(3) **Almsgiving** (*Zakat*)

Each year, all Muslims must pay *zakat* to help the poor. This is traditionally a fixed proportion of their savings (2.5 per cent) and is usually paid in money rather than in kind.

(4) **Fasting** (*Sawm*)

Ramadan

1

Each year throughout the holy month of Ramadan, the ninth month in the Muslim calendar, Muslims observe a fast. (By the Gregorian calendar the month of Ramadan moves forward eleven or twelve days each year.) The fast commemorates the month of the revelation of the first verses of the Holy Quran to the Prophet Muhammad and the victory of the Muslims over the Makkans at the Battle of Badr in AD 624. Between sunrise and sunset the Muslim abstains from food, drink and all pleasurable pursuits. This can be a great burden, especially in summer. Working hours are always curtailed during Ramadan. Naturally, a business traveller should take this into consideration when planning any visit to the Arab world. A non-Muslim visiting an Arab country during Ramadan should not eat, drink or smoke in the presence of a Muslim in daylight hours. After sunset the fast is broken with a substantial meal to which guests are frequently invited. Arab dignitaries break the fast with a light meal and then preside over a reception (*majlis*) at home with their families to which friends, colleagues and acquaintances pay brief visits. A Westerner who knows a particular dignitary should certainly consider visiting him on such an occasion. He should enter, shake hands with his host and other guests and sit down as indicated by his host. As new arrivals enter, follow the advice on *Seating* in Chapter 3. After refreshments, it is customary to leave, but you may be honoured by an invitation to stay to the second, more substantial, evening meal served towards 10 p.m. In certain cases you may find the reception combined with a meal. Ramadan ends with a festival called *Eid Al-Fitr*. Muslims wear their finest clothes and gather in the mosques to pray, after which they celebrate with visits to each other's houses and hold parties. The correct behaviour for the foreigner on this occasion is explained in Chapter 3: Etiquette.

(5) **The Pilgrimage to Makkah** (*the Hajj*)
It is obligatory for every Muslim once in his lifetime, provided that he can afford it and his health allows, to make the pilgrimage to Makkah. This takes place during the twelfth month of the Muslim year.

For the pilgrimage, the Muslim exchanges his normal dress for two plain sheets of white cloth, to demonstrate that all believers are equal before God. On arrival in Makkah he performs various ceremonies. He must first circle the Kaaba seven times. The Kaaba, an immense stone cube shrouded in black cloth with the sacred Black Stone in one corner, is situated in the Great Mosque in Makkah. It is the most important shrine in Islam. The pilgrim then moves outside the town and journeys seven times between two small hills, acting out the frantic search of Abraham's wife Hagar, hunting for water for her son Ishmael.

The Mount of Mercy in the Plain of Arafat is the next stop for the pilgrim, where he stands and meditates from midday to just before sunset. Finally, he goes to Mina to carry out the stoning of the three pillars, an act symbolic of the casting out of devils,

33

and then goes on to sacrifice an animal.

The pilgrimage ends with the most important of all Muslim festivals – the *Eid Al-Adha*, or Feast of Sacrifice. This is celebrated in the same way as the *Eid Al-Fitr* except that presents and parties are more lavish. At the time of both *Eids*, greeting cards are sent to friends and acquaintances (*see* Chapter 3). Traditionally, a sheep or goat is slaughtered in remembrance of the willingness of the Prophet Abraham to sacrifice his son Ishmael. Some of the food is shared with the poor and the rest is eaten at family feasts. A man who has performed the *Hajj* is called *Hajji* or *Hajj* (pilgrim) and may include the title *Hajj* in his name, generally as a prefix. Similarly a woman may call herself *Hajja*.

The Islamic Calendar, Festivals and the Working Week

The official start of the Muslim era is the year of the *Hijra* (meaning 'the migration') in AD 622 when the Prophet Muhammad, as a result of persecution while preaching God's message in Makkah, fled to Madinah. The Muslim calendar begins on the day after this flight. The Muslim year, known as *Anno Hijra* (AH), is based on twelve lunar months. These lunar months are shorter than the months of the Gregorian calendar and overall the Muslim year is shorter than the Gregorian by some eleven days. The *Hijra* calendar is used today for all religious purposes and in Saudi Arabia for all official purposes as well. The Muslim date is often printed beside the Gregorian date on Arab documents.

The days of the week in Arabic are:

Saturday	*Yome As-Sabt*
Sunday	*Yome Al-Ahad*
Monday	*Yome Al-Ithnain*
Tuesday	*Yome Al-Thalaatha*
Wednesday	*Yome Al-Arba'a*
Thursday	*Yome Al-Khamees*
Friday	*Yome Al-Jūm'a*

The twelve months of the Islamic calendar are:

1. *Mūharram*	30 days
2. *Safar*	29 days
3. *Rabee Al-Awwal*	30 days
4. *Rabee Al-Thaanee*	29 days
5. *Jumaada Al-Ūwla*	30 days
6. *Jumaada Al-Thaanee*	29 days
7. *Rajab*	30 days
9. *Ramadan*	30 days
10. *Shawwaal*	29 days
11. *Dhŭ Al-Qi'da*	30 days
12. *Dhŭ Al-Hijjah*	29 days

The various festivals and celebrations in the Muslim calendar are given overleaf. However, apart from the *Eid Al-Adha* and the *Eid Al-Fitr*, not all of them are celebrated in every country in the region. In Saudi Arabia, for example, only the *Eid Al-Adha* and the *Eid Al-Fitr* are public holidays.

It is traditional in the region to take one's annual holiday during the hottest part of the summer and at the same time as the schools' summer holiday. This period runs from about mid-July to mid-September. Some institutions run on caretaker management during the central part of this period.

The Muslim working week runs from Saturday to Thursday, although Thursday is a half-day for Government institutions and schools and is being increasingly regarded as a non-working day. Friday is the holy day which is the day set aside for communal worship when all Muslims attend the Mosque. For everyone living in the region it is regarded as a day of rest and one of the commonest *faux pas* for a Westerner is to ring someone in the Peninsula on a Friday.

The daily routine in the region, particularly during the summer, is to work from quite early in the morning until early afternoon, break for a siesta at lunchtime, and resume work for a few hours in the late afternoon or evening. Government offices are usually only open in the first half of the day. The above hours are often extended in the winter.

MUSLIM FESTIVALS

Annual Festival	Approximate dates			
	2000	2001	2002	2003
Lailat Al-Mi'raj (The Prophet's night journey to heaven)	25 Oct	14 Oct	3 Oct	21 Sep
Holy fast of Ramadan	27 Nov	16 Nov	5 Nov	25 Oct
Eid Al-Fitr (The end of Ramadan)	7 Jan	27 Dec	16 Dec	5 Dec
Eid Al-Adha (The Feast of Sacrifice)	16 Mar	5 Mar	22 Feb	11 Feb
Ras As-Sana (The Muslim New Year)	6 Apr	26 Mar	15 Mar	4 Mar
Ashura (A Shia festival)	14 Apr	24 Mar	13 Mar	2 Mar
Mawlid An-Nabi (The Prophet Muhammad's Birthday)	14 Jun	3 Jun	23 May	12 May

Because the Muslim calendar follows the lunar cycle all these dates will be some 11 days earlier in each subsequent year. The actual date of a festival depends on the sighting of the moon and that may vary from place to place by a day or two.

During the month-long fast of Ramadan working hours are severely curtailed, particularly towards the end of the month, and shop opening times become erratic, opening for a few hours in the morning and then for extended periods at night after the fast has been broken.

CHAPTER TWO

The Arabic Language

INTRODUCTION

Arabic is a Semitic language, the family which includes Hebrew, Aramaic (the language of Jesus), Syriac and Ethiopic. Originally confined to the northern part of Arabia its use spread during the Arab conquests to the whole of the region. There are in addition many Arabic words in Farsi (Persian), Urdu, and the languages of the Mediterranean and African countries. Familiarity with Arabic extends to the wider Muslim community in other parts of the world. The Arabic script is used with modifications in Farsi and Urdu. All are written from right to left.

As the writings of the Holy Quran were revealed by God to the Prophet Muhammad in Arabic, the language has a sacred quality for Muslims. Arabic is the official language of all the Peninsula States.

Classical Arabic

There are significant differences between written and spoken Arabic. Written or so-called literary Arabic closely resembles the classical language which is enshrined in the Holy Quran. This is the Arabic used in newspapers, books, radio broadcasts and speeches. Classical Arabic has an extensive and highly descriptive vocabulary and an attractive turn of phrase.

2

The spoken language on the other hand differs considerably from country to country, each one having its own variations or dialect. Within the Peninsula however, the variations are not as marked as between the Peninsula and North Africa. What tends to happen when two Arabs with differing dialects meet is that they revert to the literary or classical language.

Spoken Arabic

It is generally accepted that it is only possible to understand another culture if you speak the language. (Imagine how difficult it would be for a visitor to understand the British or American culture without some command of English). But few visitors to the region have the time or the opportunity for the concentrated course necessary to attain a reasonable degree of fluency. And what, some might ask, is the point of learning Arabic if English is as widely spoken as it is by the Arabs of the Peninsula?

Yet there are good reasons for mastering a little Arabic. For anyone who is serious about getting on with Arabs it gives an excellent impression. The Arabs know how difficult it is to learn and are therefore delighted when a foreigner makes the effort. It is worth learning the essential courtesies to use when meeting and greeting people and a relatively small effort can earn a disproportionate amount of kudos and appreciation. A smattering of Arabic is also useful in a taxi or the bazaar.

THE LANGUAGE OF THE ANGELS

Arabic, spoken throughout the Arab world by some 120 million people and the religious language of an estimated 700 to 800 million Muslims in 60 different countries, is enshrined in the Holy Quran, the message revealed by the Archangel Gabriel to the Prophet Muhammad. For this reason Arabic is revered by Muslims as sacred, the language of God. The classical or literary Arabic derived from the Holy Quran is rich in vocabulary, breadth of description, hyperbole, metaphor, rhythm and rhyme. When the classical language is recited from the Holy Quran, in poetry or in prose, together with its case endings (accusative, nominative and genitive), the way in which the literary eloquence and power of expression excites the senses of the Arabs has to be experienced to be believed.

Language courses

The basic pleasantries and some useful phrases are given later in this chapter and in my *Very Simple Arabic*. There are also a variety of good courses run by such institutions as the School of African and Oriental Studies (SOAS) Language Centre at the University of London, Malet St, London WCI (Contact the Language Coordinator on Tel: 020 7691 3445 or Fax: 020 7637 7355).

Any language course must be carefully structured and sympathetically taught if the student is not to be confused or demoralised. In the case of Arabic it is also better to learn a spoken form with a strong classical bias such as is used in this book.

PRONUNCIATION

Because few people have time to learn the Arabic script, most Arabic phrase books use English transliteration, and this book is no exception. All but a few Arabic letters or sounds have an equivalent in English but those which do not are shown below:

Transliteration	pronounced as
aa	a in father
ow	ow in how
ū	u in put
dh	th in the
ch	ch in Scottish loch
gh	r in French rue
ei	eye
q	a gutteral k
'(apostrophe)	a glottal stop

There is no *p* or *v* in Arabic and an Arab will substitute *b* and *f* respectively (i.e. Peters is pronounced *Beeters* and Victor is pronounced *Fictor*).

Doubled consonants should be given double emphasis. Stressed syllables are shown in bold type. The definite article *Al* is linked to its noun or adjective by a hyphen. There is no indefinite article in Arabic.

No transliteration of Arabic can ever capture the true sounds. My aim is to give as close an approximation as possible, but as in learning any language, the reader should imitate the sounds he hears actually spoken.

Most beginners are naturally shy of pronouncing words which are totally strange to them. But speak out confidently. It does not matter if you sound a bit odd; Arabs are used to hearing a wide variety of accents from within the Arab world. They will be delighted that you have made the effort. Don't take correction as criticism – it will improve your fluency and will help to

2

establish a rapport. So the general rule for a beginner is 'Have a go!'

GREETINGS AND PLEASANTRIES

Good morning

Greeting *Sabaah al-**khair*** (lit. Morning the good)
Reply   *Sabaah an-**noor*** (lit. Morning the light)

Good afternoon/
Good evening

Greeting *Masaa al-**khair***
Reply   *Masaa an-**noor***

General greeting
(at any time)

Greeting *As-sal**aam** alayk**ū**m* (Peace be with you)
Reply   *Wa alayk**ū**m as-sal**aam*** (And with you be peace)

Hello

Greeting *Mur**uhuba***
Reply   *Mur**uhuba**,* or *Mur**uhuba**tayn* (two hellos) or
          *Mur**uhuba** beek**ū**m* (Hello to you)

How are you?

Greeting *Kayf **haal**ak?* (How is your state [of health]?)
          *Kayf **haal**ik* (to a woman)
Reply   *Al-**humd**oolillah, bi**khair**!* (Praise be to God, well!)

Note 1. *Al-**humd**oolillah,* means 'Praise be to God, I am well' and it is customary to say that you *are* even if you are at death's door! The reason is that by saying so the Muslim is acknowledging God's will over all things. (Later, if pressed, he might disclose more detail of his state of health.)

Note 2.. The word *bi**khair*** is often omitted but understood.

And how are
you?

Greeting *Wa **inta**? (Wa **intee**?* to a woman)
Reply   *Al-**humd**oolillah, bi**khair**!* (Praise be to God, well!)

Goodbye

Greeting *Maa as-sal**aama*** (With the peace [on you])
Reply   *Maa as-sal**aama*** or *Allah yisullmak* (God protect
          you) or *Fee am**aan** Allah* (To God's protection [I
          commit you])
Reply   *Fee am**aan** Allah*

2

44

Greeting *Tisbah ala khair* (lit. May the morning find
           you well)   Goodnight
Reply   *Wa **inta** min ahal al-**khair*** or *Wa **inta** min ahla*

COMMON WORDS AND EXPRESSIONS

Yes	*Aiwa or Na'aam*
No	*La*
Please	*Minfudluk*
Thank you	*Shūkraan or Mashkoor*
Thank you very much	*Shūkraan jazeelan*
That's all right	*Afwan*
Don't mention it	*La shūkraan ala waajib*
	(lit. Don't thank me, it is my duty)
What is your name please?	*Shoo ismak minfudlak*

(There is no verb 'to be' in Arabic. *See* Basic Grammar below.)

My name is Mr Peters	*Ismee Meester Beeters*
Are you an American?	*Hal inta Amrikaanee?*
I am English	*Ana Ingleezee*
I am from England	*Ana min Ingletterra*
I am from America	*Ana min Amreeka*
I am French	*Ana Faransawi*
I am from France	*Ana min Faransa*
I'm pleased to meet you	*Tasharrufna* (lit. You honour me/us)
Do you speak Arabic?	*Tatakullum Arabee? Or Tahkee Arabee?*
Only a little	*Bass qaleel/Shwei*
When will I see you?	*Aymta ashoofak?*
See you tomorrow	*Ashoofak būkra*
If God wills	*In-sha'Allah*
See you later	*Il al-liqqa* (lit: To the future)
How?	*Kayf?*
What?	*Shoo? or Aysh?*
When?	*Aymta?*
Where?	*Wayn? or Fayn?*
Why?	*Laysh?*
Who?	*Meen?*
And	*Wa*
Or	*Ow*

2

Thanks be to God	*Al-humdoolillah*
Good luck/best wishes	*Fūrsa saeeda* (lit. A happy occasion)
Excellent	*Mūmtaaz*
A little	*Qoleel* or *Shwei*
Enough!	*Bass!*
Slowly/carefully please	*Shwei shwei minfudlak*
Be patient	*Khudh Baalak* or *Towwal Baalak*
Congratulations!	*Mabrook!* (lit. Blessed!)
Reply	*Allah yubaarak feek* (lit. God bless you too)
Possibly/Maybe/Perhaps	*Yimkin*
Good	*Teiyyib* or *Qwaiyyis* (feminine: *Teiyyiba* or *Qwaiyyisa*
No problem	*Mah fee mushkilla*
Not good	*Mūsh qwaiyyis(a)* or *Mūsh teiyyib(a)*
You are kind	*Inta loteef*
I understand	*Afham*
I do not understand	*Ma afham*
What do you call this?	*Ma ism haadha?*
What does this mean?	*Ma ma'ana haadha?*
Never mind	*Ma'alaysh* or *Maa yūkhaalif*
I am sorry!	*Mūtta'assif!*
Excuse me	*Ismahlee*
Pardon/Excuse me	*Aasif*
Not at all/Don't mention it	*Afwan*
I don't know	*Ana ma aaraf* or *ana ma adree*
I didn't know	*Ana ma araft*
How far is it to...?	*Ma al-masaafa ila...?*

USEFUL PHRASES

At The Airport

My name is Peters	*Ismee Beeters*
Do you speak English?	*Tatakullam Ingleezee?*
Have you anything in your bag?	*Eindak shee fee haqeebtak?*

I have this (to declare) only	*Eindee haadha foqot/bass*
I have nothing (to declare)	*Ma eindee shee*
This is necessary for my work?	*Haadha dharooree li amalee/shoghallee*
Where is the toilet please?	*Wayn al-hamaam (al-twoylet) minfudlak?*
Where is the bank please?	*Wayn al-bank minfudlak?*
Where is my case?	*Wayn shantatee?*
Hi porter!	*Ya hammaal!*
This is mine/ours	*Haadha lee/ilna*
There is a case missing	*Naaqis shanta*
How much is that?	*Kam?*
Get me a taxi please	*Ūtlub lee taxi minfudlak*
I want to hire a car	*Ūreed astajir saiyaara*
Where is the bus to the city?	*Wayn al-baas lil madeena?*
Where is the British Consulate/Embassy?	*Wayn Al-Consuleeya/ As-Sifaara Al-Bareetaaneeya?*
I want to change some travellers cheques	*Ūreed ūsruf sheekaat seeyaheeya*

In a Taxi

Taxi!	*Taxi!*
To The Bustan Hotel please	*Il Al-Fūnduk Al-Bústaan minfudlak*
Yes (Sir)	*Na'am (Seedee)*
How much?	*Kam?*
Twenty Riyals	*Ishreen riyaal*
No, that's a lot	*La, katheer*
Fifteen Riyals	*Khamsta'asher riyaal*
Good	*Teiyyib*
How many kilometres to the Hilton ?	*Kam keeloomitr illal-Hiltoon*
Ten	*'Ashara*
Go straight ahead	*Rūh mubaasharaton*
To the left here	*Il al-yesaar hina*
To the right	*Il al-yameen*
Stop there	*Woqqof hinaak*
Faster please	*Bisir'a minfudlak*
Slower please	*Bibbūt minfudlak*
Wait here please	*Intadhar hina minfudlak*

47

I will return in five minutes *Aarja' baad **kham**sa da**qaa'**iq*

In a Hotel
I have a reservation *Ein**dee** hajz*
I want a room please *Ūreed gh**ū**rfa min**fud**lak*
I want a double room *Ūreed gh**ū**rfa li*
   with a bath *shakhsayn laha ham**aam***
Is there good air-conditioning? *Hal al-m**ū**kayyif **teiy**yib?*
How much is it a day? *Kam al-ee**jaar** li **mū**ddat yome?*
   (lit: How much is the rent
   for the period of a day?)
Have you a cheaper room *Eindak gh**ū**rfa **ark**has*
   than that? *min **dhaa**lik?*
I want to see the room, *Ūreed a**shoof** al-gh**ū**rfa*
please *min**fud**lak*
No, I don't like it *La, maa ahibha*
Is there a better room? *Fee gh**ū**rfa **ah**san?*
This is fine *Haadha **teiy**yib*
Who is that? *Meen?*
(to a knock at the door)
A message for you *Ris**aala** lak*
A moment, please *Lah**dha**, min**fud**lak*
Come in! *Ta'**aal!***
For you *Illak*
Is there a reply? *Fee ja**waab?***

Calling on an Arab
Welcome *Ahlan wa **sah**lan* (a shortened
   version is *Ahlan*)
Replies *Ahlan wa **sah**lan **beek*** or
   Feek (to single host)
   *Ahlan wa **sah**lan **beek**ūm* or
   *Feek**ūm*** (to more than one
   host)
I'd like to introduce Mr Peters *Ahib **ū**qaddumlak **Mee**ster
   Beeters*
I'm pleased to meet you *Tashurru**fna*** (lit: You honor us)
   or *F**ū**rsa saeeda* (lit: A
   happy occasion)

At this early stage, the greetings appropriate to the time of day will also be exchanged and enquiries made after each person's health (*see* p. 42)

Please sit down	*Minfudlak, astarreeh* or *Tistarroh*
Reply	*Shūkraan* (Thank you)
Please have a cigarette?	*Tafuddal sigaara?*
Please have coffee/tea?	*Tafuddal qahwa/shei?*

Note 1: The meaning of the word *tafuddal* cannot be exactly translated into English. It is much used when offering or inviting someone politely to do or have something. Literally, it means 'be pleased to'.

You'll drink coffee/tea?	*Tishrub qahwa/shei?*
Reply	*Aiwa*

Note 2: Do not say 'thank you' as this is taken to mean 'no' in the same way that the French use 'merci'. It would, of course, be impolite to refuse refreshment. For further explanation *see* Chapter 3.

Enough, thank you	*Beekufee/Bass, shūkraan*
That is enough [like that]	*Haadha kifaaya kida*
Delicious!	*Lodheedh!*

When you wish to say farewell you might say:

With your permission	*'An idhnak*

The host might then say:

You have honoured us	*Shurruftna*
Reply	*Tushurruft* (I have been honoured)
My home is your home	*Baytee baytak*
I compliment your cooking	*Tislam eedayk* (to a man) *eedaykee* (to a woman)

Shopping
The market   *As-sooq*

49

How much?	*Beekam?*
Eleven dinars	*Had'ashar denaar*
No, I'll give you five dinars	*La, aateek khamsa deenaar*
No, eight	*La, Thamaania*
No, it is very expensive	*La, ghaalee jiddan*

(There is no exact Arabic translation for 'too' expensive)

Good (OK), seven dinars - my last word	*Teiyyib, saba'a deenaar aakhar kalaam*
OK, but it is expensive	*Teiyyib, laakin ghaalee*
No, it is cheap	*La, hūwa rakhees*
Is this shop open?	*Hal haadha ad-dūkkaan maftooh?*
No, it is closed [closed up]	*La, mūsakkar*
No it is closed [locked up]	*La, maqfool*
Do you want something?	*Tūreed Shee?*
No, I am only looking around	*La, atafarraj foqot*
Look! Look!	*Shoof! Shoof!* (trader's shout)
A tip! A tip!	*Baqsheesh! Baqsheesh!* (small boys' cry to tourists)

Replies:

I am in a rush	*Ana mūsta'jil* or
I have no change	*Maa eindee faqqar*
or I forgot, my wallet is in the hotel)	*Nasseet, al-mahjazza fil fūndūq*
or Run along! Run along!	*Imshee! Imshee!*
Where is the post office please?	*Wayn* (or *Fayn*) *maktab al-bareed minfudlak?*
I want to buy (a shirt) please	*Ūreed ishteree (qomees) minfudlak*

Other words from the vocabulary can be substituted in this sentence.

Sightseeing

Where is the bus station please?	*Wayn mahattat al-baas minfudlak?*

(*Al-Bass* or *As-Sayaara Al-Aam*, public car)

The first street on the left	*Awwal sharri' alal-yasaar*
Is it far from here?	*Ba'eed min hina?*
No, it is close. Only five minutes	*La, qoreeb. Khamsa daqaa'iq foqot*
Is it possible to walk?	*Mūmkin imshee?*

2

Yes, it is (a distance of) 400 metres	*Aiwa, tab'ūd ala masaafa arba'a meeat meeter*
Where is the bus to Dubai?	*Wayn al-baas ila Dubai?*
How much?	*Beekam?*
Tell me when we arrive please	*Qullee eind al-wusool minfudlak*
Where are we now?	*Wayn nehnaa alaan?*
When do we go?	*Aymta nimshee?*
After ten minutes	*Ba'ad 'ashara daqaa'iq*
Where is the best place to go?	*Wayn ahsan makaan arooh?*
Yes, come!	*Aiwa, ta'aal!*
What is there here?	*Shoo hinaak?*
Taxi! Do you know where the office of tourism is?	*Taxi! Ta'rif wayn maktab as-seeyaaha?*
I want to visit (the museum)	*Ūreed azoor (Al-Mat'haf)*

Eating Out

Is there a cafe near here?	*Fee maqha qoreeb min hina?*
A cold lemon drink please	*Laymoon baarid minfudlak*
Tea/coffee please	*Shei/qahwa minfudlak*
How many do you want?	*Kam tūreed?*
For how many people?	*Li kam nafar?*
Two please	*Ithnayn minfudlak*
Have you got Nescafe?	*Eindak qahwa neskafay?*
With milk and sugar	*Maa haleeb wa sookar*
The bill please	*Al-hisaab minfudlak*
Is there a restaurant near here?	*Fee mattam qoreeb min hina?*
Please, we would like (kebabs)	*Minfudlak nūreed (kabaab)*

Miscellaneous Phrases

Is it possible to play (tennis) here?	*Mūmkin al'ab (tennees) hina?*
Is there a swimming pool?	*Fee hammaam sabaaha?*
I want to swim in the sea	*Ūreed asbah fil bahr*
Is it possible to fish here?	*Mūmkin sayd as-samak hina?*
[Reply] Of course, certainly!	*Ma'loom!*
Is there (a barber) here, please?	*Fee (hallaaq) hina, minfudlak?*

2

EMERGENCY PHRASES

Call the Police!	*Ūtlub al-boolees!*
Call An Ambulance!	*Ūtlub al-is'aaf!*
Call the Fire Brigade!	*Ūtlub al-mataafee!*
	or *Itfaa'eeya*
Call a Doctor!	*Ūtlub al-doctoor!*
Careful (Take it easy)	*ala mahlak*
Careful! (A hole in the road)	*Ihtaris!*
Careful! (Pay attention)	*Khūdh baalak!*
Come here!	*Ta'aal!* (pl. *Ta'aaloo*)
Danger	*Khatar*
Take it easy!	*Tawwel baalak!*
Help!/Rescue me!	*An-najda!*
Fire!	*Hareeq!*
Go away!	*Insarif!*
I'm ill	*Ana mareed*
I've lost my way	*Ana tūht*
Leave me alone!	*Itrūkni li-haali!* (said with conviction)
Or if you don't, I'll call the police	*Wa Illa La, ajeeblak al-boolees*
Listen!	*Isma'!*
Look	*Ūnzūr*
Quickly	*Bi sir'a*
Stop!	*Qiff!* (or *Woqqof*)
Stop that man!	*Amsik haadha ar-rajūl!*
Thief!	*Liss!*
Is it important?	*Hoowa mūhim?*
Is it urgent?	*Haadha musta'jil?*

Telling the Time

What is the time please?	*As-saa'a kam minfudlak?*
Five minutes past twelve	*As-saa'a ithna'ashar wa khamsa daqaa'iq*

Arabs say 'The hour [is] twelve and five minutes'. This is the same for all times except quarter past, twenty past, and half past.

Quarter past twelve	*As-saa'a ithna'ashar wa ruba'*
	(lit: Twelve and a quarter)

Twenty past twelve	*As-saa'a ithna'ashar wa thūlth*
	(lit: Twelve and a third)
Half past twelve	*As-saa'a ithna'ashar wa nuss*
	(lit: Twelve and a half)
Twenty to one	*As-saa'a waahida ila thūlth*
	(lit: One less a third)
Quarter to one	*As-saa'a Waahida ila Ruba'*
	(lit: One less a quarter)
Five to one	*As-saa'a waahida ila khamsa*
	(lit: One less five)
One o'clock	*As-saa'a waahida*

BASIC GRAMMAR

Although Arabic as a Semitic language is structurally different from English, it is in many ways simpler. Firstly, it is phonetic – a word is pronounced as it is written and there are no silent letters. Secondly, the rules of grammar tend to be obeyed whereas in English there are many exceptions. Finally, although it looks complicated, the script has a rational basis with only a few more letters and sounds than in English.

Tri-literal Roots
In common with all Semitic languages, Arabic nouns, adjectives and verbs can be traced back to three or sometimes four consonants. For example, the consonant **K** plus **T** plus **B** is the root for 'writing'. By putting vowels and other consonants around this root in various combinations, it is possible to make up all the words to do with writing:

Ka**T**a**B**	=	He wrote
Ka**T**a**B**oo	=	They wrote
ya**K**T**a**B	=	He will write
Ki**T**aa**B**	=	A book
Kaa**T**i**B**	=	A clerk
ma**K**T**a**B	=	An office
ma**K**T**a**B**a	=	A library
ma**K**T**oo**B**	=	It is written

2

53

Word Order

The word order in a sentence of literary Arabic is *verb, subject, object*. In the spoken language, however, the order is as in English – *subject, verb and object*.

Numbers

It is worth noting that the grammar of numbers if particularly complex and a minefield, even for experienced Arabists.

0	*Sifr*	10	*Ashara*
1	*Waahid*	11	*Hada'shar*
2	*Ithnayn*	12	*Ithna'ashar*
3	*Thalaatha*	13	*Thalaathtat'ashar*
4	*Arba'a*	14	*Arbat'ashar*
5	*Khamsa*	15	*Khamst'ashar*
6	*Sitta*	16	*Sitt'ashar*
7	*Saba'a*	17	*Saba'at'ashar*
8	*Thamaania*	18	*Thamaant'tashar*
9	*Tis'a*	19	*Tis'at'ashar*

20	*'Ishreen*
21	*Waahid wa 'Ishreen*
30	*Thalaatheen*
40	*Arba'een*
50	*Khamseen*
60	*Sitteen*
70	*Saba'een*
80	*Thamaanee'een*
90	*Tis'een*
100	*Meea*

Numbers after 20 are made up on the following pattern:

22	*Ithnayn wa 'Ishreen*
33	*Thalaatha wa Thalaatheen*
48	*Thamaania wa Arba'een*

Unlike words or sentences, numbers in Arabic are written from left to right, i.e. 1999 =١٩٩٩. However, groups of numbers such as dates are usually written so that the groups themselves run from right to left, i.e. 21/5/1999 = ١٩٩٩/٥/٢١ .

A or An

There is no indefinite article (a/an) in Arabic and it is unnecessary to qualify a single object by using *waahid* (one). For example, *wulud* (boy), when standing on its own, means 'a' or 'one' boy.

Two

There is a special way of saying 'two' of anything in Arabic. this is know as the 'dual' and is formed by adding the ending *ayn* to the noun e.g. *wulud* means 'one boy' *wulud**ayn*** means 'two boys'. If the noun ends in 'a', add '*tayn*' to it, e.g. *ghurfa**tayn*** = two rooms.

Numbers 3 to 10

From 3 to 10 the accompanying noun is in the plural but from eleven onwards it is in the singular, e.g.

*Thal**aatha** aw**laad***	Three boys (*aw**laad*** is the plural of *wulud*)
'*Ishreen wulud*	Twenty boys

Percentages

Ten per cent is rendered as 'ten in (a) hundred' e.g.
Ashara bil meea.
Twenty per cent is   '*Ishreen bil meea*'.

Fractions

The basic fractions which you might need are:

a half	*nuss*
a quarter	*rub'a*
a third	*thūlth*

The Definite Article

This is *Al* in Arabic. In spoken Arabic, in front of words beginning with *t th d dh s sh r z n* and sometimes *g*, the *l*

2

of the article is assimilated. So *al-shams* (the sun) is pronounced *ash-shams*.

Nouns

Nouns in Arabic are either masculine or feminine in gender. Nouns referring only to females may be assumed to be feminine and so may most nouns ending in *a*. Most other nouns will be masculine - there are exceptions, of course, and these simply need to be learnt, as the adjective must always agree with its noun.

Plurals

As explained above, there are three kinds of quantity in Arabic – the singular, the dual and the plural. Plurals are formed in two ways. They are either broken plurals or sound plurals. The broken plurals are not formed on one particular pattern but are nevertheless variants of the singular and are best learnt by rote. For example:

Singular   *wulud* (boy)   Plural   *awlaad* (boys)
Singular   *bayt* (house)   Plural   *booyoot* (houses)

Sound plurals if they are feminine and end in *a* form the plural by adding *aat*:

Singular   *hukooma* (government)
Plural   *hukoomaat* (governments)

and masculine nouns referring to people form their plural simply by adding *een*:

Singular   *Muslim*
Plural   *Muslimeen*

Adjectives

Adjectives follow their noun. If the noun carries the definite article then so does the adjective, e.g.
<u>Al</u>-*wulud* <u>al</u>-*sagheer* = The small boy

Normally adjectives agree with the noun in gender and number. However, when the noun is referring to plural 'things' or 'animals' then the adjective is put in the feminine singular by adding the suffix *a*, e.g.

As-sanawaat al-akheera = The recent years

The comparative of most adjectives takes the following form:

kabeer = big	and	*akbar* = bigger
rakhees = cheap	and	*arkhas* = cheaper
katheer = many	and	*akthar* = more

Verbs

Arabic has only two tenses – one denoting completed action, and the other incomplete action. In simple terms this means a past tense and a present tense. The present tense is also used to cover the future. For example:

Katab = He wrote (past)
Yaktub = He is writing (present) or He will write (future)

The verb 'to be' does not exist in the present tense. For example:

Al-wulud sagheer = The boy is small ('is' being understood)

In colloquial Arabic, 'there is' and 'there are' are translated by the word *fee*, followed by the noun in the singular or plural:

Fee hallaaq hina = There is a barber here
Fee booyoot hinaak? = Are there houses there?

'There was' and 'there were' are translated by the words *kaan fee*.

He was = *Kaan*   She was = *Kaanat*   I was = *Kūnt*.
He will be = *Yakoon*   She will be = *Takoon* I will be = *Akoon*

Simple regular verbs in Arabic consist of a root of three consonants and when an Arab refers to a verb he uses the third person singular:

Katab = He wrote (i.e. to write - there is no infinitive in Arabic)

The Past Tense
This is formed by attaching suffixes to the root *Katab.*

Katabt	I wrote	*Katabna*	We wrote
Katabt	You (masc.) wrote	*Katabtoo*	You (pl.) wrote
Katabtee	You (fem.) wrote	*Kataboo*	They wrote
Katab	He wrote		
Katabat	She wrote		

Note that the subject pronoun (I, you, he etc.) is normally omitted in Arabic.

The Present and Future Tense

This is formed with a prefix (and sometimes also a suffix) to the modified root and by changing its second vowel:

Aktūb	I write	**Naktūb**	We write
Taktūb	You (masc.) write	*Taktūboo*	You (pl.) write
Taktūbee	You (fem.) write	*Yaktūboo*	They write
Yaktūb	He writes		
Taktūb	She writes		

Although the final vowel change varies and must be learnt for each verb, the same format is used for most regular verbs.

The Imperative
This is formed on the following pattern:

Singular	*Ūktūb!*	Write!
Plural	*Ūktūboo!*	Write!

The Negative
This is formed by putting *maa* in front of the verb:

*Maa kat**abt***   I did not write
In sentences without the verb 'to be', the word *mush* is used:

Ana mush min London I am not from London

The imperative is negated by prefixing *Laa* to the present tense:

*Laa t**ūkt**ūb!*   Don't write!

Personal Pronouns
These are as follows:

Ana	I	*Nehna*	We
Inta	You (masc.)	*Intum*	You (pl.)
Intee	You (fem.)	*Hum*	They
Hoowa	He/it		
Heeya	She/it		

Possession and Object of a Verb
This is denoted by attaching suffixes to the noun:

-ee	my	*-na*	ours
-ak	yours (masc.)	*-kum*	yours(pl.)
-ik	yours (fem.)	*-hum*	theirs
-oh	his		
-ha	hers		

e.g. *bayt* + *ee* = my house

When a noun has a feminine ending *a*, then *t* is put in front of the suffix:

seiyaara   = car,   and   *seiyaaratee* = my car
e.g. *Seiyaara* + *t* + *ee*

The object of a verb is also denoted by using the same suffix, with the exception that *ee* becomes *nee*:
He struck me = *Darubnee*

To have

This is expressed in Arabic by adding the same suffixes to the word *Eind*. For example:

Eindee = I have   *Eindak* = You have

But there is a Special Rule of Possession in Arabic called the construct state: 'The house of the boy' is not translated as such. In Arabic this would be:

Bayt al-wulud = (The) house (of) the boy

The definite article is dropped from the first word and 'of' is understood. Names are considered definite and so:

Bayt Mohammed = Mohammed's house

Questions

To ask a question, use the same intonation as in English:

Eindak qahwa? = Have you (got) coffee?

There is much more to Arabic grammar than this but it is hoped that these simplified rules will be a helpful introduction.

THE ARABIC SCRIPT

One of the reasons people consider Arabic a difficult language is the complicated appearance of the script. But it is not that difficult if you analyse it.

Arabic script is written from right to left and is cursive, meaning that most of the letters in any word are joined together.

The twenty-nine characters of the Arabic alphabet are given below. All but three have an equivalent sound in

English. There are no capital letters in Arabic. Each letter has a slightly different form depending on its position in a word, but the basic characteristic of the letter is nevertheless recognisable wherever it is:

Name of letter	Pronunciation	Form depending on position		
		End	Middle	Beginning
أ *alif*	a as in apple	ـا	ـا	أ
ب *ba*	b as in ball	ـب	ـبـ	بـ
ت *ta*	t as in top	ـت	ـتـ	تـ
ث *tha*	th as in thin	ـث	ـثـ	ثـ
ج *jeem*	j as in job	ـج	ـجـ	جـ
ح *ha* (hard)	h as in hoot	ـح	ـحـ	حـ
خ *kha*	kh as in loch	ـخ	ـخـ	خـ
د *daal*	d as in day	ـد	ـد	د
ذ *dhaal*	th as in then	ـذ	ـذ	ذ
ر *ra*	r rolled as in roar	ـر	ـر	ر
ز *za*	z as in zebra	ـز	ـز	ز
س *seen*	s as in sit	ـس	ـسـ	سـ
ش *sheen*	sh as in shine	ـش	ـشـ	شـ
ص *sawd*	s as in sword, said with emphasis	ـص	ـصـ	صـ
ض *dawd*	d as in door, said with emphasis	ـض	ـضـ	ضـ
ط *to*	t as in taught, said with emphasis	ـط	ـطـ	طـ
ظ *dho*	th as in then, said with emphasis	ـظ	ـظـ	ظـ
ع *'ein*	like a glottal stop	ـع	ـعـ	عـ
غ *ghein*	like the r in French 'rue'	ـغ	ـغـ	غـ
ف *fa*	f as in feed	ـف	ـفـ	فـ
ق *qaaf*	c as in caught or in some countries a glottal stop	ـق	ـقـ	قـ
ك *kaf*	k as in kite	ـك	ـكـ	كـ
ل *lam*	l as in let	ـل	ـلـ	لـ
م *meem*	m as in met	ـم	ـمـ	مـ

2

Name of letter	Pronunciation	Form depending on position		
		End	Middle	Beginning
ن noon	n as in net	ن	ـنـ	نـ
ه ha(soft)	h as in hear	ـه	ـهـ	هـ
و wow	w as in well	ـو	ـو	و
ي ya	y as in yet	ـي	ـيـ	يـ
ء hamza	glottal stop (gentler than the 'ein)			

Short Vowels

There are three short vowels which are sounded but are normally omitted in writing. Exceptions are the Holy Quran and in calligraphy.

ˊ written above the word, sounds like the 'a' in pat

ˏ written below the word, sounds like the 'i' in pit

ˀ written above the word, sounds like short 'u' in root

Long Vowels

These are formed by following a short vowel with the letter associated with it:

آ sounds like an 'a' in pass

وُ the short 'u' plus a *wow* sounds like an 'oo' in root

يِ the short 'i' plus a *ya* like an 'ee' in feet

Diphthongs

These are formed by combining short and long vowels:

وَ the short 'a' vowel plus a *wow* sounds like 'ow' in cow

يَ the short 'a' vowel plus a *ya* sounds like 'ay' in 'hay'

Dots
These are often joined in handwriting:

    ت handwritten looks like   ﺖ

    ث handwritten looks like   ﺚ

    ي handwritten looks like   ﯽ

Special 'a'
In some cases the ى without the dots at the end of a word is pronounced as a long 'a' sound. These have to be learnt by experience.

Ta marboota
The letter ﻩ is often found at the end of a word with two dots above it: i.e.   ﺔ   This is a common form of feminine ending. It is usually pronounced as an 'a' sound. When followed by the definite article it is pronounced as a 't'. It is called a *ta marboota*.

Orthographic Signs
The most common are:

   °   used to mark a consonant without a vowel

   ٵ   at the end of a word, giving the sound 'an'

   ّ   above a letter, has the effect of doubling it

Examples
By referring to the alphabet it should be possible to decipher the following words. (Remember to read from right to left.)

كَتَب = ب + ت + ك   spells *Katab* and means 'he wrote'

أَلْبَيْت = ت + ي + ب + ل + ا   spells *al-Bayt* and means 'the house'

هَدَف = ف + د + هـ   spells *Hadaf* and means 'target'

Examples of Common Signs

مطار	Airport	متحف	Museum
اسعاف	Ambulance	ممنوع الدخول	No entry
القادمون	Arrivals	ممنوع الوقوف	No parking
بنك	Bank	ممنوع المرور	No thoroughfare
حلاق	Barber	ممنوع التصوير	No photography
مكتبة	Bookshop	جوازات	Passports
مقهى	Café	خاص	Private
مركز (ل)	Centre (for)	طريق خاص	Private road
سينما	Cinema	اسحب	Pull
الجمرك	Customs	ادفع	Push
خطر	Danger	مطعم	Restaurant
دائرة	Department	يمين	Right
المسافرون	Departures	طريق	Road
مدخل	Entrance	مدرسة	School
مخرج	Exit	قف	Stop!
للاجرة	For hire	شارع	Street
للبيع	For sale	خياط	Tailor
ممنوع	Forbidden	تاكسي	Taxi
مستشفى	Hospital	تلفون	Telephone
فندق	Hotel	تواليت (دورة مياه)	Toilet
يسار	Left	رجال	Men
منطقة عسكرية	Military area	سيدات/نساء	Ladies
صراف	Money changer	جامعة	University
خطر الموت	Mortal danger	سيدات/نساء	Women
البلدية	Municipality		

CHAPTER THREE

Etiquette

INTRODUCTION

There is a strict code of social conduct or etiquette throughout the Peninsula and it is possible for a foreigner who is ignorant of it to give offence, although it must be said that the Arabs are generally very tolerant of foreigners who are clearly unaware of it. Arab courtesy is such that even if someone does transgress they must never be allowed to know it. Nevertheless, it is a decided advantage to understand the basic rules, and the purpose of this chapter is to explain the key common denominators of etiquette pertaining to the region as a whole. Once you understand them do not be over-confident. Some of the worst howlers are committed by those with a little knowledge who imagine they can extrapolate from it to meet an unfamiliar situation. Only practise what you know to be correct.

3

ARAB COURTESY

No visitor to the Arabian Peninsula can fail to be impressed by the friendliness, courtesy and unfailing hospitality of the Arabs and the most important characteristic for personal success is to be well-mannered. As Sir Donald Hawley writes in his book *Manners and Correct Form in the Middle East*, 'The ill-mannered man is not forgiven, and, however well-intentioned he may be, he will fail.' The best advice to someone visiting the region is to be polite, patient and as considerate as the Arabs are themselves.

CALLING ON AN ARAB

The Arab Perception of Time

The first hurdle in a foreigner's understanding is likely to be the Arab perception of time. It is quite different to that in the West. One should always be on time for any

Appointments

appointment but be prepared to wait, sometimes for a long time, or even to have a meeting postponed or conceivably cancelled. On the occasions when this happens it is not necessarily bad manners or forgetfulness but of necessity. The person you are visiting will have acted for reasons which may not seem justified to you but which are perfectly valid in his culture. His presence may have been requested at short notice by a more senior person or for important family business. You should resist the inclination to feel frustrated or slighted and accept the situation with good grace. As you become more familiar with the culture you will begin to understand.

Shaking Hands

Shaking hands

Whenever you greet or take leave of someone always shake hands and only with the right hand. Try not to use too firm a grip. On entering a room full of people, shake hands and exchange greetings first with the person on whom you are calling and then with as many others present as seems appropriate, i.e. those in the immediate vicinity of your host. It is customary to shake hands even if you have not been formally introduced. Once an Arab feels he knows you do not be surprised if he holds on to your hand as a mark of friendship or occasionally taps you on the arm during conversation to emphasis a point. Arabs are more tactile than Westerners. *See also* Chapter 1 - *Values.*

One exception to the rule of shaking hands is that it is not normal for a man to shake the hand of an Arab woman unless she follows the Western custom and specifically offers it.

Greetings

It is particularly important to give a person on whom you are calling his correct name and title. Detailed advice on Arab names and forms of address are given later in this Chapter under *Forms of Address.* Although Arabs are only too conscious of the difficulties of their language and will almost certainly greet you in English,

you may sometimes gain enormous kudos if you are
able to master one or two of the basic pleasantries in
Arabic. The standard greetings are given in Chapter 2 ,
but the most common general greeting in the Peninsula
is:

Greeting *As-Salaam alaykum*
(Peace be on you)

Reply *Wa alaykum as-Salaam*
(And on you be peace)

An Arab may also say to you *Ahlan wa sahlan!*
(Welcome!)

To which the reply is *Ahlan wa sahlan beekūm!*
(And to you!)

Enquiries are then always made into each other's
health; a formula which is invariably observed no
matter how frequently you meet someone or talk on the
phone. Even if you ring an Arab say, twice in one hour
it is still considered important to ask how he is before
mentioning the subject of your call. When you get to
know an Arab better, you might also ask after the well-
being of his family. Enquiries about the family are
restricted to the collective family and children. Because
of the greater privacy accorded to women in the Arab
world one should never enquire after an Arab's wife,
unless you or your wife know the family very well.

Taking a Seat

When you enter the office of an Arab for a business
meeting do not be surprised to find it full of other
visitors. A senior Arab figure will routinely receive large
numbers of people each day who may call to enlist his
help or simply to greet him. When you introduce yourself
to your host you should, unless it seems inappropriate,
give him your card. If you intend to be a regular visitor
to the region this should be printed in Arabic as well as
English.

A seat will then be indicated to you, possibly with the
word *tafuddal.*

69

Ta*fud*dal

The meaning of the word cannot be exactly translated into English but is the term used when offering a seat or ushering someone through a doorway. Literally translated it means 'be pleased to' or 'be so good as to' (go first). If the room is crowded the seat will probably be on the immediate right or left of your host and this position is usually reserved for the most important visitor. In other words, because you are the latest arrival you are considered most important - for the moment anyway. When someone else arrives you should stand up, shake hands with the newcomer and be prepared to vacate your seat for him. Watch your host and take your lead from him.

The Sole of the Foot

A traditional custom in the Arab world which is still observed today is to avoid presenting the sole of your foot directly at another person. The sole of the foot was traditionally considered unclean and this used to mean, and still does in some countries, that you are intentionally insulting that person. So to be on the safe side it is advisable to sit with both feet on the floor and not cross your legs unless your host does so and even then to avoid presenting your sole directly to him. If you are fortunate enough to be invited to an Arab meal sitting on the floor the same rule applies. Shoes are removed and the soles of the feet tucked in underneath or kept behind you.

Refreshments

When you visit an Arab he will invariably offer you refreshment, normally tea or coffee, and it is usual to wait for this to arrive before mentioning the purpose of your visit. However, it is becoming increasingly common in some circles to dispense with such formalities and start talking seriously as soon as greetings have been exchanged. Your host's manner and general comportment will usually tell you what type of person he is. If he abides by the traditional custom, the initial greetings will be followed by a period of silence or confined to general enquiries after your well-being or journey until a servant enters with tea or coffee.

You can be offered a variety of refreshments. In many places in the region you will still be offered Arab coffee (*gahwa*) in the Bedu tradition. It would be impolite to refuse. Arab coffee is pale, bitter and often flavoured with cardamon and other spices. A small amount is poured from a long spouted brass coffee pot into a small handleless cup which should be taken in the right hand, even if you are left-handed. Only the right hand should be used when drinking, eating, smoking or offering anything to another person (even for waving in welcome). Drink as many cups as you like but not a lot more than your host or others present. Two or three is usual.

The signal to show that you have had enough is to give the cup a quick twist or shake when handing it back. If it is handed back without doing this the server will simply continue to refill it. It is not done to *say* that you have had sufficient - just indicate by shaking the cup. You may also be offered dates with the coffee. You could also be offered thick, strong, Turkish coffee (in a small cup) after being asked whether you take it without sugar, medium or sweet but this is a custom more common to the Levant and other Arab countries outside the Gulf region. It may be accompanied by a glass of water to quench the thirst. Turkish coffee should be sipped, being careful to leave the thick coffee grounds in the bottom of the cup. Another refreshment offered is tea in the Arab style which is sweet, without milk and served in a small glass cup and saucer

These are the most common refreshments but it is becoming increasingly common in large establishments with perhaps a lot of expatriate employees to serve instant coffee and tea or a soft drink or a glass of water.

Smoking is becoming less popular in the Middle East, as elsewhere, and one should only smoke if invited to do so, or following the host's lead.

Shaking the coffee cup

3

Broaching the Subject of Your Visit

Generally speaking, once refreshments have been served, the moment should be opportune for you to consider raising the subject of your visit. However, it is usually best to wait until you are invited to do so or to have a clear sign from your host that he is willing for it to be introduced. You must be particularly sensitive to the mood and circumstances of the meeting and not force the pace. Give your host long enough and he will normally give you an indication. The last thing you should do is to show impatience. In the event that you are clearly discouraged from talking seriously, do not be tempted to persist. There is likely to be a good reason. You should also avoid discussing your business in front of others. Simply ask if you can meet again.

Never expect a topic to be raised, discussed and a decision taken on your first visit. An Arab will not only wish to get to know you, but also consider the matter you are bringing to his attention; it would be quite wrong to push him just because your time is limited. It should be his concept of time that matters rather than yours.

Communication

As has been said, many Arabs speak good English. Nevertheless, as a general rule you should bear the following points in mind:

Make due allowance for a limited knowledge of English. A limited vocabulary may make a person's meaning obscure. If you are in any doubt it is prudent to rephrase it back to him diplomatically to confirm. The limited command of a language can also make a phrase sound unintentionally rude. An example of this can be seen when a customs official at the airport says to you 'Give passport!' because those are the only words he knows in English.

Use simple English. Native English speakers use the vernacular without thinking and it can be particularly

Getting to the point

Plain English

3

difficult to understand if English is not your mother tongue. Use short sentences rather than long ones for additional clarity.

Make your point briefly and succinctly. When the opportunity arises to mention the subject of your visit, for example a business proposal, do not wrap it up with a long lead in or a detailed explanation. At an initial meeting a brief and succinct description is far more likely to elicit interest and hopefully, the dialogue will proceed from there.

Avoid discussing politics, religion and women. Suffice it to say that these are delicate and often emotive subjects. Refer to the Gulf and not the Persian Gulf (*see* Chapter 1 - *Historical Summary*). Respect Islam but don't be tempted to comment on it. Finally, women in the Arab world enjoy an altogether more secluded position than in many other cultures and a male visitor should avoid mentioning them. Asking an Arab if he has children on the other hand can open a topic of genuine mutual interest.

Conversational *Faux Pas*

Be careful with humour. Arabs have a great sense of fun. Do not be afraid to show that you have a sense of

THE ARAB SENSE OF HUMOUR

There is an old story of a ruling Arab Sheikh who, in the early days of the development of the Peninsula states, asked a British official to send him an 'expert'. The British offical readily agreed but asked what the expert's specialisation was to be. The Sheikh replied that he did not want the official to invent problems, just to provide him with an expert. "Right, Your Highness!' said the British official and took his leave. As he reached the door, the Sheikh called out, "And another thing, let him have only one arm." "Only one arm, Your Highness?" queried the official. 'Yes," said the Sheikh, "I want none of this, 'on the one hand...and on the other hand'!"

humour but do not attempt to entertain an Arab with jokes until you are quite sure what he does or does not appreciate. Never use sarcasm or irony. It is likely to be misunderstood or regarded as unkind.

Do not worry about pauses in conversation. Silences are not embarrassing to an Arab. He does not feel the need as we do to maintain a steady flow of conversation. Indeed, lengthy silences are often the norm in Arab social gatherings. They will often simply take pleasure in each other's company.

Be diplomatic. Nothing you say or do must in any way be construed as critical, disapproving or patronising about the Arab world.

In short, be careful what you say. Avoid going to extremes. Don't bore your host with the merits of your own country, government or systems. He may take it as implying criticism of his own. You should aim to demonstrate that you are a straightforward but discreet person with balanced personal views, whom he can trust.

Interruptions
You may be fortunate in being alone with your host but you should not be thrown if there are others present and the meeting is subject to interruptions. Because of the open-door policy of the Arab culture anyone, particularly an important person, may call on your host at any time and each new arrival will receive the same courteous welcome as yourself. The telephone or an intercom may also interrupt the dialogue. Having said that, an Arab appreciates privacy as much as you do and if he likes you, the initial contact usually leads to a private meeting. But it is your host who will determine that. You may hint that you have something confidential or important to impart and even invite him for a private meal in a restaurant or hotel but usually it is he who will make the first steps towards meeting in a more private venue.

3

Open door
policy

Personal Relationships
As emphasised in Chapter 1, the Arabs set great store by
personal relationships. You will always be greeted
courteously but beyond that you may or may not detect
that an Arab is holding back until he is clear what sort of
person you are, if he considers he can trust you or if he is
interested in conducting business with you. Your
demeanour must be open, friendly and polite but not
over-familiar or ingratiating. A relationship of trust on
both sides will take time to establish. As a general rule,
the degree of mutual trust will be commensurate with the
number of times you have met.

Rapport

Cancelled Meetings
As mentioned earlier, do not show any sign of
annoyance or frustration if a meeting is cancelled or
interrupted, when, for example, your host's presence is
demanded elsewhere, sometimes at short notice.
Practical difficulties and misunderstandings do occur.
In order to succeed one must be able to accept such
situations with equanimity, however inconvenient,
demonstrating a calm and relaxed attitude. See *The
Arab Perception of Time* above.

3

Taking Your Leave
Initial visits are usually short. Do not attempt to
achieve significant results at a first meeting. It is quite
enough to introduce yourself and perhaps the subject of
your visit. Overstaying your welcome could jeopardise
your chances later on. If you are a businessman, you
might leave a brochure or briefing document with your
card. On leaving, if possible remember the phrase for
'Goodbye':

Farewells

Greeting   *Maa as-salaama* (Lit. With the peace [on you])
Reply   *Maa as-salaama* or *Allah yisullmak* (God
             protect you)

If, on leaving an office or Arab house, your host escorts
you to the door he will invariably stand on your left and

75

invite you to go through the door first, usually with the word *tafuddal*. It is considered polite to demur once or twice before accepting. The reverse would apply if you were the host and then your guest would politely refuse once or twice before accepting.

RECEIVING AN ARAB

When receiving an Arab in your own office or home country, extend him all of the foregoing courtesies in return:

- A warm welcome, handshake and seating
- Enquiries after his health, general wellbeing and exchange of pleasantries
- Encouragement to raise the subject of his visit, unless it is a social call, but without undue haste
- Offer further hospitality if appropriate - e.g. if he is visiting for a period of time
- On departure, escort him to the front door of your premises and to his car

ENTERTAINMENT

A Meal in An Arab House

A visitor may be fortunate enough to be invited to an Arab meal or party (*hufla*). Invitations are very often issued at short notice.

Arrive shortly after the time on the invitation and dress in a suit and tie or open-necked shirt depending on the circumstances. One should get local advice on what is appropriate. Most parties to which businessmen are invited are all-male affairs. However, if, exceptionally, it is the sort of party where wives are included, then it may be polite to take a bouquet of flowers for the hostess. Again, take local advice.

On arrival, the guests are ushered into a reception room where the host will introduce them to those already present, starting with the most important. If the party is a family affair then family elders will come into this category and a foreign visitor should show them due deference and attention. It is the general custom to remove one's shoes, either on arrival or, if the meal is to be eaten at floor level, certainly on entry to the dining room. Follow the lead of your host.

After a period for liquid refreshment the guests are shown into the dining room where the meal will be set out either on tables or at floor level. Meals served at table usually follow the general international pattern, i.e. soup, followed by a main course and then a variety of sweetmeats or fruit. A good host will ply you with more and more food, and it is the custom to leave a little food on your plate to indicate that you have had enough. If the meal is served on the floor be careful not to present the soles of your feet to other people. If the meal is eaten in the traditional way there will be no knives or forks except perhaps for a knife which the host or a helper will use to cut meat from a joint or carcass. Use only the right hand for eating. Some people sit on their left hand as a reminder! The main course is generally rice with chicken or lamb. The host will sometimes offer a tender piece of meat or fruit to a guest and this should be politely accepted although, since all etiquette is exaggerated, some guests may out of politeness refuse before accepting. (A simple refusal is often not taken at face value.) Contrary to popular Western belief, sheep's eyes are not considered a delicacy.

Traditional meals

When the meal is over, the guests wash their hands and return to the reception room where coffee and possibly more sweetmeats or dates are served. Incense is often brought round at this point. It is polite to take your leave shortly after drinking coffee, and certainly after the incense. Your host may at some point invite you to smoke a *nargeela* (hubble-bubble). This has a long pipe and the smoker draws the tobacco smoke through scented water.

The hubble-bubble

Formal Receptions
These are an increasingly common feature in the modern official and business life of the Peninsula. Foreigners normally wear a suit. Receptions are usually held in the

early evening and last for a couple of hours. The period is sometimes stipulated on the invitation, eg. 6 to 8pm. One should arrive fairly promptly, five or ten minutes after the time on the invitation. The host and his colleagues usually position themselves near the entrance to the reception room and greet the guests on arrival. Snacks or a buffet will be available at side tables or brought round by waiters. Again, only use the right hand for drinking, eating and smoking. Wives and other ladies may be present at this sort of function but often form a group among themselves. It is better to avoid engaging an Arab wife in conversation alone. At the appropriate hour the guests take their leave, saying farewell to the host and other dignitaries positioned at the entrance.

As well as giving the usual greeting, you might congratulate your Arab host if the party is being given to mark a special occasion, such as a National Day. The appropriate Arabic word is *mabrook*! (congratulations!).

Entertaining in a Peninsula Country

Entertaining

The majority of entertainment arranged by foreign visitors in the region is in the form of the formal reception above or a meal in a restaurant or hotel. Sometimes functions are held on a motorised dhow which should have toilet facilities and adequate protection from the weather. All of these venues have the added advantage that the local hotel manager is likely to be well versed in the correct form for such occasions.

Any party should be in keeping with local custom i.e. sexes should be segregated, pork products should not be served and a careful decision whether to serve alcohol should be made. A Muslim is forbidden by the laws of Islam to eat pork or drink alcohol and all meat must be *halaal,* i.e. permitted and slaughtered in the prescribed manner.

Invitations

For formal functions an invitation card should be produced in English and, in certain circumstances, in Arabic as well. Local advice should be sought on what is appropriate. An Arabic card can be produced in the country concerned, or by one of the many good Arabic printers in the West. The more important the function, the more elaborate the card. It would usually include the company logo.

The guest list should be completed with care to ensure the inclusion of the correct levels and numbers for your purpose. It is always best to seek informed advice on any guest list, and the embassy or local adviser can usually help. A high ranking Arab will be particular about who else is attending the function and his secretary will often ring the host to find out. Invitations are not always acknowledged and you should not read any special significance into non-attendance.

In the more conservative states, Arab women may not as a rule attend mixed functions unless they are private family affairs and the hosts are close friends. They more usually attend a gathering at which only ladies are present.

Ideally, Arab food should be provided, but the international cuisine produced by most of the first-class hotels is fast becoming acceptable, and even the norm. Because the Arabs are so hospitable and spare no expense or effort to entertain their guests, a foreigner should, within reason, do the same. In addition to the obvious requirement for good food in pleasant surroundings you could also consider other ideas that will make the occasion enjoyable e.g. a corner of the reception room could be set aside for an exhibition of paintings, a short film shown or a local musical group could play at the entrance to the reception. At a business function the guests are sometimes given a small memento on departure.

FESTIVALS

A number of religious festivals *(Eids)* are celebrated each year in the Muslim calendar (Details of Muslim festivals are given in Chapter 1). The foreigner really need only pay special attention to two of them, the *Eid Al-Adha a*nd the *Eid Al-Fitr.*

Eid Al-Adha
Eid Al-Fitr

79

The *Eid Al-Adha* comes at the end of the Hajj pilgrimage and the Eid Al-Fitr at the end of the month-long fast of Ramadan. As explained in Chapter 1 under *The Five Pillars of Islam - Fasting*, during this fast, all Muslims (with some exceptions such as travellers, the sick and small children) are required to abstain from food, drink, tobacco and all other pleasurable pursuits between sunrise and sunset. This can be a great burden especially if the month of fasting falls in summer. Naturally foreigners should be considerate in Ramadan and during daylight hours refrain from smoking, eating or drinking in the presence of Muslims or in public places. In any case, in most countries of the region it is a punishable offence to do so. It is also incumbent on foreign women to dress respectably during Ramadan.

Eid Cards

3

Greeting cards

On the occasion of both the *Eids* it is customary to send cards of congratulation to your Arab friends and colleagues and if you are an official or a businessman, to those people with whom you frequently deal. The cards contain an appropriate greeting and message of congratulation in Arabic, some being suitable for both Eids and others being specific to a particular Eid. These cards can either be bought locally or at an international Arabic bookseller. Some large institutions and companies often have their own cards specially printed which include their logo and perhaps the name of the executive who will sign it, printed in Arabic. It is the custom to sign the card and it should be dispatched to arrive a day to two in advance of the Eid. The approximate dates of Eids are given in Chapter 1 - *The Muslim Calendar*.

The recipient of an *Eid* card will occasionally return the compliment by sending a card of thanks, also signed. You could use the same type of card to thank an Arab for his card at Christmas. It is becoming an accepted custom to send 'Seasons Greetings' cards at Christmas but this is normally done by a Muslim to a Christian and not the other way round.

Verbal *Eid* Congratulations

When meeting an Arab on the day of an *Eid* or in the days closely following it, it is customary to shake hands and offer the following congratulatory greeting:

Greeting	*Eid mubaarak!* (Congratulations on the *Eid!*)
Reply	*Allah yubaarak feek* (And to you)

Eid Calls

In addition, at the time of the *Eid* it is customary for prominent citizens to receive callers in their homes and palaces. A foreigner living in or visiting the region at this time should certainly consider calling on an Arab he knows well. Take local advice on the most appropriate time to call. The visit is brief unless you are asked to stay on for a meal. You enter the reception room, congratulate your host on the *Eid* as advised above and take a seat. Provided that it does not detract too much from the ceremony being conducted by the host, you may also congratulate others present – senior members of your host's family or someone you know. There then follows some general social conversation, coffee is served and after a short pause you should depart saying goodbye to your host and whoever else seems appropriate.

Arab families also visit each other at *Eid* time. If you know an Arab family well you would be welcome to call, perhaps taking a small gift for his children but, again, seek local advice on what is considered appropriate in a particular circumstance. Finally, it is customary to give your servants a reasonable gift of money at the time of each Eid. (*See* Chapter 5 - *Servants.*)

MISCELLANEOUS CUSTOMS

Admiration

Exercise care in admiring anything belonging to an Arab. If you do so too effusively, it is traditional for him to be honour bound to offer it to you as a gift, and even if you succeed in refusing it, it will take a long time!

3

Gifts

An Arab may not proffer thanks for a formal gift. This is a traditional custom, although it is changing and is coming more into line with the international practice of expressing thanks. An Arab may politely refuse a gift, indicating that you should not have taken the trouble. This refusal may be repeated but it is correct to insist on acceptance.

Thank you

Sometimes when an Arab says 'Thank you' he means 'No', for example when replying to an offer of refreshment, etc. This works in much the same way as *merci* used in French. If you wish to accept when something is offered simply say 'Yes'.

Animals

Whereas Arabs love horses, and hawks, and have a great respect for the camel, dogs are generally considered unclean and will not be approached or touched (except perhaps for the Saluki - the Arabian gazelle hound).

Congratulations

Congratulations should be offered to an Arab on the occasion of any achievement such as a promotion and it always gives a good impression to say this in Arabic:

Greeting   *Mabrook!* (Congratulations)
Reply   *Allah yubaarak feek* (God bless you)

Public Prayers

It is not done to take undue notice of or interfere with someone who is praying in a public place such as an airport lounge, or in the market place (*souq*). It is also best to avoid walking in front of someone while they are praying.

Beckoning

One should never beckon anyone by using the forefinger of the right hand. This gesture has an offensive connotation in the Arab world (as it generally does in Mediterranean countries). It is better not to beckon at all, but if you do, then put all the fingers of the right hand downwards and pull the hand towards the body saying *'ta'aal'* (come).

ARAB NAMES

The first thing to do when writing to an Arab or meeting him is to get his name right. Arab names can be complicated to spell and may be transliterated from Arabic into English in a number of ways. The best solution is to use the version written by the Arab himself, e.g. on his card or letter heading. Note that two names may sound the same but there may be slight, but important differences: **Moham**med is different from Mah**mood**, **Maa**jid different from Maj**eed**, and Sal**eem** different from **Saa**lim. In addition, Mohammed is sometimes shortened to Mohd., and the apostrophe is used to represent a glottal stop, e.g. Sa'aad.

Arab names / margin note

Arab names usually consist of three names – the individual's name followed by that of their father and grandfather or possibly the family name. The names are sometimes linked by *bin* or *ibn* meaning 'son of' or, in the case of a woman, by *bint*, meaning 'daughter of' or 'girl'. For example, a man's full name might be Ali Mo**ham**med **Has**san or Ali bin Mo**ham**med bin Hassan. He would probably not use all of the names being commonly known as Ali Mohammed. His sister in the same way would be called **Faa**tima bint Mo**ham**med bint **Has**san. Many Arab women do not use their husband's name but in certain circumstances, for example if an Arab is living in a Western country, a married woman may use her husband's last name and call herself, for example, Mrs **Has**san. If you need to know a woman's name, it is best to enquire what form she uses.

Certain Arab names are compounded with a prefix or a suffix:

* *Abdul* in front of a name, meaning literally the 'servant of', which is followed by an attribute to God,

83

such as Abdul-Rah**maan** meaning 'servant of the merciful'. Aways refer to him by his full name, Abdul-Rah**maan**, and never simply 'Abdul'.

- *Abu* meaning 'father of'. A man may be known as Abu Mohammed, – 'the father of Mohammed'. It is only applied to the first born son and would be used particularly for the first few days after the birth. *Abu* is sometimes used figuratively, e.g. Abu Shanab meaning 'father of the moustache'. Sometimes a nickname such as Abu Nimr (father of the lion) takes the place of the real name.

- *Umm* meaning 'mother of' is used by a woman as part of, or in place of, her real name; e.g. Umm Kalthoom, the mother of Kalthoom, was a famous Egyptian singer.

- *Al* or *El* in front of the family name, often hyphenated. It is generally used to indicate a royal or distinguished family, e.g. Al-Nahyan, the ruling family of Abu Dhabi.

- The suffix *Ad-Din* (pronounced Ad-Deen), also written *Eddin*, means 'of the faith', e.g. Salah Ad-Din (Saladin) meaning 'the rightness of the faith'.

The above explains why, when you visit the region, the immigration forms ask you for your own name, your father's name and your family name.

FORMS OF ADDRESS AND OFFICIAL CORRESPONDENCE

You should address an Arab in speech or in writing by using his first name with the appropriate prefix, if there is one, for example, 'How do you do, Shaikh Mohammed?' In writing, foreign correspondents tend increasingly to follow the Western practice of addressing 'Dear Mr Mohammed', or 'Dear Mohammed', if you know him well. When an Arab travels abroad he would usually conform to Western practice by booking himself into an hotel as Mr Al-Kitbi or Mr A. Al-Kitbi.

Foreigners in the Arab world are referred to in the same way as an Arab would be, thus Mr James Peters would find himself addressed as Mr James rather than Mr Peters.

If you wish to call to someone or attract their attention it is not considered polite to call their name baldly. In this circumstance all names, titles and ranks are prefixed by *Ya* which can be literally translated as 'Oh'! Therefore if you called Ahmed you would say *Ya Ahmed*. This is used even in intimate speech to a friend, who would for example be addressed as *Ya Akhi*! ('Oh brother!').

Forms of address are generally more formal in the Arab world than in the West, with greater deference and respect being shown to those in authority or to senior members of the family. A guide to the various forms of address is given below.

Titles

Title	*English*	*Arabic*
Ambassador	Your Excellency	*Ya Sa'aadat As-Safeer* (initially) *Sa'aadatak* (thereafter)
Amir (Kuwait, Bahrain & Qatar)	Your Highness	*Ya Sumoo Al-Ameer*
Crown Prince	Your Highness	*Ya Saahib As-Sumoo*
Deputy (i.e. MP)	Your Excellency	*Ya Sa'aadat An-Na'ib* (initially) *Sa'aadatak* (thereafter)
Director or manager of a firm	Mr (Abdulla Fahid)	*Ya Sa'aadat Al-Mūdeer* (initially) *Sa'aadatak* or *Ya Mūdeer* (thereafter)
Doctor	Dr Ahmed	*Ya Doktoor Ahmed*
Engineer	Engineer Ahmed	*Ya Mūhandis*
Imaam	Your Eminence	*Ya Fadeelat Al-Imaam*
King(Jordan)	Your Majesty[1]	*Ya Jalaalat Al-Malik* (initially) *Ya Jalaalatkum* (thereafter)

3

Titles

Title	English	Arabic
Minister (of government)	Your Excellency	*Ya Ma'aalee Al-Wozeer* (initially) Sir (thereafter)
Mohammed (familiar)	*Ya Mohammed*	*Ya Mohammed*
Mr Mohammed (formal)	Mr *Mohammed*	*Ya Seiyyid Mohammed* or *Ya Seiyyid*
President (of a State)	Mr President	*Ya Fakhaamat Ar-Ra'ees*
President (of a company or organisation)	Mr President	*Ya Sa'aadat Ar-Ra'ees*
Prime Minister	Prime Minister	*Ya Dowlat Ar-Ra'ees*
Prince (Royal)[1]	Your Royal Highness	*Ya Sahib As-Samoo Al-Maliki*
Princes (Other)	Your Highness	*Ya Saahib As-Samoo*
Private citizen	Mr Mohammed Hassan	*Ya Seiyyid*
Professor or learned person	Professor	*Ya Ūstadh* (also *Ūstaz*) (initially) *Seedee* (thereafter)
Ruling Shaikh (and some immediate family)	Your Highness	*Ya Samoo As-Sheikh*
Shaikh (others of ruling family)	Shaikh... (name)	*Ya Samoo As-Sheikh*
Shaikh (not hereditary)[2]	Shaikh ... (name)	*Ya Sheikh... (name)*
Stranger	No equivalent	*Hadritak* or *Seeyaadatak*
Sultan of Oman	Your Majesty	*Ya Jalaalat As-Sultaan*
Waiter or servant	Waiter	*Ya Akhi* (lit: Oh Brother)
Woman	Mrs Hassan	*Ya Saiyyida* or *Ya Sit*

Note 1. In Saudi Arabia sons and grandsons of King Abdul Aziz ibn Saud are addressed as 'Your Royal Highness'.

Note 2. *Shaikh* or *Sheikh*. Besides being a hereditary title used by members of the ruling families of the Arab Gulf states it is also given to the leaders of tribes, senior members of leading families, religious leaders, and judges. Also to those who have achieved distinction in the community, usually in later life, as a mark of popular respect. It has also the literal meaning in Arabic of 'an old and revered person'.

Military and Police Ranks

For reference purposes, the most common Arabic words used for military and police ranks are:

Fareeq Awwal - General
Fareeq - Lieutenant-General
Liwa - Major-General
Ameed - Brigadier
Aqeed - Colonel
Mūqoddam - Lieutenant-Colonel
Raa'id - Major
Naqeeb - Captain
Mūlaazim Awal - Lieutenant

Mūlaazim Thaanee - Second-Lieutenant
Wokeel Awwal - Warrant-Officer Class I
Wokeel - Warrant Officer Class 2
Raqeeb Awwal - Staff Sergeant
Raqeeb - Sergeant
Areef - Corporal
Wokeel Areef - Lance-Corporal
Jundee - Private

Military titles

Official Correspondence

A letter to an Arab may be written in English. In some circumstances (particularly in Saudi Arabia) it is best to write both in Arabic and English. The form it takes depends upon the exact situation and it is advisable to seek expert advice on this important topic. Be sure that your adviser is fully conversant with local usage, as terms and form can differ from country to country. (Guidance on translation services is given in Chapter 6.) As an example, a formal letter to a senior figure would open:

Letters

> Your Excellency,
> After greetings
> I am honoured to inform you etc

and end, if a business letter, with for example:

> Finally, Your Excellency, please be assured
> of our best attention at all times.

CHAPTER FOUR

Visiting the Peninsula

INTRODUCTION

The purpose of this chapter is to provide essential advice and a check-list for the planning and conduct of a visit to the region. Points applicable only to business travellers are included in Chapter 6.

TIMING A VISIT

Climate

The climatic conditions vary between countries and even within a country, depending on the height above sea level and distance from the coast. The best time to visit is in the spring or autumn, but high summer temperatures are not necessarily uncomfortable, particularly if the atmosphere is dry - as it is for example in Riyadh. But if the heat is accompanied by high humidity, as in most coastal areas, the combination can be unpleasant. Heat and humidity may both be largely irrelevant, however, if you intend to spend most of the time in air-conditioned hotels, offices and cars – which are now the norm throughout the region. Details of climate are included in the Country Annexes at the back of the book.

Heat and humidity

The Calendar

As well as the time of year and the climate, consider the Muslim calendar and the effect of visiting during Ramadan when the normal routine of life can be disrupted, the major festivals and the annual summer holidays from the end of July to the beginning of September. A visit at festival time can, however, be an interesting experience. The approximate forecast dates of the major religious festivals are given in Chapter 1, and national holidays in the Country Annexes.

Ramadan

Clothing

It would be wrong to imagine that it is always very hot in the region. In winter it is often cold, windy and wet and at such times European clothing is entirely appropriate. It is best to double check just before your visit. In the

91

summer months, a range of lightweight clothing is necessary, preferably made of cotton, since other materials such as man-made fibres can irritate the skin. Appropriate items include lightweight suits and cotton shirts, underclothes and socks. It is particularly important that shoes are loose-fitting and made of leather since feet swell appreciably in the heat, and need to breathe.

For men, the appropriate dress for official visits to an Arab in his office or when attending a formal function is a suit and tie. For less formal occasions, an open neck shirt and slacks are suitable. For casual wear sandals or desert boots (fawn coloured suede with rubber composition soles) are popular and can be purchased locally. Good walking shoes or boots may also be useful. Even in summer the evenings can be quite cold and you may need light wollen jumpers, or a shawl for a woman.

For a woman, cotton dresses or skirts and tops are probably the most suitable summer wear, but these should conform with the advice given on *Standards of Dress* below.

Hats have long ceased to be an article of formal attire but anyone who intends to spend a lot of time at a beach club or shopping would find one necessary to protect themselves from the effects of the sun, particularly in summer.They can easily be bought locally. Sunglasses are advisable for every visitor.

It is possible to get clothes tailor-made at reasonable prices in the region. It is common practice to ask a local tailor to copy an existing suit or dress, and this they often do very well. Long term visitors in particular should seek first-hand advice in this regard when putting their wardrobes together. Beautiful kaftans and shawls can also be bought in the bazaars.

Standards of Dress

Foreign visitors should always be sensitive to local sensibilities in this regard. Custom varies considerably within the region. In Saudi Arabia, for example, women are required to cover their arms and legs in public (*See* General Comments in Saudi Arabia Annex), while in other countries

Dressing for the occasion

4

of the Peninsula modest Western dress would be the norm. As a general rule, male visitors should wear long trousers (shorts are not approved of) and a shirt with a collar in public places, and women should wear a modestly cut dress with sleeves and a skirt covering her knees. Whatever the country, Arab men and women are genuinely offended when they see foreigners dressed in scanty and provocatively cut clothing in such public places as the bazaar. For the same reason it is not acceptable for a man to strip to the waist. Finally, one should not wear swimming costumes away from the immediate vicinity of the beach or pool.

Anyone visiting the region in a professional capacity will find that the Arabs they meet are always immaculately attired in the traditional long flowing robe or Western-style suits and they naturally expect foreigners who claim their attention to be equally well dressed. Appearances count for a lot.

Finally, for foreigners to wear the traditional Arab dress is not regarded with favour, as it is fast becoming the dress which distinguishes a national citizen. It would cause offence, and in Oman it is against the law. For similar reasons the foreigner should not carry prayer beads unless he is a Muslim.

HEALTH

Vaccinations and Immunisation
Before you travel check which vaccinations are necessary, if any. Vaccinations must always be spaced out, so you should consult a doctor or vaccination clinic at least two months prior to departure, particularly if children are involved.

Malaria
There is a risk of infection in some parts of the region. Your GP can obtain advice on the prophylactic appropriate to each area from the Malarial Reference Laboratory at the London School of Hygiene and Tropical Medicine. Anti-malarial tablets are taken prior to, during, and after a visit, as prescribed by a doctor,

4

BEWARE OF THE HEAT!

SUNBURN

Even mild sunburn can be uncomfortable. To avoid being burnt, start by exposing the body for a strictly limited period each day; ten minutes is enough on the first day. Use protective lotions and avoid the heat of the day from roughly 11 a.m. to 3 p.m., even on cloudy days when the sun's rays still penetrate.

PRICKLY HEAT

Increased exposure to sunlight combined with perspiration and tightly fitting clothes can cause a red itching rash known as prickly heat, which is cured by showering regularly, drying thoroughly and applying powder.

HEAT EXHAUSTION AND HEAT STROKE

In the summer heat it is important to consume adquate amounts of water and salt. A person working in the open needs up to 12 pints a day. Add sufficient salt to your food so that you can taste it, and always drink water with your meal. Salt tablets are not recommended. Dehydration of the body, producing listlessness, headaches, dizziness, nausea and a high temperature are indicative of heat exhaustion. In extreme cases of dehydration, a person will pass out, run a high temperature and stop perspiring. This condition is extremely serious and is termed heat stroke, and can cause permanent damage if left untreated for long. In the case of both heat exhaustion and heat stroke the immediate treatment is to reduce the body temperature by any means possible, concentrating particularly on the head. One way is to apply a cold wet towel or ice and ensure that the patient is in a cool shady place. The next step is to increase the body's salt and water content by administering a saline drink. In the case of heat stroke, however, professional medical assistance should be always be sought as soon as possible. (The risk of dehydration is increased by drinking alcohol.)

so check well in advance of your visit.

Keep exposed parts of the body covered out of doors after sunset and use an insect repellent ointment or spray. Unless you are sleeping in air-conditioning, close the windows of your bedroom before sunset and spray the room with insecticide spray. For added protection, sleep under a mosquito net or burn a mosquito coil or tablet - a vapour-emitting impregnated substance heated by an electrical element. The latter are perfectly safe although the vapour emitted can be a little strong for some. A new version of this electrical device is now available, and uses an odourless clear liquid in place of the traditional tablets. All of these can be bought locally.

Insect repellants

Travellers under Medication
Pharmacies in the region are invariably well stocked. However, travellers under special medication may be advised to take essential supplies with them with a spare, signed prescription as an additional precaution. Medicines should be clearly labelled with their pharmaceutical name and it is prudent in these days of sensitivity to the carriage of drugs, particularly in Saudi Arabia, to carry a certificate from a doctor explaining the situation. Restrictions exist on the importation of a range of drugs into Saudi Arabia, including tranquillisers and sleeping pills. For advice in the UK, call the Home Office Drugs Branch on telephone 020 7273 3806. Finally, the trade names of some drugs differ from country to country, so it worth checking before you travel if you are likely to need a specific branded medicine.

4

Medical Insurance
It is essential to take out full medical insurance when visiting the region. Although medical facilities (doctors, hospitals, clinics and pharmacies) are extremely good in all countries except the Republic of Yemen, there is no reciprocal health-care agreement between the countries of the Peninsula and the UK, and visitors will have to pay for treatment, which can be costly. Insurance should be

Health insurance

comprehensive and include repatriation to your home country in case of need. Check whether your insurance cover stipulates that you pay when receiving treatment and reclaim the cost later, or whether payment is made by the insurance company direct to a hospital or doctor.

Medical Emergencies

As has been mentioned, the medical facilities in the region – doctors, dentists, hospitals and the ancilliary services – are of a generally high standard. In the event of an emergency you can seek treatment at any clinic or hospital. However, these facilities are not always free for foreigners and you should indicate your willingness to pay a fee and carry evidence of any medical insurance to ensure you receive prompt treatment.

ENTRY REQUIREMENTS

Visas

All countries in the region require the visitor to have a valid passport which for some countries must extend for six months after the intended visit. Some Arab countries also object to evidence of a visit to Israel, and all but the United Arab Emirates and Bahrain require an Entry Visa or No Objection Certificate (NOC). Visas are obtained from relevant embassies and consulates by applying in person, by post or through your travel agent. Details of the current requirements for each country are contained in the Country Annexes.

Passports

A visa application form is usually presented with a passport, one or two photographs and a small fee. Visa requirements, particularly health regulations, change from time to time and the responsible embassy or travel agent will update you. If you attend the embassy in person you will be given a receipt for your passport, or a paper with a reference number on it, and you will be asked to call back later for your visa - anything between two days and two weeks, depending on the time of year.

When you receive your visa make sure you understand the exact extent of its validity. If you are

4

landing or transiting through a third country on the way to your main destination, a transit visa may also be required.

CURRENCY

Except in the Republic of Yemen (*see* Country Annex) travellers' cheques, the currency of major Western countries and major credit cards (e.g. Visa and Mastercard) are readily accepted throughout the region. Most British debit cards can be used to obtain funds from banks and ATM outlets. As elsewhere in the world the exchange rate in an exchange bureau is likely to be better than with an hotel cashier. Always check carefully the figures on the various denominations of notes and coins to avoid expensive mistakes. The Arabic for 50, for example, is very similar to 500 and unfortunately the larger denomination notes are often smaller than those of lesser value, as is true of some coinage. Arabic numerals are illustrated in Chapter 2.

Cash and credit cards

There are restrictions on the amounts of currency that can be taken into some countries of the region and it is wise to check this at the time you apply for your visa. Be careful not to break any currency rules as such offences are taken very seriously.

PROHIBITED GOODS

There are restrictions on a number of imports to the region, with each country having its own rules. The main prohibitions are covered below and details are included in the Country Annexes, but the latest regulations should be checked with the relevant embassy or travel agent.

Banned imports

Drugs
Drugs offences are viewed as extremely serious crimes throughout the region, and in Saudi Arabia and UAE can carry the death penalty (*see* Country Annex on Saudi Arabia). Care should be taken to ensure that prescribed medications are not confused with illicit drugs (*see Travellers under Medication* above).

97

Alcohol

Alcohol is strictly forbidden in Saudi Arabia, Kuwait and Sharjah (UAE). In Bahrain, Oman and the UAE, visitors are permitted to bring in a small quantity of duty free alcohol (Oman by air only). In these countries and in Qatar, alcohol is available in some hotels, and non-Muslims and expatriates are allowed a quota for personal consumption on being granted a special license. Penalties for alcohol-related offences are severe in all countries, in particular in Saudi Arabia. *See* Chapter 5 - *Local Laws and Customs*, and the country annexes.

Food

Import of pork is also forbidden on basic religious grounds.

Publications and Videos

Avoid carrying any magazine or book of a politically controversial nature, or non-Muslim religious material may be confiscated. In a very different field, care must be taken over what is considered in the region as pornographic literature. Men's magazines of the *Playboy* type fall into this category. Any publication with nude pictures may gravely offend a Muslim's religious sensibilities. Western publications on sale in the region and in particular in Saudi Arabia are censored. Videos are regarded with suspicion by the customs authorities and may be confiscated. In Saudi Arabia the authorities will insist on viewing them before allowing them to be imported. It is most unwise to attempt to conceal them on arrival.

ARRIVAL

Immigration Forms

Because of the way Arab names are written, an immigration form will ask for your own, your father's and your family name. You should simply equate this to your first name, any second name and your surname. The form will also ask for your address in the country and your sponsor. Put your hotel or if you have no pre-arranged accommodation, your Embassy and your sponsor/agent's address.

4

Customs Formalities

It is not unusual for the customs officials in a Peninsula country to carry out a search of your baggage on arrival and in Saudi Arabia it is always done. The official will first request your passport and then ask you to open each item of luggage, which he will systematically search. You should appreciate that the official is required to ensure that no drugs or prohibited items are imported into the Kingdom. He is aware that the majority of foreigners are unlikely to transgress the local laws and if you are polite and cooperative, the search will often only be a cursory one.

Transportation

If possible, arrange to be met and taken direct to your accommodation. Anything that cuts down the hassle and time taken in battling out of an airport is a good thing. However, buses, taxis and self-drive cars are available at all the region's airports. Taxis are generally cheap but it is best either to go by the meter or to agree the price before the start of a journey to avoid any argument later over the fare.

Car hire and taxis

Although cars can be conveniently hired and insurance cover is adequate, an accident does result in delays and other complications (*see Emergencies and Car Accidents* below). It is, for example, necessary to stay at the scene of an accident until the police arrive in order to establish blame - which may take some time. For this reason, on a short visit it may be better to use taxis or hire a car with a driver.

If you do hire a self-drive car, you will need either a Western driving licence or an International Driving Licence. The regulations differ from country to country and it is advisable to check with the hire company at the time of booking. An International Licence can be obtained from the AA or RAC in UK on production of two passport photographs, a current UK licence and a small fee. Ensure you fully understand the local traffic procedures and laws and what action must be taken by the driver in the event of an accident. Check the extent of cover provided by the insurance in respect of the vehicle, passengers and third parties. Also check the extent to

Driving licences

4

99

which an accident might delay your return home.

Security

Arab countries are, by and large, very safe places to visit and live in but, like anywhere else, theft does occur. It is best to lock valuables in a safe place and avoid either carrying a large sum of money or leaving it lying around in a hotel room or on a beach. Keep a photocopy of the main pages of your passport and any important personal documents. Carry your passport or some other means of identification with you in a secure place during any excursion outside your hotel.

Photography

Although cameras and camcorders are permitted in places of architectural interest, elsewhere they must be used with care. It is forbidden to photograph military installations and this includes airfields, ports and even bridges. Some people also object to being photographed, and you should ask permission first. You should always avoid photographing women. A Polaroid camera can be a novel way of getting on with people you meet on desert trips in remote areas, but you should always explain or illustrate the device before photographing them.

Visiting Mosques

In a few Arab countries foreign visitors are permitted to enter mosques. However, it is obligatory to be soberly dressed, to remove your shoes (slippers may be provided) and for women to wear a head scarf.

Bargaining in the Market (*Sooq*)

Bargaining is in the Arab blood. It has been described as the art of compromise without backing down or losing face. Many foreigners either find bargaining tedious or else are ignorant of how to go about it but in the Peninsula it is a way of life. Some shops, especially if they sell basic commodities, have fixed prices but market stalls do not and the seller and the buyer will haggle to

4

get the best price possible. Sellers are often surprised – and, one suspects, a little disappointed – when a foreigner pays the asking price without a quibble.

BARGAINING POWER

To bargain you need time. You will compare the asking price with the going rate for an article. If you don't know it, as is likely, then decide what you are willing to pay. It is then necessary to convince the seller that you are quite prepared to do without the item and are willing to walk away. If you show that you are in any way keen to buy something the seller will hold out for a high price - and get it! If the shopkeeper quotes a price of 10 Dinars for example but you decide it is worth 7, then offer him 5. He may come down to 8 and you can then rise to 6, letting him push you to 7. If you stick out for a low price do nevertheless leave him some room for manoeuvre or he will not be able to meet your offer without losing face. Perhaps the most important aspect of any negotiation is to remain on good personal terms with the other party at all times. The haggling may become heated, but if it become personal, or the shopkeeper decides he does not like you, he may well decide not to deal with you, in spite of the fact that it is to his detriment. Personal relationships are again all important and you should not be surprised if a shopkeeper offers you tea and is not at all offended if you leave without buying.

General Emergencies and Car Accidents
(*See also* Medical Emergencies above)
If you are involved in some kind of emergency such as an infringement of the law or a car accident, the cardinal rule is to remain calm, polite and at all costs avoid a confrontation, however unpleasant the situation and however strong the provocation. Once you have lost your dignity, offended a local inhabitant or member of the police, it can take a long time to re-establish a sensible dialogue. It may be difficult to make yourself understood to a local who speaks little or no

English but keep calm and use the Arabic emergency phrases given in Chapter 2 which are designed to cover the most commonly experienced situations.

Car accidents

In the event of a car accident, you are required by law in most of the Peninsula countries to remain at the scene of the accident until the arrival of the traffic police. However slight the damage,never move the vehicle. The police will make out an accident report which will usually apportion blame and will give you a copy which it is necessary to have before the car can legally be repaired. If someone is killed or injured, the police usually arrest or detain the driver and possibly the passengers, until blame is established and legal proceedings are completed. For this reason it is vital not only to carry your passport at all times but also a list of emergency telephone numbers, such as your embassy consul, sponsor or hotel.

Drunkenness

The law in the Peninsula countries is particularly strict with regard to displays of drunkenness in public places and in the case of drink-driving the police will immediately imprison you until you come before a judge. This may take several days and punishments are severe – either a heavy fine or prison sentence and, in Saudi Arabia, possibly corporal punishment as well.

You may also appeal for assistance and advice to your local sponsor or the Consul at your embassy. An explanation of UK Foreign and Commonwealth Office Consular Services Abroad is summarised in the Annexes.

DEPARTURE

Many Arab countries impose an airport tax on departure, usually payable in the local currency. It is wise to keep back a small amount of local currency to pay this.

4

CHAPTER FIVE

The Expatriate

INTRODUCTION

This chapter gives guidance on the essential considerations for those contemplating taking up residence in the Peninsula. It outlines the main types of expatriate employment, how to assess and prepare for the post, and some of the major facets of expatriate life.

Many thousands of expatriates are employed in the Gulf countries and Saudi Arabia, the result of rapid development and a shortage of qualified labour, among other factors. Broadly speaking, it is mainly Europeans and North Americans who fill the managerial and specialist posts while those from the Far East, the Indian sub-continent, Africa and other Arab countries work mainly in the service industries. The majority of expatriates are male but there is a significant number of females working as nurses, teachers, house servants etc. Understandably, the policy in all the Peninsula countries is to reduce their reliance on foreign labour and increase employment for Nationals, an aim which is being slowly but steadily achieved.

Expatriate life can be an enjoyable and rewarding experience, particularly when shared with one's family. For those employed by a Western-based organisation or large Arab institution such as a national government or oil company, expatriate employment means tax-free pay, generous benefits and a higher than usual standard of living. Housing, home leave and other benefits are typically provided free of charge or there will be allowances in lieu. Most Western expatriates have a house servant and lead an active social life, and there is generally ample scope for leisure and sporting activities.

The expatriate working for a private Arab company, perhaps as a professional advisor or employee, may find that although the contract, terms and conditions and lifestyle will usually be similar to other categories of expatriate, his employment may be less secure and success will depend very much on the personal relationship with the Arab employer.

Finally, it is worth emphasising that while the Peninsula

5

Nationaliities

countries have much in common, living conditions, and therefore expatriate life, differ significantly from country to country and within countries themselves. Life in Dubai, for example, which caters for Western tastes in a number of ways, contrasts markedly with Saudi Arabia, where alcohol is forbidden and the way of life is much more conservative. Even within Saudi Arabia itself conditions differ, and expatriates will find life in Jeddah more relaxed than in Riyadh. The general characteristics of each Peninsula country are described in the Country Annexes but advice is given in this chapter on researching the detailed, up-to-date, situation in each country.

CULTURE SHOCK

Culture shock is a perfectly natural phenomenon which affects us all when making a major move into an unfamiliar environment. It occurs to some degree or other when you move home in your own country, but the move to such a fundamentally different culture as the Arabian Peninsula, combined with the inevitable stress of reorganising your personal life, can be traumatic. If often affects wives more than husbands, since a husband's work takes his mind off other things. A husband needs to be particularly sympathetic in this regard. The reaction from culture shock is a negative one, varying from mild to serious, and everyone experiences it, even if they do not care to admit it. However, if it is not to spoil an otherwise enjoyable experience in one's life, it is important to take positive steps to combat it. Among the proven measures are: to be well briefed, to understand and rationalise the cultural differences, and to make sure that you are well equipped for your hobbies, sporting and leisure activities. Perhaps the single most important step to take, particularly for a wife, is to talk to someone who lives, or has lived, in the country you are going to. Personal advice from a sensible, experienced expatriate is invaluable.

ASSESSING AND PREPARING FOR A POST

Everyone going to the region for the first time experiences something of a culture shock and some find that they are not suited to expatriate life. The successful expatriate needs to be adaptable, with a measure of self-reliance and also a sensitivity to life in a completely different culture. A study of the preceding chapters will help to explain what is entailed in this regard. It must be said that anyone with a short temper, which is bound to be exacerbated by the hot climate and the inevitable frustrations, will almost certainly fail.

Adapting to the life

The cost of failure can be surprisingly high; not only will it adversely affect the company's business but an individual's career and well-being, not to mention that of his family. When it happens that a person is clearly wrong for a particular job it often transpires with the value of hindsight, that the individual or the recruiter failed to make an accurate assessment beforehand.

It costs a Western company in the region of £100,000 a year to appoint and maintain a senior manager in the Peninsula and so it is worth making as thorough an appraisal as possible.

5

The main points for consideration in assessing an expatriate post are outlined below.

Briefing

Most Western expatriates in the Peninsula are recruited by a commercial company or recruitment agency with experience of the region. They should provide the expatriate with an adequate job specification, the terms and conditions of employment, and information on the expatriate lifestyle, the bad points as well as the good. It is vital to be well informed and if possible you should obtain the views of at least one independent source with recent experience.

Preparation courses

Ideally, an expatriate, along with his spouse and any teenage children, should attend a course of preparation such as those run at the Centre for International Briefing at Farnham Castle in Surrey. Scheduled courses for countries in the Middle East are run every five weeks and cover the complete range of information required to achieve a speedy and effective transition to the new role for the assignee and his/her family. It also offers the opportunity to meet and network with other assignees moving to the same region, or very often the same country. Courses can be tailor-made, and give comprehensive information on the political, economic, social life and laws of the country they are going to and include talks by expatriates with recent experience. Contact details: The Registrar, The Centre for International Briefing, The Castle, Farnham, Surrey GU9 OAG. Tel: 01252 721194; Fax: 01252 711283; Website www.cibfarnham.com; E-mail: info@cibfarnham.com

Contract, Salary, Terms and Conditions.

If the post is accompanied, the minimum term of contract will usually be two years, and a minimum of one year if the post is bachelor status. It is important to get the terms of the contract correct at the outset, when one is in a stronger negotiating position, as it is difficult if not impossible to improve on it later on. Concentrate on the essential elements rather than niggling over details, although occasionally these can be important. It will be helpful, for instance, to ascertain how the contract compares with those of other expatriates of a similar status. Also consider what financial and other safeguards are included if, through no fault of your own, you do not complete the predicted period of your contract.

If considering a post working directly for a private Arab company you should acquaint yourself with local employment law and the safeguards it provides. A local lawyer will advise you. Your embassy can usually recommend one specialising in this field.

Judge the salary and benefits offered against the local cost of living. Double check the cost of living with someone who is living in, or has recent experience of, the country you are going to. You will be paid in the local currency which is either directly linked to or tends to follow the US dollar. You will therefore need to follow the value of the local currency against the dollar, in relation

5

Financial safeguards

Exchange rates

to local spending power and funds you intend to repatriate. Most Peninsula currencies do not fluctuate a great deal against each other or the US dollar, although it could be a significant consideration if your contract were to run for several years. It is as well to have a contingency arrangement in place from the outset.

Finally, consider your overall financial situation. The advice of an accountant well versed in finance for expatriates is vital. Consider your qualification for UK tax-free status and the ramifications of returning to the UK before the end of the period stipulated by the Inland Revenue. Also consider the effect, if any, on pensions, UK property, investments (particularly offshore), overseas banking, National Insurance Contributions, payment of VAT and duty on overseas purchases such as cars. Recruiters often offer comprehensive information on all these aspects but it is still sensible to obtain independent advice. Yemen is the only Peninsula country to levy income tax at present.

Tax and investment

Benefits and Allowances

Multinationals usually provide their expatriates with furnished accommodation, electricity, water, housing maintenance, children's education, and sometimes transportation to work as well as a servant, although the latter may depend on the seniority of the appointment. Also provided may be family membership of a recreational club, which is often the only activity available to Western expatiates and can be expensive.

The benefits mentioned above will either be provided by the employer or an allowance up to an agreed ceiling will be paid in lieu.

Removals

Assuming that fully furnished accommodation is provided, removal will normally only amount to transporting personal effects. A weight and capacity allowance will be given for removal by air or sea. Packing and insurance should be included. A modest increase in the return allowance is usually given to cover some purchases made during the tour.

5

Travel to and from Post and Leave

A two-year accompanied contract will certainly include free air travel to and from the Peninsula at the beginning and end of a tour and for annual leave. Tickets will be provided for the expatriate, his wife and any children accompanying him. One or two return tickets per year will also be provided for children at boarding school in their home country to visit their parents. Single expatriates will receive the same free travel to and from the Peninsula country and for annual leave. Bachelor status (married unaccompanied) expatriates will usually be given more frequent leave, again with air travel paid for, to compensate for separation from their spouses. The class of air travel varies according to the seniority of appointment. Some employers allow their expatriates to take cash in lieu of tickets, but experience has shown that it is never a good idea to forego one's leave entirely to save money. A break is essential.

Accommodation

Expatriates are usually provided with a fully furnished flat or villa or an allowance in lieu. In the Gulf countries and Saudi Arabia this can cost several thousand pounds a year and the rent is sometimes required to be paid a year in advance. Electricity is usually provided free, since running air-conditioning is an expensive but essential facility. Other living expenses however, such as home contents insurance and private telephone bills are met by the expatriate. Insurance is easily arranged locally.

Cars

Western companies usually provide cars on the same basis as at home. Local Arab organisations may also provide transportation, and certainly to and from work for bachelor status posts. As far as personal vehicles are concerned, most makes of car can be purchased in the region but it may not be possible to buy and run a right-hand drive vehicle. Four-wheel drive vehicles are popular - and for desert trips are essential . Visits to the desert are a favourite expatriate pastime in the spring and autumn. Car maintenance facilities are generally good and fuel, as one might expect, is extremely cheap.

It is necesssary to have a residence permit before being legally permitted to obtain a local driving licence or purchase a car, and most people hire one in the interim. A local licence is usually granted on production of an International Driving Licence and/or a national one. (*See also* Chapter 4 - *Transportation.*)

Driving licenses

Health Care

Most Western employment contracts include the provision of free local private medical and dental care and repatriation to the home country in the event of serious illness for expatriates and their dependants. The employer may well provide this through local or international medical insurance. Full medical and dental checks should be carried out prior to departure.

An expatriate arriving in the summertime should avoid strenuous exercise until fully acclimatised. This can take anything from a week to a month.

Children's Education

In countries where there is a sizeable British, American or International community there will be fee-paying English-language and other primary schools of a reasonable standard, but secondary schools are less common. An expatriate contract often includes the cost of local education at these schools. Expatriates with older children sometimes arrange boarding-school education in the home country, in which case the contract usually covers the cost of air fares for at least two school holidays for children to visit their parents.

Arrival in a Peninsula country

Most employers arrange for the reception of their expatriates, usually through the company's local sponsor or representative office, and place them in a hotel or in temporary accommodation until a suitable villa or flat is ready. Then it will be necessary to tackle the (usually lengthy) administrative formalities, such as organising

Documents to

5

legal residence etc. Take with you all personal documentation such as birth, marriage, health, driving licences and, depending on the appointment, original certificates of education qualifications (e.g. your degree), plus a copious quantity of passport-sized photographs for yourself and your family. Photographs are needed for most applications. Local documentation includes a residence permit or visa, driving licence, a permit to purchase alcohol (in some countries) and possibly an identity card.

EXPATRIATE LIFE

Western expatriates have traditionally been highly regarded in the Peninsula countries. Their professionalism, integrity and ability to get on with the nationals is widely recognised.

A Representative Appointment

If an expatriate has been appointed to represent a Western company or organisation in the Peninsula he or she will have the task of reporting the local situation in terms which the parent company can understand. The views of the homebased head office will, of course, be based on their own priorities and business culture. They will usually have limited understanding of the Arab concept of time, the difficulty of access to those in authority, the local decision making process, the influences at work in society or indeed, the Arab culture generally. This should not become a consuming issue. However, it is incumbent on the expatriate representative to do all he can to meet the aims of his head office, intelligently interpreting their requirements and adapting them to suit the local scene. He should report back in as much detail as necessary but must never be tempted to colour information to justify bad news or to enhance his position. Honesty is the best long-term policy even if it is not fully understood or appreciated. It helps if one enjoys a close relationship with one's boss and is confident of his or her full support.

Reporting to HQ

5

Medical and Dental Treatment

The expatriate should sign-on with a doctor and dentist immediately on arrival. Most medical and dental care is a mixture of private clinics and government hospitals and some foreign firms issue their expatriates with a medical identification card to ensure cover in an emergency. Notes on health care are included in Chapter 4.

Local Laws and Customs

Most expatriates happily abide by local laws and customs and lead an enjoyable and trouble-free existence. Nevertheless, particularly in the more conservative countries of the Peninsula, problems arise either because expatriates are ignorant of local laws or, less frequently, because they disregard them.

It is important to realise that expatriates have no special legal status in an Arab country. They are subject to the law like everyone else. Diplomatic immunity is only granted to officially accredited diplomats. If an expatriate breaks the law and is arrested, his own embassy or government may petition on his behalf but would have no power to demand their release. An explanation of UK Foreign and Commonwealth Office Consular Services Abroad is summarised in the Annexes.

Most legal problems are connected with driving, drink and drugs.

On driving, follow the advice given in the previous chapter under *Transportation*. It is usually best to travel as a passenger for the first week after arrival in order to get used to the local driving conditions and traffic regulations.

The laws on the consumption, possession and manufacture of alcohol are strict in all the Peninsula countries. In Saudi Arabia the penalty for the possession and consumption of alcohol is imprisonment, possible corporal punishment (flogging) and deportation. Alcohol is also forbidden in Kuwait, Yemen and Sharjah and in Qatar except for non-Muslims. In some Peninsula countries Westerners are allowed to purchase alcohol in major hotels and to buy a quota for personal

Legal status

5

Alcohol

113

consumption. However, the misuse of this privilege, such as over-indulgence in public or the consumption of alcohol while driving will lead to immediate arrest, a fine and possibly imprisonment. Expatriates need to make themselves fully aware of the latest local rules and regulations on arrival in a country. An outline of the current laws are contained in the Country Annexes.

Drugs

The laws relating to drugs are the most draconian. In Saudi Arabia and the UAE some drug-related crimes are a capital offence. Every visitor to Saudi Arabia will see a warning to this effect on his immigration entry form. In other Peninsula countries, it is regarded as a serious offence punishable by imprisonment and eventual deportation.

Working Hours and Recreation

Leisure time

The working week is from Saturday to Thursday lunch time although Thursday is increasingly becoming regarded as a holiday. In most Arab countries the working day starts early in the morning, finishes at 1 or 2 pm, and, after lunch and a siesta through the hottest part of the day, resumes in the late afternoon until around 6 or 7 pm. This leaves plenty of time for sport - tennis, swimming, sailing or water-skiing. In Peninsula countries there are social and sporting clubs with facilities for all these activities. Sometimes the membership is restricted to Westerners in order to protect the culture and values of the local Muslim community. Friday, the holy day of the week, is universally treated as a holiday. In some countries the offices of foreign institutions such as Western embassies, are increasingly choosing to work on Thursday but take a two-day weekend on Friday and Saturday, which has the advantage of bringing their working week more into line with the head office in their home country.

Weekends

Servants

Many expatriates have a servant of some sort, a nanny, cook or someone to help with housework. The servants are expatriates themselves, coming mostly from Africa and Asia. Servants are not as much of a luxury as they may sound and many people consider the climate is debilitating enough to make them a necessity.

You may take on a good servant from your predecessor or a friend, but otherwise you will have to recruit one. You should check the local employment laws with regard to employee rights, repatriation to their home country etc. An insurance policy of some sort is usually necessary to cover accidents in the home. Employ a new servant on a strictly probationary arrangement at the outset, e.g. on a month's trial.

Make sure you establish and maintain a correct relationship. Over-familiarity leads to a lack of respect and encourages a servant to lower standards and often to take advantage of their employer. The best sort of relationship is one of semi-informality - courteous and considerate but correct and always keeping one's distance.

Because some servants are Muslims and their religious beliefs must be respected, do not ask a cook to prepare pork unless you are sure that they are happy to do so. Make every allowance during the month-long fast of Ramadan when they will be short of sleep, hungry during the day and not able to work as hard or as long hours as usual. Servants, in common with all Muslims, have a holiday over the period of the *Eid Al-Adha* and the *Eid Al-Fitr* and should be given a reasonably generous gift of money for each *Eid*.

Never in their presence lose your temper or your dignity. Once you have shown a lack of control and probably wounded his pride as well, it will be difficult to re-establish an effective working relationship. There is one other danger which old hands will readily acknowledge. Think twice before blaming a servant if something goes missing or gets broken – remember that an accusation is impossible to retract and harder to redress if it proves unjustified.

Finally, sacking an incompetent or dishonest servant can be a tricky business. It is best to talk it over with an

5

Making allowances

experienced colleague to minimise any personal animosity, safeguard your possessions and comply with local regulations. It is always preferable to pay money in lieu of notice.

The Embassy

Your Embassy or Consulate sometimes becomes the focal point for expatriate social life (and the business life as well, in some cases). The facilities of the Embassy – the garden, swimming pool, tennis or squash court or club bar – are frequent venues for diplomatic receptions as well as numerous social, charitable, cultural and commercial functions. Expatriates and their wives are invariably involved in such activities. However, the primary functions of the Embassy are to represent the home Government to the host Government and to protect the interests of its citizens and it must not be regarded as existing largely for the benefit of the expatriate. community.

Finally, if you are going to stay in a country for any length of time, you should register at the Consul's office in your Embassy.

Embassy facilities

5

THE FEMALE EXPATRIATE

The situation of the female expatriate deserves special consideration during the assessment of a post in the region. She needs to be just as adaptable, sensitive and self reliant as her male counterpart, if not more so. If she is a wife and does not have a job then some sort of social activity or interest such as charitable work is essential. The opportunities for employment in what are viewed as appropriate occupations for women expatriates differ from country to country. Nursing and teaching are open to women in all countries, as is secretarial work, except in Saudi Arabia.

Some expatriates choose to move only in their own circles in the Peninsula but a foreign woman certainly does not have to remain isolated from Arab women. Provided she has the opportunity, feels comfortable doing so, and is

Expatriate women

sufficiently sensitive to the difference in culture, making contact with Arab women can be a most rewarding experience. She is likely to make many firm friends.

On arrival in an Arab country the female expatriate must learn the limits of her freedom. In most countries she will enjoy complete freedom to travel and shop although there will always be male preserves such as coffee houses which are barred to her. In Saudi Arabia, at present, a women may not drive a car and therefore must employ a driver. Furthermore, apart from her driver, a woman in Saudi Arabia may not appear in public accompanied by a man other than her husband or close blood relative such as her father or brother. She is also required to cover her arms and legs and most Saudi Arabian women wear an *abaya* and head shawl. In other countries (and in some cities of Saudi Arabia) the code of behaviour is more relaxed, but there are nevertheless standards of dress applicable to women. (*See* Chapter 1 - *Arab Women* and Chapter 4 - *Standards of Dress*).

Relationships

A word of warning is necessary concerning relationships with Arab men. The freedom with which Arab men are able to talk to expatriate women is in complete contrast to the relationship which custom demands they enjoy with their own womenfolk. Foreign women must be alive to this, behaving with decorum; encouraging the wrong attitude in an Arab male risks offending the Muslim code of conduct.

Islamic law and the Muslim code of conduct strictly forbid relationships outside marriage, whether as partners or extramarital. If such a situation comes to the attention of the authorities, it could well result in deportation, and in some cases imprisonment.

DESERT TRAVEL

One of the most popular recreational pastimes for the expatriate is to visit the remote, unspoiled and beautiful areas of desert, mountains and oases that lie in the hinterland of all the Peninsula countries. Even in the desert, there is a surprising wealth of flora and

Desert trekking

fauna. However, for the uninitiated the desert can also be a potentially dangerous place. People have become lost, been caught in flash floods and have died from thirst or heat stroke – even on quite short journeys of up to 15 miles. Any forays into the desert must be taken seriously and organised with care. The suitability of your vehicle, its equipment, spares, fuel, water and medical supplies are some of the many considerations. Seek expert advice, take a guide if possible and make sure someone staying behind knows where you have gone and when you are coming back.

Good books on desert travel and camping are on sale in local book shops. Particularly useful is Jim Stabler's *The Desert Driver's Manual* (Stacey International, 1997)

Essential precautions will include:

- Always take more than one vehicle. Air-conditioned four-wheel drive are best.
- Vehicle equipment of spare wheel (two for long trips), tyre pressure gauge and foot pump, fan belt, tool kit, spare ignition key, spare fuses, tow rope, jack, wooden jacking block, wheel brace, sand channels, shovels, jumper leads, spare oils and fire extinguisher.
- Desert driving uses more fuel than on roads; allow half as much fuel again, plus a reserve.
- Plenty of water and food plus a reserve in case of a breakdown.
- Comprehensive medical kit and knowledge of the treatment for commonly experienced emergencies such as heat stroke (*see* Chapter 4 - *Health Care*).
- Water sterilisation tablets and insect repellent.
- Prior and continued protection against malaria if prevalent in the areas you are visiting.
- Sleeping bags. Even in summer the desert is very cold at night.
- Map, binoculars, compass and a GPS system if you can afford it.
- Mobile phone if coverage is available.
- Knowledge of the desert, as well as desert and

mountain driving.
- Rules for travel and camping, e.g. getting lost, flash floods, stagnant water.
- Never travel in a sand storm or at night.
- Beware of camels which stray on to roads and can be difficult to see at dusk and dawn.
- Car insurance cover. International boundaries are not always clear and it is prudent to have cover for both sides of any borders.

5

CHAPTER SIX

The Business Traveller

INTRODUCTION

The conduct of business in the Peninsula countries may best be described as gentlemanly, tricky and time-consuming. The influences at work are rooted in the local culture. Personal relationships are of paramount importance, social and business etiquette must be observed and religion plays a part. Negotiating and striking a deal are conducted on well established lines and the pace is a good deal slower than in the West.

Business etiquette

Today, operating successfully in the Peninsula is a matter of personality and professionalism. Personality amounts to being open, friendly and non-judgmental, able to adapt to the Arab way of doing business, to cope with the heat and frustration and, overall, to display a mixture of endless patience and dogged perseverance. Professionalism means efficient market research and business operation and a thorough understanding of the Arab culture, the market and the way business is conducted.

THE MARKET

One occasionally hears the market in the Peninsula portrayed as difficult or depressed. But this is to paint a totally false picture. In spite of the fluctuations in the price of oil, it continues to be a growth market in both the public and the private sectors. It is one of the West's major trading partners, providing excellent opportunities for exporters of the right products and services.

The transformation of the infrastructures of the Gulf States in the 1970s was followed by a period of consolidation and the diversification of their economies - including Arabisation wherever possible. The reduction in the price of oil was perhaps the beneficial shock that encouraged the move in this direction. But the development of their industrial bases continues. The traditional markets for defence products, luxury goods and consumer goods remain unchanged and new markets are emerging in any number of new fields such as communications, tourism and manufacturing. All the Peninsula countries also have a keen

The emerging markets

123

interest in agricultural development and there is a continuing need for education and training in technical fields.

At the same time the large imbalance of trade with the West, combined with tighter budgets, has brought reforms in economic outlook and particularly in the way that large projects are financed.

Niche markets

For small and medium sized companies approaching this market however, such considerations may not necessarily apply. For them it is very often a question of identifying a niche market and having the right product to fill it. If some areas of the market are unpromising others are growing. The expansion of the population in the Peninsula States is around 3.5% per annum, and with 50% of the population under the age of 16, there is a rising the demand for housing, consumer products, education, employment and leisure activities.

MARKET RESEARCH

The importance of market research cannot be over-emphasised. It should include a study of :

- *Product and service requirements*: What is wanted and why. Gaps in the market. Competition.
- *How business is done*: Representatives, agents and consultants.
- *The decision-making process*: Who takes the decisions, who influences the decision makers, and the procurement system.
- *Finance*: Loans, credit, counter-trade agreements, offset, joint ventures.
- *Plan of campaign*: A detailed plan of action including estimated timescales.

Assistance with Market Research

In the UK, the business traveller can look to the following organisations and agencies for assistance with market research:

- British Trade International (BTI) Arabian Peninsula Section. Provides advice and assistance to exporters to the region, and offers a wide range

6

of free written material including a yearbook, *Gulf Spotlight,* introductory guides to each market (updated every six months) and summaries on key sectors.

The BTI

- BTI also supports many official trade missions to the region every year – an excellent way to make a first visit in a protected environment.
  Contact numbers are:
  Saudi Arabia: 020 7215 4839; UAE: 020 7215 4246
  Oman and Bahrain: 020 7215 4388
  Kuwait and Qatar: 020 7215 4811

- BTI Export Promoters. Senior managers seconded from industry with specialised knowledge of the territories to which they are appointed, whose job it is to promote UK exports including advice and assistance to UK exporters.
  Contact Tel: 020 7215 8328.

- BTI Export Market Information Centre (EMIC)
  This is the BTI's free self-service reference library for exporters. EMIC's collection includes statistics, directories and multilateral aid projects. Open 0900 - 2000 Monday to Friday and 0900 -1730 Saturday.
  EMIC, Kingsgate House, 66-74 Victoria Street, London SWIE 6SW. Tel: 020 7215 5444/5; Fax: 020 7215 4231; E-mail: EMIC@xpd3.dti.gov.uk; Internet URL: www.dti.gov.uk./ots/emic.

- For the latest information and details of BTI support, visit the BTI website at: www.brittrade.com. BTI support includes access to the TradeUK Export Sales Lead Service and National Exporters Database and Grant-Supported Trade Fairs and Exhibitions.
  Contacts for first-time exporters are:
  - England. One of the network of Business Links. Tel: 0345 567765 or visit the Business Link Signpost website at: www.businesslink.co.uk
  - Scotland. Scottish Trade International. Tel: 09141-228 2812/2808 or www.sti.org.uk
  - Wales. Welsh Office Overseas Trade Services. Tel:01222 825097 or www.wales.gov.uk

6

125

▸ Northern Ireland. Industrial Development Board for Northern Ireland. Tel: 02890 233233; or website: www.idbni.co.uk

COMET

◆ Committee for Middle East Trade (COMET) COMET is a BTI advisory group for the Middle East whose main purpose is to assist in the formulation of Government trade policy and to seek out and promote ways of improving UK performance in the region acting as an interface between Industry and Government. Its staff can provide briefing for UK firms on individual Middle East markets and can advise on more specialised information sources available to the exporter. It works closely with such organisations as the Middle East Association, CBI and Chambers of Commerce. Bury House, 33 Bury Street, St James's, London SW1Y 6AX. Tel: 020 7839 1170/1191; fax: 020 7839 3717; website: www.comet.org.uk E-mail: enquiries@comet.org.uk

DESO

◆ Defence Export Services Organisation (DESO). DESO is part of the Ministry of Defence and aims to assist UK industry in the promotion of defence and related equipment and services to overseas governments. It works closely with other government departments including the Foreign and Commonwealth Office and British Trade International and such organisations as the Defence Manufacturers Association (DMA). The Division of DESO responsible for the Peninsula countries is The Regional Marketing Directorate 1 (RMD 1). Contact details: DESO, Ministry of Defence, Metropole Building, Northumberland Avenue, London WC2N 5BL. Tel: Switchboard: 020 7218 9000; Fax: Direct 020 7807 8307.

MEA

◆ Middle East Association. An independent non-political, non-profit making organisation financed by its members' subscriptions and whose purpose is to promote trade between UK and the Middle East. Offers members practical help towards expanding their business with these markets.

Membership is open to companies in the UK and the Middle East and to certain individuals. Close contact is maintained with Government departments (especially BTI, FCO and COMET) The MEA is involved in sponsoring (with BTI funding) organising and managing trade missions to the Middle East , participates in exhibitions in the region and holds regular receptions for commercial and diplomatic guests and UK Government officials and frequent seminars and discussion meetings with expert speakers. Middle East Association(MEA) Bury House, 33 Bury Street, St James's, London SWIY 6AX. Tel: 020 7839 2137; Fax: 020 7839 6121; E-mail: mail@the-mea.demon.co.uk

- Arab-British Chamber of Commerce (A-BCC)
  Founded in 1975 under licence from the UK Department of Trade, the A-BCC is an organisation devoted to promoting commercial, industrial, tourist and financial relations between the Arab countries (except Egypt) and the UK. It provides the following services, some of which are available to members only: certification service (certificates of origin and other commercial documents); legalisation service (if required by an Arab embassy); business inquiry service; trade information bulletin (weekly); visa service; seminars on specific countries; translation, typesetting and printing services; reference library; Arabic and English courses and various publications on commerce in the region. A-BCC, Belgrave Square, London SWIX 8PH. Tel: 020 7235 4363; Fax: 020 7245 6688.

A-BCC

6

All of the above offer advice to individuals, hold regular conferences on specific markets and organise trade missions to the region.

Valuable marketing advice and assistance can also be provided by:

Further

- The Commercial Sections of British Embassies abroad including locally engaged staff who, through long service in the various countries, have a wealth of information on local markets.

- British Business Groups which are established in all major cities of the region.
- Local banks.
- UK chambers of commerce
- Professional trade associations in specialised fields.
- The British Council. On educational and cultural matters.
- Arab Embassies in London,

Background Publications

Publications distributed by The British Trade International's (BTI) Export Publications Unit:

- *'Hints to Exporters Visiting the Arabian Peninsula'* Provides practical information for the potential exporter and the international traveller on all the Peninsula countries. Topics include preparation for a visit, travel and currency information, social customs, economic factors, import and exchange regulations, methods of doing business and a wealth of contact points including useful Internet sites.
- *Sources of information.* Provides a list of useful contact points for further information covering all aspects of doing business in a market. (BTI).
- *Sector reports and general reports.* Market research reports on sectors/areas where exporting opportunities for UK business have been identified.(BTI)
- *Project Lists.* Produced by the commercial staff of the Foreign and Commonwealth Office (FCO) based overseas it identifies opportunities for UK exporters in major projects and contracts overseas.
- *Countertrade and Offset - A Guide for Exporters* Explains the basic forms, including barter, tolling, counterpurchase, offset and buyback with case histories for each. Discusses the issues to be considered in negotiating countertrade deals, provides information on the offset policies of more than 80 overseas markets. Gives a list of 135 contacts as well as details of companies who can

offer expert help - including traders, bankers, insurers and consultants.

For all the above publications contact the BTI's Export Publications Unit on Tel: 0870-1502 500 or visit the Export Publications website at www.dti.gov.uk/ots/publications.

Other useful publications:

- *MEED (The Middle East Economic Digest) Ltd* publish:
  - ▶ MEED (weekly) The leading English-language business magazine on the Middle East which gives comprehensive coverage of all economic developments in the region as well as regular special reports on individual countries.
  - ▶ MEED Money (weekly) The Middle East financial markets magazine
  - ▶ MEED Profiles on Saudi Arabia, Qatar and UAE.
  - ▶ A series of investors guides giving information on publicly listed companies.
  - ▶ MEED Quarterly Report on Saudi Arabia.
  - ▶ Middle East Business Finance Directory. Of the top 500 companies in the region.

  Contact information. MEED, 21 John Street, London WC1N 2BP Tel: 020 7505 8000; Fax 020 7831 9537 or on their website www.meed.com.
- *The Economist Intelligence Unit.* Quarterly and annual country reviews and country reports going back over the last 5 years. Also periodic publications on telecommunications, health care, the automotive sector, financial services and human resources (recruitment). Contact details: The Economist Intelligence Unit, 15 Regent Street, London SW1Y 4LR. Tel: 020 7839 1997; Fax: 020 7491 2107; E-mail: london@eiu.com or The Economist Building, 111 West 57th Street, New York, NY 10019, USA. Tel: 1 212 554 0600 Fax: 1 212 586 1181 Email: newyork@eiu.com
- *Major Companies of the Arab World.* A comprehensive directory published by Graham and Trotman Limited, Sterling House, 66 Wilton

6

129

Road, London SWIV IDE. Tel: 020 7821 1123

♦ *The Exporter's Guide to Trading in The Gulf: Legal Aspects.* A guide to commercial agency law produced by Nabarro Nathanson in conjunction with the BTI's Arabian Peninsula Section. Obtainable free from Nabarro Nathanson Tel: 020 7518 3630 or BTI Tel: 020 7215 8192/8271.

A resumé of Department of Commerce support available to US companies wishing to access the Peninsula markets is given in the Annex.

PRODUCT REQUIREMENTS

When identifying opportunities or gaps in the market, due consideration should be given to what is needed as well as what is wanted. They may not always be the same thing. Some products introduced into the region create more problems than they solve; for example if they require highly skilled operation or complex maintenance. Any sales package therefore should be completely comprehensive and cover installation, training, management, spare parts and maintenance support.

Contracts can be won for a variety of often complex reasons. As a rule, products are attractive if they are the best at the right price and in most cases can be demonstrated to be the latest on the market. They must be 'proven'. The fact that the product has already been purchased by another prestigious customer or, in the case of Defence equipment, is in service with the British Armed Forces, is an added selling point if not essential. The introduction of a new product, service or technique must take account of traditional and Islamic beliefs. The successful introduction of a new toothpaste acceptable to Muslims, containing no animal fat, is a good example. Finally, attempt to establish what competition (foreign or otherwise) you face in your product range.

There are a number of ways to bring a new product or service to the attention of the Arab market and one should seek advice from the BTI in this regard. One way is through the Central Office of Information (COI) whose

The sales package

6

purpose is to project British industry abroad. British Embassies overseas also seek to place stories with newspapers, trade and technical press and possibly local radio and television as well. A leaflet entitled Worldwide Export Publicity explains the process and is obtainable from: Client Services Group, COI, Hercules Road, London SEI 7DU. Tel: 020 7928 2345

Financing

As mentioned, the large imbalance of trade with the West combined with tighter budgets has brought reforms in economic outlook and particularly in the way large projects are financed. Major deals contingent on credit, privatisation, public flotation, BOOT (build, own, operate and transfer) schemes, counter trade, offset, technology transfer and the formation of joint ventures are increasingly being proposed. It is sensible for foreign companies to consider these options at the planning stage. Proposals which include such an element may stand a greater chance of success and often attract certain incentives.

Loans and credit

All the advisory organisations mentioned earlier in this chapter under market research can also supply information on funding, i.e. the international aid programmes, government loans, extended credit facilities, etc. They will also be aware of banks specialising in various project fields.

Export Credits Guarantee Department (ECGD)

ECGD is a Government department which offers industry and exporters of goods and services a wide range of financial assistance including insurance, protection and credit. The complete range of its facilities may be obtained from ECGD at: PO Box 272, Aldermanbury House, Aldermanbury, London EX2P 3EL. Tel: 020 7382 7000

MARKETING PLANS

In the majority of cases the need to establish a personal relationship and mutual trust means that any sales campaign must be staged over a period of time. There

131

will, of course, be notable exceptions - like the salesperson travelling to the Peninsula for the first time as a member of a trade mission with a luxury product for which there was little competition and doubling annual sales in a week! But the successful negotiation of a major export project, perhaps against active competition, is generally a lengthy and often tortuous process, taking months and in some cases years to accomplish. This may be obvious to the experienced business traveller in the region but not to his boss at home, and any sales plan should have a realistic time frame. If the market research is thorough, the Arab decision-maker and those who influence him have been clearly identified and the right person chosen to represent the company, then a visit will not be wasted. You must also always be prepared, however, for business to be concluded in an unorthodox way. Contracts can be won or lost for a wide variety of complicated reasons. Be prepared to think laterally as well as analytically. The preparation and conduct of your visit should take account of the guidelines and advice below.

Thinking laterally

QUALITIES OF A SUCCESSFUL BUSINESS TRAVELLER

Two of the qualities necessary for success in the Arab world have been mentioned earlier – endless patience and dogged perseverance. Similarly important are the ability to establish a rapport with others at all levels, to have a friendly and open disposition, and show integrity. Finally, it is important to be able to adapt to the way the Arab people do business, behaving with sensitivity towards their culture. The Arab is calm and dignified in his speech and actions and is unfailingly polite. So must you be. Be respectful but not subservient. If necessary, you must be prepared to stand your ground and to refute any unjustified allegation in a calm but diplomatic way and with good humour. The Arabs can be great teasers and do not respect those who rise to the bait or are easily rattled.

Establishing a rapport

The importance attached to personal relationships is very relevant to commercial life. Like you, an Arab will wish to establish whether you can be trusted. This takes time, and the degree of that trust may be directly related to the number of times you have met, but once established, is of great value. *See* Chapter 3 for more information on personal relationships.

Business life in the Arab world is also conducted mainly on the basis of who you know and it pays therefore to get to know as many people as possible. A foreigner will find he is more readily accepted and trusted (and more likely to obtain information) if he is friendly with everyone he meets. That includes the hotel staff, the agent's chauffeur

---

TRUST AS THE BASIS OF BUSINESS

There is the salutory lesson of an Arab client wishing to invest with an English merchant banker whom he knew well and trusted. The Arab visited his friend's bank and offered to invest a large sum of money in whatever his English friend advised. There was no more to be said, but the Englishman decided, for form's sake, to introduce this important new client to his Managing Director. The Managing Director was delighted but, unaware that the deal had been struck on the basis of trust, thought to reinforce the Arab's decision to invest with a short discourse on how successful the bank had been that year. By the end of the speech, the Arab was so suspicious about the Managing Director's need to justify the investment that he withdrew his offer.

---

and the client's clerk. It is customary to shake them by the hand on first meeting in the morning and on saying farewell. But don't be over familiar or too friendly or pry, as it may well be reported back.

It is sometimes said that because the Arabs respect age the older business traveller is likely to be more successful. This is not true. What matters more is an appreciation of the culture and business methods. As a general rule, the

133

ambitious, go-getting, 'time is money' breed of businessman will not succeed. Although there is a generation of bright young Arab executives coming to the fore in some countries who may follow some of the modern dynamic business methods, they are as yet a minority. There will be, of course, the odd occasion when an Arab customer needs something by *yesterday*. If he knows you, he will turn to you for help and you must be prepared to move fast and on a basis of trust, possibly with only a verbal agreement.

Sometimes an Arab acquaintance will make a personal request which has nothing to do with your commercial dealings. Although this is unusual in Western culture, it is wise to try and help.

Finally, an Arab does not like dealing with an underling or with constantly changing faces, a complaint often directed at foreign companies. The person he deals with must have the authority to negotiate without constantly referring back to his superiors. For these reasons an early decision has to be taken as to who will authoritatively represent a Western company for a particular sales campaign and, once appointed, that person should remain the principal point of contact. Since the establishment of trust is so important, it would be wise to introduce any standby representative at an early stage. Of course, as a project develops it will be necessary for the company to deal at whatever level is appropriate. An Arab Minister, for example, would expect to see the Company Chairman at the proper time.

Finding the right level

Businesswomen

Although the field of commerce in the Peninsula is male-dominated, there are nevertheless a number of highly successful Arab businesswomen who control large enterprises although they personally adopt a low profile. Others conduct business in an exclusively female environment.

Foreign businesswomen have not found it difficult to do business in the region and in several fields they are more successful than men. In the more conservative Arab

6

countries, however, a businesswoman must expect to find that men are less at ease with her than they would be with a man, although she will always be treated with the utmost courtesy. For her part, the foreign businesswoman should dress soberly, not exaggerate her femininity and, most importantly, she should adopt a polite, straight-forward and businesslike approach without being in any way aggressive or assertive. In Saudi Arabia a businesswoman should be escorted by a local representative or sponsor, who should also be a woman, and she should not forget that it is customary for men to walk ahead of women.

VISIT ADMINISTRATION

Follow the advice in Chapter 4 - *Visiting The Peninsula*. Additional points for business travellers are set out below.

Business Cards

These are normally printed in English on one side and in Arabic on the other. A company logo is best left untranslated but the subtitle beneath, if there is one, should be translated into Arabic. The card may need to be larger than normal to accommodate the Arabic script. It is also worth discussing in detail the meaning that your name and company appointment will have when they are translated to make sure it conveys the correct impression to an Arab customer. You should avoid describing yourself as an 'Assistant' or 'Deputy', even if that is correct in English, as Arab customers do not like to feel that they are dealing with an underling. But also consider how this affects the translation of the cards and titles of any colleagues who may become involved at a later stage. Finally, avoid any obvious misrepresentation. There is a well-known story of a salesman from a large multinational corporation who asked his translator to give him a title that was impressive in Arabic to avoid undue delay in getting to see the right people on his trips to the region. He found he was always given immediate access to the most senior people, but only discovered

Dual-language cards

6

135

why later when someone asked him about his role as the President of his corporation.

Business Correspondence

It is becoming increasingly common for customers in the region to correspond by fax, e-mail or telephone rather than by letter. When writing is appropriate however, use headed notepaper with an address in Arabic. For some governmental institutions, the extra expense of having dual English/Arabic language letterhead may well be justified. If a brochure is enclosed it must be in Arabic as well as English. The material should be self-explanatory (no obscure abbreviations), of the highest quality - coloured photographs, maps and diagrams - and not too wordy. For advice on correspondence with Saudi Arabia, see below.

Brochures

The person representing a Western organisation should also be the correspondent with the customer. Nothing is more confusing or annoying to a customer than to receive correspondence from several different people on the same topic. Unfortunately, it is not an uncommon practice, especially in large Western corporations. For legal reasons a Western company may issue a contract under the name of the Commercial Director, for example, but it should be sent to the customer under cover of a letter from the main representative.

Use plain English. Idiomatic and flowery turns of phrase will not be understood or appreciated. Write in the active rather than the passive voice. If any action is being requested in the letter then make a clear statement to that effect, leaving it to the end for emphasis. Finally, in promoting a product or a project, do so in such a way that no criticism is made or implied of any existing system in the Peninsula. (*See also* Chapter 3 - *Forms of Address and Official Correspondence.*)

Translations into Arabic

Documents produced in Arabic are often vital to a sales campaign. In most Peninsula countries brochures should be in English and Arabic and at least the

Executive Summary of any proposal should be as well. The Arabic and English are usually arranged either alongside one another or with Arabic at the front and English at the back. In Saudi Arabia all official correspondence is required by law to be in Arabic as well as any other language, such as English, and it is advisable to produce separate Arabic and English (or other) doucmentation.

Good translators are not cheap, partly because they are much in demand and take trouble to impart the true meaning of a document to the reader. Translating documents is usually the last thing people do to prepare for a visit to the region but you will negotiate a better price if you do not ask for a rush job.

A good translator will also advise on the general effect and presentation of any documents. English trade names and the vernacular, if put directly into Arabic can turn out to be meaningless or even offensive. The word '*zip*', for example means 'penis' in Arabic, and a phrase like 'top of the range' would be meaningless if directly translated.

Making yourself clear

Translating documents

6

LOST IN TRANSLATION

What the Arabs see as an over-emphasis on sex in advertisements and the use of peculiarly English puns or colloquialisms do not come across well. A shipment of litter-bins to one Peninsula country turned out to have an inscription describing them as pigs' litters. Simpler mistakes have included a batch of signs which should have warned of camels straying *onto* the road but which showed the camels walking *off* the road – since traffic drives on the right in the Peninsula, the signs are also positioned on the right of the road!

Ideally any correspondence, brochure or advertisement should also be relevant to the Arab culture.

There are a number of firms offering a professional

translation service. Once such is Intonaton: Contact St Alphage House, 2 Fore Street Moorgate, London EC2Y 5DA. Tel: 020 7920 9322; fax: 020 7920 9323.

Details of other firms providing similar services may be obtained from The Institute of Translating and Interpreting, 377 City Road, London EC1V 1NA. Tel: 020 7713 7600; Fax: 020 7713 7650.

Visit Visas

Passports

Because of the time taken to obtain visas, regular travellers often apply for an additional passport, and one with 94 pages rather than the customary 30 pages is particularly useful. However, if two passports are used make absolutely certain that the same passport is always used for the same country. To be discovered using a second passport would present major problems and a possible charge of misrepresentation. It is possible for a frequent traveller to obtain a multi-entry visa. Good travel agents and some chambers of commerce provide a visa service for their members for which they make an administrative charge.

Entry visas

Some countries have special entry requirements. For Saudi Arabia, for example, a visa application must be accompanied by a letter of invitation from a Saudi sponsor. Regulations of this sort vary from country to country and are, of course, liable to change. Sometimes they can be eased or speeded up if you have the right contacts. *See* the Country Annexes for details.

Hotels in the Peninsula

Hotel addresses, telephone and fax numbers in each of the Peninsula countries are given in the BTI booklet *Hints to Exporters Visiting The Arabian Peninsula*. However, it should be possible for your travel agent, local sponsor or agent to negotiate special rates.

Dress and General Appearance

Pay attention to your appearance – you will be judged on how you look. A business traveller should be smartly but soberly dressed - a good-quality suit (lightweight in

summer) and a tie for a man and a formal suit or dress
for a woman.

Security During Overseas Visits

Cooks Travel Service provide advice for businessmen on
security during trips abroad. The sort of concern that a
businessman dealing in defence or security products
might have, in the unlikely event of hijack, is to avoid
carrying evidence of the nature of his business. On
commercial confidentiality it is also best to have a pre-
arranged business code for use when communicating
with the UK from an Arab country, especially when
discussing prices.

Business Samples

Business samples are best accompanied by a certificate
explaining that they are of no commercial value and are
being carried as an essential part of your work.

PREPARATION AND TIMING OF A VISIT TO THE REGION

In addition to the advice given in Chapter 4, plans should
take account of:

- Appropriate preparatory action having been taken
  by a local agent, the Commercial Officer or the
  Defence Attache (in the case of Defence sales) of your
  Embassy, if you have enlisted their help.
- The availability of all those you wish to see; Arab
  clients, agents, British Ambassador, Commercial
  Officer or Defence Attaché, etc.
- The time of year. The summer months of July and
  August and school holidays tend to be times when
  Arab customers take holidays abroad, and the hotter
  months are generally less conducive to doing
  business.
- The holy month of the fast of Ramadan is best
  avoided. Working hours are curtailed, particularly
  towards the end of this month. The dates, which are

139

different each year by the Western calendar, are forecast at the end of Chapter 1.

- The main Muslim festivals are also best avoided if they are holidays in the country you are visiting. In Saudi Arabia only the *Eid Al-Adha* and *Eid Al-Fitr* are celebrated as holidays. The dates, which again change each year are also forecast in Chapter 1.
- National Days (dates are given in the Country Annexes). Also note any holiday observed by Embassies, such as the British Embassy's Queen's Birthday celebrations.
- The Pilgrimage. Flights to the region and particularly to and within Saudi Arabia can be very crowded during the period of the run up to, and end of, the annual Hajj pilgrimage.
- Consider the working week and business hours. For details see Chapter 1 and the Country Annexes.

THE CONDUCT OF BUSINESS

The Embassy

The first port of call, unless you have been advised otherwise, and particularly on your initial visit to a country, will probably be the Embassy. This is not only a basic courtesy but good sense as their assistance and advice can be invaluable. It may be best not to highlight any link with the Embassy to your Arab customer until you are sure of his attitude, in case it offends his sense of confidentiality.

The Commercial Section of the Embassy exists to promote trade. An Ambassador holds frequent receptions for visiting trade missions or important commercial initiatives to which he will invite influential local dignitaries, heads of industry and commerce, and local businessmen. The Commercial Officer, his staff and the Defence Attaché will also be involved. Such functions can provide invaluable access to local businessmen and the decision-makers.

Local Agents, Sponsors, Consultants and Advisers

Large numbers of agents, sponsors and consultants operate in the Peninsula, their role being to facilitate transactions between foreign businessmen and their customers. They are paid a fixed fee or a percentage of any business and their services usually amount to the promotion of goods to local customers, identifying market opportunities and gaining access to the decision-makers. This system, although strange and even repugnant to some Westerners, is a legitimate and often essential business practice in the region. Any business traveller who has spent countless hours in the outer office of a Shaikh or waited for days in a hotel for a telephone response, is grateful for it. What is not to be countenanced is the man who, hearing of a contract in the offing, threatens to spoil it unless he is cut in on the deal; i.e. he claims the ability to bring the deal to a successful conclusion, with the clear implication that without him the deal won't go through. This is a difficult situation which must be dealt with in the light of the circumstances but your agents, consultants, professional bodies or local Embassy will provide good advice.

Never confuse the payment to an agent or consultant for legitimate business services with a bribe. You may hear a number of stories about bribery and corruption and it may be suggested that such practices occasionally oil the wheels, but bribery is a serious offence in all states of the region and the penalties are severe.

Although it is usual to use sponsors and local representatives it is not always obligatory and it is even forbidden for certain types of business. Nevertheless, most Western companies feel the need for a local adviser of some kind and they usually make a major contribution to success. The problem invariably lies in choosing the right one. It is an important and tricky subject and one on which a businessman should get as much good advice as he can before committing himself.

The type of arrangement you make will depend on the nature of your business. Regulations on the necessity for sponsors and agents or otherwise vary from country to

Representations

6

Agent's fees

country and depend on whether, for example, you are exporting, setting up a representative office, business or joint venture operation and who is the customer. If you are involved in the latter two activities then a sponsor is likely to be obligatory. For some Western exports it would not be essential and in the field of Defence it is expressly forbidden and companies awarded a contract are asked to sign a statement to the effect that no commission has been paid to a third party. It is advisable to visit a local lawyer at an early stage in any campaign and obtain a briefing on the options available and the legal and other implications of each option. Your embassy and local lawyers are usually well briefed in these matters. If agents are expressly forbidden in any field or for any other reason it is never worth trying to get round the law.

Commission

Thoroughly research the suitability of an agent and be as certain as possible that they have the necessary influence to ensure access, can obtain a favourable response from the decision-makers, and can provide good market intelligence including information on the competition, before signing up with him. These are the main requirements of a good agent and it is prudent to have some proof of his effectiveness from himself and others. Asking a third party about him calls for discretion. He may have a record of success but can he sustain it? Is he seen in the community as benefiting so much, say, from a particular business that the decision-makers deliberately decide to place the contract elsewhere? Any agreement with an agent should be drawn up in writing which must be fair to both sides. He will want you to make enough of a commitment to justify his efforts and you will want to safeguard yourself against an ineffective agent. The agreement should specify the field of operation in detail and have a time limit. Local laws should be carefully considered. It always pays to take advice from a local lawyer. In some countries and in some circumstances it is extremely difficult to sack an ineffective agent once he has been appointed and local court cases can be expensive, embarrassing and detrimental to one's business.

Agreements with agents

Finally, although it might appear to the newcomer to the Arab scene that progress without local help is impossible, and agents do often have an important role to play, their activities should never be allowed to become a substitute for your own direct contact with the customer.

The Decision-making Process

The decision-making process, particularly in the public sector, is often dominated by a small number of powerful individuals. Authority to take decisions may not be delegated in our bureaucratic way but all decisions, large and small, are often referred back to the top. This has the advantage on occasions that major decisions are taken remarkably quickly and with the minimum of fuss.

However, the decision-makers also rely on the increasing use of expert consultants, advisory committees and boards, not only for major projects but also for product purchase. A formalised system of procurement is an established feature of all the Peninsula Defence Forces, large entities such as national oil companies and most departments of government. You are likely, therefore, to have the effectiveness and value of your product examined by a number of highly competent experts and government officials who then report on it to the decision-maker. One of the important aims of market research is to ascertain who makes the final decision.

Dealing with commercial firms is slightly different. The centuries-long tradition of trade in the Arab world has brought certain families to prominence. The private sector is still largely dominated by family business. The heads of these large trading families, some of which are more reminiscent of empires, are much respected figures of the establishment and again the decision-making is confined to relatively few people.

Middle management has an important role to play and should not be ignored or consciously by-passed. Bear in mind that a special feature of the region is that a strong bond of loyalty links the middle manager to his boss. This bond will be strengthened rather than weakened if the middle manager is an Arab expatriate. In Saudi

Family businesses

Middle management

143

Arabia and some of the Gulf States many of them will be Lebanese, Egyptian or Palestinian by origin.

Access

One particular hurdle for any international businessman is gaining access to the decision-makers. In spite of the traditional custom of approachability – or perhaps because of it – it is often difficult for a foreigner to do this and the more senior the person the more difficult the access. It is generally far too time-consuming to work one's way up. The organisations mentioned above under Market Research will usually give good advice. Often your local Embassy can help, the Defence Attaché in the case of Defence products or the Commercial Counsellor in the commercial field.

Defence
sales

In the case of Defence products, the Defence Attaché will advise (and update) you on the procurement process, staff lists, locations of military personnel and security regulations and procedures which you are likely to encounter when dealing with the military in a particular Peninsula country. In the commercial field Western companies usually employ the services of a sponsor or agent, which is generally not permitted in the field of defence sales.

Whatever assistance you receive, access is always a problem. Because the decision-making process is centralised in a few hands, the decision-makers are much in demand not only from foreign visitors but also those both above and below them.A minister may be sent for by a ruler at short notice and detained, sometimes for an extended period. An Arab's commitment to his family or friends may make similar demands on his time. In spite of the fact that the pace of life is ever quickening, Arabs do not naturally make appointments to see each other on a routine basis and do not like to plan their schedules too tightly or too far into the future. It is therefore not sensible for a foreign visitor to request an appointment more than say a week or so in advance or to be inflexible over the date or timing if something should force a change. Having said that, if the request for access is clearly beneficial to an Arab as well as the visitor an Arab will often go out of his way to grant it.

Confidentiality and Integrity
As a basic principle it is always best to keep your dealings strictly confidential. In an area where competition is keen and everyone is intensely interested in everyone else's business an Arab customer will expect you to obey what is sometimes termed 'The Third Party Rule', i.e. never repeat to a third party what an Arab has told you. Also avoid mentioning to an Arab what someone has said to you, or he may think you are repeating what he says in the same way.

Business Etiquette
Follow closely the general advice given in Chapter 3. If you are invited to mention the subject of your visit during an initial meeting and other people are present, give only enough information to interest the Arab in granting you an exclusive interview at a later date when the matter may be discussed in more detail. He may well suggest the venue or he may accept an invitation to a meal in a local hotel, perhaps in a private room or, failing that, to discuss matters with one of his trusted subordinates.

Formal Presentations
Any presentation in this highly competitive market must be efficiently produced. However, the facilities in a client's offices may not always be extensive. Plan to overcome any limitations and consider the following guidelines:
  ♦ Language. Most presentations in the region are given in English but if it is clear that it would be better to communicate in Arabic choose a good interpreter. It is usually possible to hire someone locally. He should be intelligent enough to earn the respect of the Arab customer and speak in an acceptable dialect, i.e. either the local dialect of the country you are in or classical

6

Arabic. Egyptian and Palestinian Arabic is universally understood. If the presentation is in English then follow the advice on Communication given in Chapter 4.

* Rehearse well. Keep it straightforward with the minimum of abbreviations and mnemonics.
* Take it slowly, allow questions during your dialogue and pauses for customer participation.
* The script of the presentation (attractively bound) may also be provided for the clients - in Arabic and English together with a copy of any film or video.
* Support it if possible with slides, a film or a video.
* Always have a spare projector on hand.
* If the product is portable it should be taken to the presentation.
* The length of a presentation should normally be 20 minutes at most with time for questions.
* Do not imply criticism of any existing facility or Arab organisation when plugging your own product.
* Brochures should be produced to a high standard. The language (Arabic and English) must be easily understood with no inexplicable abbreviations. Technical detail is best left as an annex to the main document.

Demonstrations and Trials

It is best to establish at the planning stage of any project whether a demonstration or trial will be necessary. They are however, often extremely time-consuming and costly. (Will the customer contribute?) A successful demonstration, particularly of defence equipment, calls for the highest degree of professionalism. The following matters should be addressed:

* Several rehearsals under conditions identical to the final demonstration. Anticipate everything that could go wrong.
* A backup or duplicate at every stage to replace anything that does go wrong.
* Simplicity of presentation.
* Translated speech in the dialect of the Arab customer.

- An illustrated written record of the demonstration.
- A film or video to augment the demonstration (perhaps including any feature that could not, for safety reasons, be demonstrated).
- Use local Arab operators but make sure they are trained, rehearsed and controlled.
- Availability of the decision-makers and their attendance.
- That extra idea to make an impact.
- A memento of the occasion as a gift to the principal person or persons present.

Demonstrations

Promotional Gifts

As in any commercial dealings, promotional gifts such as diaries (which can be produced including the *Hijra* calendar), calendars, pens or paperweights, and other gifts are always acceptable and serve to keep a firm's name prominent in the client's mind. Gifts should always be carefully chosen to reflect the relative importance of the recipient, e.g. the Arab Director General of an Organisation should be given a more prestigious gift than a member of his staff. It is wise to record the giving as it is often difficult to remember a year later what you gave and when. It should also be remembered that gifts need to be appropriate for the recipient. In countries such as the Gulf states where luxury goods are commonplace the expense of a gift to a senior citizen or Shaikh can be considerable. It would be better to do it properly or not at all. A newcomer is advised to seek advice from an experienced colleague.

Subsequent Visits and Refusals

The rule is to visit often. Arabs are justifiably cynical about single visits, broken promises, and a lack of a commitment on the part of the Western businessman. Arab courtesy is such that you will never receive a directly negative response to a business proposal. If you have failed to get a response and the Arab in question has clearly had every opportunity to give one, then you have to be able to recognise the signs that clearly point in the

147

direction of rejection or a change of circumstances (which can amount to the same thing). All too often one hears of the frustrated foreigner who says "I have heard absolutely nothing. I have no idea what they think!" But if you suspect you have failed, it is not a good idea to embarrass an Arab by pressing him to clarify his position.

Negotiations

As has been said in Chapter 3 under *Bargaining,* foreigners often find bargaining tedious, but to the Arabs of this part of the world it is second nature and is bound to be a major feature of any business deal. It is wise to be well prepared. It should be approached as the art of compromise without backing down or losing face. To negotiate a good deal is a matter of pride to an Arab and it will be very important to achieve it if he is dealing on behalf of himself, his organisation or his Government. This being the case, for you to make a significant reduction in price during a negotiation without reason (as sadly is sometimes done) is to encourage the belief that you were significantly overcharging. Therefore at each stage of a negotiation there must be a meaningful reason for reducing a price or changing a position. Plan at the outset to leave room to manoeuvre in any contract, both for reducing the price a number of times (perhaps by removing optional elements) but also to offer some added attractions to compensate for sticking at your original price. Always try to keep something in reserve because it will certainly be needed!

Leaving room for manoeuvre

THE ARAB NEGOTIATOR

Commerce has been a part of the Arab way of life for centuries, and they are past masters at negotiation. There is the apocryphal story of a Lebanese schoolboy who, when asked what two and two made, said, "Am I buying or selling?"

Negotiations can be tough, heated and with unusually forthright statements being made by the Arab customer, some of which may shock you. In some instances this is a deliberate negotiating technique. Keep your cool, firmly refute any unjustified statement and, above all, do not allow any altercation to become personal.

As well as striving to maintain a pleasant relationship with an Arab customer it is important to be especially sensitive and responsive to what he says during your dealings. He may sometimes give you genuinely helpful advice. He may do this obliquely. In doing so he may be compensating for the gap in culture and understanding between you and because he likes you. The words may sometimes be intended for your ears only. It has happened more than once in my experience and it pays to listen very carefully to what he says - such hints are often missed.

Verbal Agreements and Records of Meetings

There is a strong tradition in the Arab world of concluding agreements verbally. Modern bureaucracy demands that they now be put in writing, but even today some Arabs will regard an oral agreement as binding. Arabs pride themselves on having prodigious memories for every detail in even the most protracted negotiations and it is very important not to make an oral commitment or a promise that you cannot keep. It is always sensible to write to an Arab customer following a meeting, thanking him and at the same time confirming your understanding of any important conversation or decision. Although it is often tiresome to do so, it confirms the situation to both parties, flushes out any misunderstandings and prevents any change of mind which one side or the other could later seek to introduce.

It is wise to be aware of the Arab characteristic of adhering to the letter of any agreement as well as necessarily to the spirit of it. If both sides have established a genuine rapport, however, then written agreements are usually consigned to the filing cabinet and the parties proceed on the basis of mutual trust, a situation much preferred in Peninsula countries.

Listening to the customer

6

Arab memory

149

Contracts

Detailed advice on the content of contracts can be obtained from your company or local lawyer, the Embassy Commercial Section or from the BTI. Whereas a Western company may wish a contract to conform to the laws of its home country, this may not be acceptable to the Arab customer who may wish his own jurisdiction to apply. It is sensible for foreign companies to take both home-based and local legal advice for large contracts to safeguard their interests, although they may sometimes have to accept that this may not be entirely to the extent that they would wish.

In all the capitals of the Peninsula countries there are representative offices of leading Western legal firms, generally in partnership with local firms. There are also excellent local firms. Many of the Western and other lawyers have extensive experience in commercial contract work as well as the formation of joint ventures, public floatation counter trade and offset etc.

As a general principle contracts should always be kept as simple as possible. The language must always be straightforward, bearing in mind that it will be translated into Arabic. For clarity, use short sentences and relegate detailed or technical data to an annex. Finally, avoid introducing later amendments, or your integrity may be called into question!

Legal assistance

6

Licences

The export of all Defence equipment, dual use goods and certain others are subject to the granting of a government licence. The control and licensing of products for export is the responsibility of The Export Licensing Branch (ELB), a division of the Department of Trade and Industry. The Export of Goods (Control) Order 1994 (available from HMSO, Tel: 020 7873 0011 and Fax: 020 7831 1326) lists those goods which are subject to export control and an application should be made to the ELB as soon as an order is received from an Arab customer. It will be necessary for the exporter to declare the intended use of the goods and for the

Arab customer to provide an 'End User Statement' certifying the intended use of the goods. The process of approval takes about twenty working days. For further details contact ELB Helpline on Tel 020 7215 8070 or the ELB Website on www.dti.gov.uk/export.control Scroll to the 'What's on' site for the control list.

Export licenses

Western VIP Visits to the Arab World

A visiting businessman or resident expatriate representative should ensure that any senior executive of his company who visits the Arab world is well briefed on the customs of the region. There is more than one story of a senior businessman flying out to clinch an important deal, who unwittingly commits a *faux pas* with an Arab official or ruler and suddenly finds, inexplicably, that the deal is not confirmed.

The VIP should be made aware in particular of the importance of personal relationships in commerce. The fact, for example, that one reason for winning a deal will be that the Arab customer likes and trusts the person who has been representing the company.

Finally, the visiting VIP should be warned of the necessity for extreme flexibility with his programme, and that nobody can visit the region on a tight schedule with guaranteed appointments.

Islamic Attitudes to Commerce

It is as well to be aware of the Islamic view of commerce. The writings of the Holy Quran look with favour on commercial activity. It specifically condemns fraudulent practice. Unlike Christianity, however, nothing is said against the accumulation of wealth and possessions (Arabs traditionally dislike anyone who boasts of a lack of them), but Islam does lay a duty on the rich to use their wealth for the common good and specifically to give alms (*zakat*) to the poor. *See* Chapter 1, Islam.

The writings of the Holy Quran are also clearly opposed to any gain accruing from chance, and usury is expressly forbidden. These beliefs have been interpreted

151

to take account of modern commercial practice. Insurance was also originally frowned upon by orthodox Islamic opinion because it was seen as an attempt to frustrate the will of God – if God wills a man to suffer loss, he must do so and not seek compensation. However, the huge sums invested in projects today have made such a strict interpretation impractical.

A local lawyer will advise on the extent to which the *Sharia* law applies to a Western businessman's dealings in the Peninsula.

Entertaining an Arab Customer in UK

Follow the advice given in Chapter 3 under *Entertainment*. In addition, if you invite an Arab client to the UK it is important to make it clear what your invitation entails. The value of the exercise might be totally negated if there is, for example, a misunderstanding as to who pays what bill. Some commercial companies might invite an Arab client to London, offering to pay the air fare and/or the hotel bill, together with all transportation and entertainment for a specified period and leave it to the client to stay on longer at his own expense if he or she wishes. You might also consider asking the client if he/she would mind settling their own telephone bill. Finally, you should confirm that the hotel understands what it means to cater for the needs of a Muslim guest. Most large London hotels are fully aware of the requirements, but provincial hotels may not be.

Be as generous in your hospitality as your Arab guest would undoubtedly be if he were the host. If the visit is to London, then one of the modern luxury hotels in the area of Hyde Park or Knightsbridge would be appropriate accommodation. Pay constant attention to his needs without being over-attentive. If feasible, you should allocate a private Prayer Room at each venue for your guest together with a compass to indicate the direction of Makkah and quietly inform him that this is available if required.

The schedule should not be too crowded. Allow some

time for relaxation, sightseeing and shopping and possibly a private social engagement.

Follow the advice given in Chapter 3 under *Receiving an Arab* and *Entertaining*.

6

ANNEXES

REGIONAL ORGANISATIONS

REGIONAL ORGANISATIONS

The Arab League
Formed in 1945, The Arab League exists to co-ordinate policies and activities towards the common good of all Arab states. All the Arab states of North Africa and the Middle East are members including those of the Arabian Peninsula. A large number of committees attached to the council deal with a variety of sectors of interest to the League such as political, economic, cultural, social, financial and legal affairs. The Arab Monetary Fund set up by the League in 1977 provides financial assistance to member states. The permanent headquarters is based in Cairo and the League has representative offices in a number of Western countries and at the United Nations.

The Gulf Co-operation Council (GCC)
The GCC is a council of six of the Peninsula countries, the States of Kuwait, Bahrain and Qatar, the Kingdom of Saudi Arabia, the UAE and the Sultanate of Oman, It was formed in 1981 to strenghten relations between its members and to co-ordinate and unify policies in all fields including politics, economics and defence. It is the vehicle for establishing similar systems in the GCC in such areas as finance, education, communications, travel, legal, customs and trade affairs. Its permanent headquarters is in Riyadh, Saudi Arabia.

GCC

The Organisation of Arab Petroleum Exporting Countries (OAPEC)
The states of Kuwait, Bahrain, Qatar, The Kingdom of Saudi Arabia, the United Arab Emirates and other Arab oil producing countries of the Middle East formed this organisation in 1968 with its headquarters in Kuwait. Its

OAPEC

157

aims are to safeguard the interests of its members and organise co-operation in various fields of the petroleum industry.

OPEC

Note 1: Saudi Arabia, the UAE, Qatar and Kuwait are also members of the wider grouping the Organisation of Petroleum Exporting Countries (OPEC).

OIC

Note 2: All the Peninsula States are also members of the Organisation of The Islamic Conference (OIC) of Islamic nations whose Secretariat is based in Jeddah, Saudi Arabia and which promotes Islamic values and among other activities provides aid to Muslim communities in need.

REGIONAL ORGANISATIONS

BAHRAIN

STATE OF BAHRAIN

Geography
The island State of Bahrain, situated midway down the
Arab Gulf about 29 kms from the coast of Saudi Arabia,
consists of an archipelago of 33 low-lying islands with a
total area of 691 sq kms. The largest island, also called
Bahrain, is about 50 kms long and 16 kms wide. Manama,
the capital city and main commercial centre, is linked to
the second largest town and international airport,
Muharraq, by a causeway and bridge. Another causeway
links Bahrain island with mainland Saudi Arabia. The
main port is Mina Salman. Industrial development is
concentrated on Sitra Island. Other major towns are
Jiddhafs, Rifa'a, Isa Town and Awali.

Climate
Pleasant from November to March, warm by day and
cool by night with temperatures varying between 14 and
24°C. From June to September it can be extremely hot and
humid with temperatures averaging 36°C by day.

History
In ancient history, Bahrain (in Arabic meaning 'two seas')
was the site of Dilmun and part of a great civilisation and
trading empire. As well as having a strong trading
heritage the island was known for its lush vegetation,
plentiful sweet water and pearls. One of the first
territories outside the Arab mainland to accept Islam, it
later formed part of the Umayyad and Abbasid empires
and thereafter was frequently fought over by a succession
of powers seeking influence in the Arab Gulf. Following
Britain's withdrawal from the region the country declared
full independence in 1971. A constitution was introduced
in 1973 which provided for an elected assembly but this

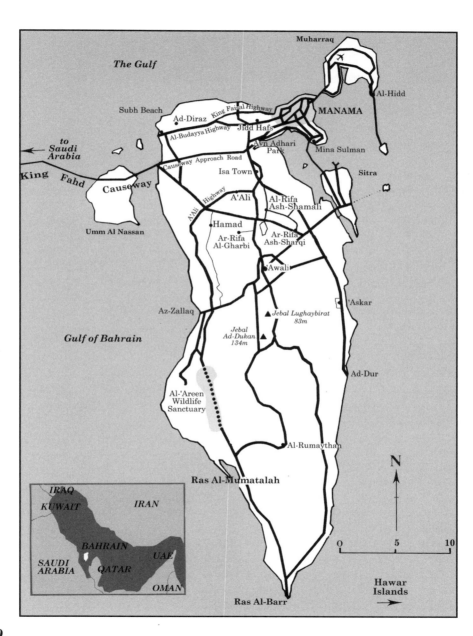

The Gulf

Muharraq

Al-Hidd

MANAMA

Subh Beach

Ad-Diraz

King Faisal Highway

to
Saudi
Arabia

Al-Budayya Highway

Jidd Hafs

Ayn Adhari
Park

Mina Sulman

King Fahd

Causeway

Causeway Approach Road

Isa Town

Sitra

A'Ali
Highway

A'Ali

Al-Rifa
Ash-Shamali

Umm Al Nassan

Hamad

Ar-Rifa
Al-Gharbi

Ar-Rifa
Ash-Sharqi

'Awali

'Askar

Az-Zallaq

▲ *Jebal Lughaybirat*
83m

Gulf of Bahrain

Jebal
Ad-Dukan
134m

▲

Ad-Dur

Al-'Areen
Wildlife
Sanctuary

Al-Rumaythan

N

Ras Al-Mumatalah

IRAQ

KUWAIT

IRAN

BAHRAIN

SAUDI
ARABIA

QATAR

UAE

OMAN

0   5   10

Hawar
Islands
→

Ras Al-Barr

B
A
H
R
A
I
N

was dissolved in 1975. A Consultative Council was appointed in 1992 and enlarged in 1996.

Government
Bahrain is an absolute monarchy. The ruler, the Emir, His Highness Shaikh Hamad Bin Isa Al-Khalifa is a member of the Al-Khalifa family which has ruled the country since 1783. The Emir governs by Emiri decree through the Prime Minister Shaikh Khalifa Bin Salman Al-Khalifa, an appointed Cabinet of ministers and the Consultative Council.

Economy
Based on oil, with limited local production but significant refining of Saudi oil. Bahrain has succeeded in diversifying its economy into aluminium smelting, manufacturing, financial services, commerce and tourism. Traditional industries such as dhow building and agriculture play a small part. A number of incentives have been introduced to encourage inward foreign investment. Although it is not obligatory, goods are normally sold through a local agent.

Population
Approximately 620,000, of whom around 30% are expatriates. Projected Bahraini National growth rate is 1.6% per annum. Most Bahraini Nationals are Arabs but a large number are also of Iranian ancestry.

Religion
The state religion is Islam, 85% of the population being Muslim, approximately two thirds Shia and one third Sunni. The ruling family and many of the leading merchant families are Sunni. There are also indigenous Christian, Jewish, Hindu, Parsee and other minorities.

Official Language
Arabic. English is widely spoken in business and official circles and by expatriates working in the service sector.

B
A
H
R
A
I
N

National Flag
Red with a broad serrated white stripe along the hoist.

Visas
Those with British passports showing place of birth as UK do not require a visa for visits of up to one month. Those whose occupation in their passport is shown as journalist or publisher must obtain prior permission to enter the country from the Ministry of Information. There is an Airport Departure Tax of BD3. It is forbidden to import cultured pearls. The possession of a video camera may be recorded in one's passport to ensure it is re-exported.

Alcohol
Non-Muslims may import up to two litres of alcoholic beverage. Alcohol is available for non-Muslims in certain hotels, and may be purchased at registered outlets. However, prices are high.

Local Time GMT + 3 hours, EST + 8 hours

Dialling Code 00 973

Public Holidays
All Muslim Festivals (*see* Chapter 1); New Year's Day -1 January and National Day - 16th December.

Working Hours (approx)
Government offices: 0700-1415 Saturday to Wednesday. *Banks:* 0730-1200 and 1530-1730 Saturday to Wednesday; 0700-1100 on Thursday. Business hours: either 0800-1530 Saturday to Wednesday or 0800-1300 and 1500-1730 Saturday to Wednesday.
Shops: 0830/0900-1230 and 1530-1730 Saturday to Thursday with extended hours for superstores, shopping malls and the *sooq*.
British Embassy: 0700-1400 Saturday to Wednesday. The working week and working hours are sometimes extensively amended during the holy month of Ramadan.

Currency
Bahraini Dinar (BD) divided into 1,000 Fils. At the time of going to print, the exchange rate was BD .6120 = £1 sterling and BD .3770 = US $1. Credit cards are widely accepted and most major banks are linked to at least one international ATM network.

Income Tax
There is no personal taxation.

Electricity Supply
230 volts, except Awali town which uses 110 volts. There are various plug fittings usually three-pin flat type.

Transportation
Most hotels have an airport pick up service on arrival in Bahrain. Taxis have meters. Check that they are set before your journey. Taxi fare to the city centre from the airport about BD 5. International Driving Licences must be verified at the Ministry of Interior Traffic Headquarters before use. The national airline is Gulf Air owned jointly by Bahrain, Qatar, Abu Dhabi and Oman.

Tipping
Taxis - tips appreciated. Hotels normally add 15% service charge (as do restaurants) and a 5% tax to their bills. Tips in such cases not expected. Airport porters, 100 fils per item of baggage.

Embassies
Embassy of the State of Bahrain in Britain:
98 Gloucester Road, London SW7 4AU.
Tel: 020 7370 5132/3; Fax: 020 7370 7773
Embassy of the State of Bahrain in the US:
3502 International Drive NW, Washington DC 20008
Tel: 202 342 0741.
British Embassy in Bahrain:
 21 Government Avenue, Manama 306.
Postal address: PO Box 114, Manama, State of Bahrain.
Commercial Section: Tel: 00 973 534 404;

Fax: 00 973 536 109; E-mail britemb@batelco.com.bh
US Embassy in Bahrain:
Shaikh Isa Bin Salman Highway, Al-Zinj District,
Manama. Tel: 00 973 273 300.

Tourist Sites

Sites include the National Museum on Al-Fateh
Highway; the Heritage Centre on Government Avenue;
Wind Towers (several locations); Bab-Al-Bahrain (City
gateway); the *Sooq*, Beit Al-Quran on Government
Avenue (Museum and Research Centre); The Friday
Mosque on Al-Khalifa Avenue; the Dhow Building Yards
near Pearl Monument roundabout; Al-Fatih Mosque on
the coast south of Manama and the Bahrain Craft Centre
on Isa Al-Kabeer Avenue. Al-'Areen Wildlife Sanctuary
(controlled access).

General Comments

Although Bahrain is a very liberal country by Arab Gulf
standards, it is nevertheless a very conservative society.
Visitors should dress soberly, particularly in public places
and in rural areas. When visiting mosques it is obligatory
to remove one's shoes and women are expected to cover
their heads. As in all Gulf countries, care should be
exercised with photography; obtain permission when
photographing men and do not photograph women.

BAHRAIN

THE STATE OF KUWAIT

THE STATE OF KUWAIT

Geography

Kuwait is situated at the north west head of the Arab Gulf. In area about 7,818 sq kms, it is mainly dry and flat, or gently undulating gravelly desert. It has a 224 km-long coastline with Kuwait Bay in the centre. The islands of Bubiyan and Failaka lie off the north-east shore. Al-Mutla Ridge runs along the northwest side of Kuwait Bay and Kuwait City, the capital and commercial centre, is located on the southern shore. Kuwait borders Iraq in the north and west and Saudi Arabia in the south. Major towns are Ahmadi, centre of the oil industry, Fahaheel and the historical town of Jahra (Al-Jahra). Industrial areas are located at Shuaiba and Mina Abdullah on the southern coastline and at Shuwaikh near Kuwait City. Shuwaikh includes the port.

Climate

The temperature during the winter months (November to March) is generally pleasant but it can also be very cold particularly at night. Daytime temperatures vary between 14 and 24° C. Rainfall, usually falling in winter, averages 100 mm to 370 mm. In summer, (June to September) it is very hot and humid although not as much as Bahrain or Abu Dhabi. Temperatures average 36°C by day. Sandstorms often occur in early summer.

History

The origins of 'Al-Kuwait' or 'little fort' in Arabic, go back to a settlement some three hundred years ago but the island of Failaka is known to have been inhabited during the bronze age and a Greek colony was established there in 2nd century BC. Its importance grew, slowly at first, based on trade and pearling until in recent

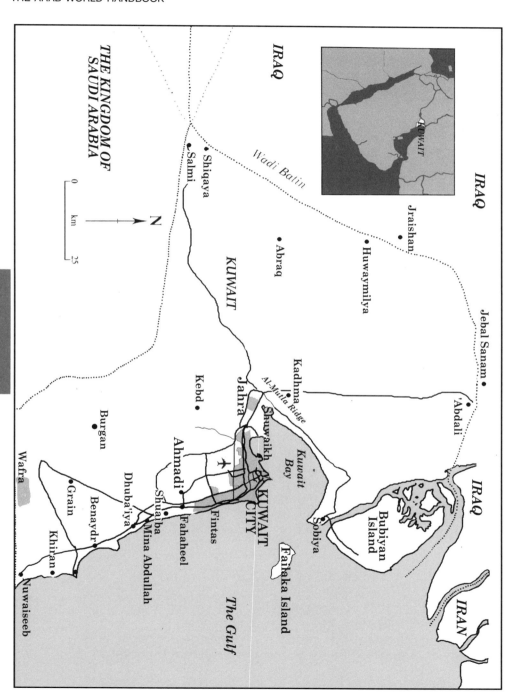

history it has become an immensely rich oil-producing state, accounting for 3% of the world's production and 9.3% of total world reserves. A long period of protective treaty relations with Britain came to an end in 1961 when Kuwait became an independent state. In 1990 Kuwait was invaded and occupied by Iraq until being liberated by an international coalition in 1991.

Government

The Head of State, the Emir, His Highness Shaikh Jabir Al-Ahmed Al-Jabeer Al-Sabah, is a constitutional ruler of the Al-Sabah family who have ruled in the region since 1756. The Emir rules through the Prime Minister, the Crown Prince and an appointed cabinet. A partly-elected National Assembly makes a critical examination of Government. No formal political parties exist although there are a number of informal groupings.

Economy

Oil production and the petrochemical industry account for about 90% of Kuwait's export revenues. The country has long sought to diversify its economy in areas such as agriculture, light industry of various kinds, manufacturing and financial services and has carried out significant investment abroad. Kuwait has been a major foreign aid donor to other Arab countries and the developing world. Almost all trade is conducted through Kuwaiti nationals and Kuwaiti companies. There is an active British Business Forum.

Population

2.2 million comprising approximately one-third Kuwaitis, one-third other Arabs, and one-third other nationalities including Westerners and Asians. Annual growth rate for Kuwaiti Nationals is about 2.7%. More than half the population live in Kuwait City and its environs, in Ahmadi (264,000) and Jahra (224,000).

K
U
W
A
I
T

Religion

The state religion is Islam. Almost all Kuwaitis are Muslims. The majority are Sunni Muslims but there is a sizeable Shia minority. There are small communities of other religions and a number of churches cater for expatriates.

Official Language

Arabic. English is widely spoken in business and diplomatic circles and by expatriates working in the service sector. Farsi (Persian) is also widely understood.

National Flag

A horizontal rectangle divided into three horizontal stripes of green, white and red (top to bottom). The side on the hoist forms the base of a black trapezoid set into the stripes.

Visas

British nationals require an entry visa obtainable from the Kuwait Embassy in London and the application generally has to be supported by a Kuwaiti sponsor. Most large hotels can act as a sponsor in support of an application. The hotel will require a faxed copy of your passport, the dates of arrival and departure and general reason for visiting, such as 'business'. The visa usually takes 3-4 days to process and must be collected from the Kuwait Embassy. Single entry visas are valid for one month and cost £30. Multi-entry visas cost more, depending on the period required. Visas cannot be issued on arrival in Kuwait. Visa regulations change from time to time and visitors are advised to check well in advance if possible. Passports must not contain evidence of a visit to Israel and visitors who have should seek advice from their nearest passport issuing office. There is a KD 2 airport departure tax.

Alcohol

The importation of alcohol is forbidden. The prohibition of alcoholic beverages in Kuwait is strictly enforced. The use of or dealing in drugs will incur severe penalties of imprisonment or fines.

Local Time GMT + 3 hours, EST + 8 hours

Dialling Code 00 965

Public Holidays
All Muslim Festivals (*see* Chapter 1); New Year's Day - 1 January and National Day - 25 February.

Working Hours
Normal working week is Saturday to Wednesday and half-day on Thursday. Business hours are from 0830-1230 and 1630-2000 in winter. Some offices work only from 0700-1400 in summer.
Government offices: 0730-1330 Saturday to Wednesday and 0730-1130 Thursday in winter, and 0700-1300 Saturday to Wednesday and 0700-1100 Thursday in summer.
Oil companies: 0800-1500 Sunday to Thursday.
Banks: 0800-1200 Sunday to Thursday and some branches open in the afternoons.
British Embassy: 0730-1430 Saturday to Wednesday.
The working week and working hours are sometimes extensively amended during the holy month of Ramadan.

Currency
Kuwait Dinar (KD) divided into 1,000 Fils. At the time of going to print, the exchange rate was KD 0.4938 = £1 sterling and KD 0.3042 = $1 US. Credit cards are widely accepted.

Income Tax
There is no personal taxation.

Electricity Supply
240 volts AC. Plugs flat-pin British type.

Transportation
The taxi fare from the airport is KD 5. There are standard fares in Kuwait City. A number of highly efficient taxi companies can also arrange a luxury limousine to pick you up from anywhere in the city within minutes of calling. Be wary of the orange airport taxis which are old and battered

K
U
W
A
I
T

169

and generally demand a higher fee. Agree the price before your journey. The national airline is Kuwait Air.

Tipping
Tips are expected by airport and hotel porters but not by taxis. Hotels and restaurants normally add a service charge. Tipping is only customary in the more expensive restaurants.

Tourist Sites
There is no official tourism in Kuwait and the only company offering tours is Orient Tours. Places of interest include Kuwait Towers, the City's main landmark on the coast road which has an observational deck, coffee shop and restaurant; Tareq Rajab Museum; the National Museum; the Old City gates; the former British Political Agency building and the Exhibition of Kuwaiti Sailing Ships.

Embassies
Embassy of the State of Kuwait in UK
2 Albert Gate, Knightsbridge, London SW1X 7JU.
Tel: 020 7590 3400; Fax: 020 7259 5042.
Embassy of the State of Kuwait in US
2940 Tilden St NW, Washington DC 20008
British Embassy in Kuwait (Commercial Section)
Arabian Gulf Street, SAFAT 13001, State of Kuwait. Tel: 00965 2403334; Fax 00965 2407395.
E-mail: britemb@ncc.moc.kw and tradeukw@ncc.moc.kw
US Embassy in Kuwait
Al-Masjid Al-Aqsa Street, Plot 14, Block 14 Bayan.
Tel: 00 965 242 4151.

General Comments
In spite of extensive mine clearing operations following the Gulf War there are still large numbers of unexploded mines and other weapons in many areas, even those marked as 'cleared'. Mines can also be washed ashore on the beaches or uncovered in the desert. When travelling outside Kuwait City and on the offshore islands it is strongly advisable to stick to paved roads and certainly not to handle any suspect object.

THE SULTANATE OF OMAN

THE SULTANATE OF OMAN

Geography

Oman occupies the south-eastern corner of the Arabian Peninsula. Its diverse territory covers about 320,000 sq kms and has a 1,700 km-long coastline. Oman also includes the isolated Musandam Peninsula overlooking the Strait of Hormuz which together with another small enclave, Madha, lie within the UAE. There are a number of islands, the largest of which is Masirah. The northern coastal strip, on the Gulf of Oman, consists of a sand and gravelly plain known as the Batinah Coast. Beyond this to the southwest lie the Hajar Mountains with the highest peak being the Jebel Akhdar (9,957 feet), or 'Green Mountain', although this name is also used to refer to the complete Hajar range. Further to the southwest, Oman borders Saudi Arabia on the edge of the vast desert of the Rub' Al-Khali or 'Empty Quarter'. The remainder of Oman's territory includes two large areas of salt flats in the central region, a long southeastern coastline on the Arabian Sea and the fertile Dhofar region and mountain range in the south where Oman borders the Republic of Yemen. The interior and coastline of Oman are very beautiful. The Government implements an active programme to protect and enhance the environment. The capital, commercial centre and main port of Muscat (pop. 550,000) is situated on a rugged part of the north-east coast. It comprises the districts of Muscat, Ruwi and Muttrah and is often referred to as the 'three cities'. Other major towns are Sur (south of Muscat), Nizwa (13,000) in the interior, and Salalah (50,000) in the south.

Climate

Like its geography, the climate in Oman is varied. In winter, from October to March, Muscat and the coastal

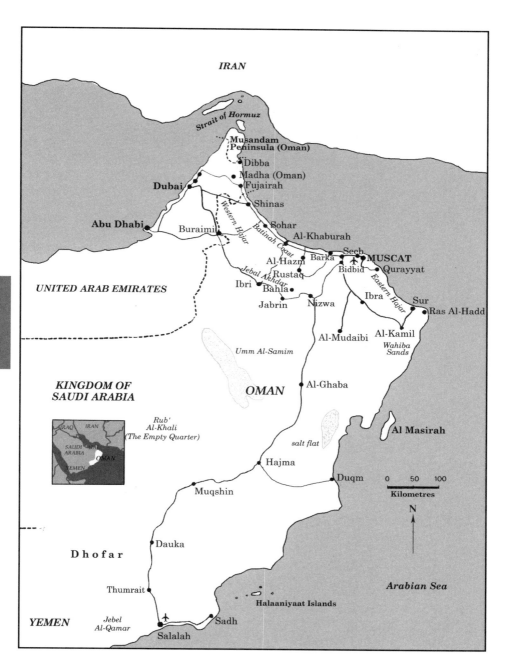

region is pleasantly warm with temperatures between 16 and 32 degrees centigrade. In Salalah however, it is humid with temperatures at the top end of this scale. In the summer months from April to September the coast is hot and very humid. Highest temperature and humidity (May to July) reaches 47°C with 85% humidity. The interior is generally hot and dry except at altitude. Rainfall is low except for Salalah and Dhofar where light monsoon rains fall from June to September.

History

The earliest settlements in Oman can be traced to the 3rd millennium BC and it was also known to have been an important independent copper-producing state. Following a period under Persian rule it achieved further importance as the main source in the world of frankincense. Converting to Islam at an early stage, the area finally came under the influence of the Portuguese. However, the Portuguese were evicted in 1650 and for two centuries Oman itself became an imperial power in the region. In 1646 and again in 1798, Oman entered into long-standing and friendly treaty relations with Britain and these continue to this day. Since becoming Head of State in 1970, the present ruler, His Majesty Sultan Qaboos Bin Said Al Said has presided over the exploitation of the country's oil resources, creating a modern state while at the same time preserving Oman's unique character and heritage.

Government

Oman is an absolute monarchy and His Majesty Sultan Qaboos rules through a Cabinet of Ministers. The Sultan is a member of the Al Bu Said dynasty who have governed in the region since 1749. There is also a Consultative Council, the *Majlis Ash-Shura*, which is an elected legislature. The Sultan maintains a personal style of government, touring the country for several weeks each spring to meet his people. The Government has followed an active Omanisation programme to replace expatriates with Omanis and this has had a large measure of success.

Economy

Oman's economy is essentially dominated by oil which provides 99% of the country's export revenues although production is modest compared with the Arab Gulf. Since production began in 1967 oil revenues have been used to establish an efficient infrastructure including a road network, housing and electricity. A priority has also been placed on defence. In 1975 the Government defeated an eleven-year-long armed revolt in the southern region. Oman is successfully diversifying its economy by exploiting gas, copper and other mineral deposits, expanding the agricultural and fishing industries, and industrial development.

Population

Roughly 2 million, predominately Arab but with Baluchi, Lawati and Gujarati communities as well. Most of the population live in Muscat and in the Batinah Coastal Plain. The growth rate of Omani nationals is around 3.6% per annum. There are about 400,000 immigrant workers from the Indian sub-continent and the Far East.

Religion

The State religion is Islam. Most Omanis are Ibadhi (Sunni) and Sunni Muslims. There is a small number of Shia Muslims in the capital area.

Official Language

Arabic, but English is widely spoken. Swahili, Farsi, Urdu, Baluchi and a number of Indian languages are also commonly spoken.

National Flag

A vertical red band on the hoist within the top of which is superimposed a white *khanjar* (or *khanja*) (the traditional dagger of the region) and crossed swords. To the right of the red band are three horizontal bands of white (top), red and green (bottom).

O
M
A
N

Visas

Visas (No Objection Certificates) are required. Business and tourist visas can be obtained by applying to Omani Embassies abroad and the process takes up to six working days. Visitors must have the support of an Omani sponsor and it is possible for four and five star hotels to act as sponsors for a single entry visa application. The sponsor will explain the procedure to be followed. On application it is necessary to determine the cost, period of validity and duration of use of the type of visa required. A number of passport photographs are needed. Visas can usually be collected on arrival although it is necessary to have the visa number and if possible a photocopy of the visa which must have been lodged by the sponsor with airport immigration. Passports must not contain evidence of a visit to Israel and visitors whose passports have been marked should seek advice from their nearest passport issuing office. There is an airport departure tax of RO5.

Alcohol

Permitted to non-Muslims in certain hotels. Non-Muslim visitors arriving by air are permitted to import one bottle of alcoholic beverage. This is not, however, permitted when entering by road. Non-Muslim residents may apply for an alcohol allowance.

Local Time   GMT + 4 hours, EST + 9 hours.

Dialling Code   968

Working Hours (approx)
Business: 0800-1300 and 1530-1830 Saturday to Thursday.
Government offices: 0730-1430 Saturday to Wednesday.
Banks: 1800-1200 Saturday to Wednesday and 0800-1130 Thursday.
Shops: 0800-1300 and 1600-1800 Saturday to Wednesday and 0800-1300 Thursday.
British Embassy office hours: 0730-1430 Saturday to Wednesday. The working week and working hours are

O
M
A
N

sometimes extensively amended during the holy month of Ramadan.

Public Holidays
Most Muslim festivals (*see* Chapter 1); National Day and the Birthday of HM The Sultan - both on 18 November.

Taxation
There is a double taxation agreement between Oman and UK, but personal income is not taxed in Oman.

Currency
Omani Riyal (RO) divided into 1,000 Baizas. At the time of going to print, the exchange rate was RO 0.6250 = £1 sterling and RO 0.3850 = US$1. Major credit cards are accepted.

Electricity
220/240 volts. Plugs either 2-pin or 3-pin flat British type.

Transportation
Seeb International Airport is located 40 kms west of Muscat. Taxis do not have meters or fixed fares. Fares should be negotiated in advance. The fare to Muscat from Seeb International Airport is around RO 8. The national airline is Gulf Air owned jointly by Bahrain, Qatar, Abu Dhabi and Oman.

Tourist Sites
Although Oman is now officially open to tourism, there are as yet no tourist offices. However, a number of tour companies and the larger hotels offer tours. There are an almost overwhelming number of sites of interest in Muscat, Nizwa, Salalah and the mountains, oases and farms in the interior with their unique *falaj* or irrigation channels. Sea and coastal trips, diving, visits to the principal museums, the *souqs,* the forts and other national buildings make Oman one of the most interesting tourist locations in the region.

Tipping
Taxis are not tipped. In restaurants, if there is 10% service charge, tipping is not necessary. A Government tax of 17% is added to all hotel bills.

Embassies
Embassy of the Sultanate of Oman in UK
167 Queens Gate, London SW7 5HE
Tel: 020 7225 0001; Fax 020 7589 2505
Embassy of the Sultanate of Oman in US
342 Massachusetts Avenue, NW, Washington DC, 20000.
Tel: (202) 387 1980/1.
866 United Nations Plaza, Suite 540, New York NY
Tel: (212) 355 3505.
British Embassy in Muscat
PO Box 300, Muscat 113, Sultanate of Oman.
Tel:00 968 693086; Fax: 00 968 693088
E-mail: becomuegto.net.om
US Embassy in Muscat
Jameat A'Duwal Al-Arabiya Street, Medinat Qaboos
Diplomatic Area. Tel: 00 968 698989.

General Comments
Although to a Western visitor Oman may appear an open and liberal society and the Omanis in the Capital area cosmopolitan by Gulf Arab standards, the underlying culture is nevertheless conservative, particularly in rural areas which have only been open to foreigners in the last fifteen or twenty years. For this reason one should be careful to dress soberly. It is not permitted to visit mosques. As in all Gulf countries care should be exercised with photography. Omanis are very sensitive about security and one should always obtain permission to take photographs of all but obvious tourist sites. Finally, as elsewhere, do not photograph women.

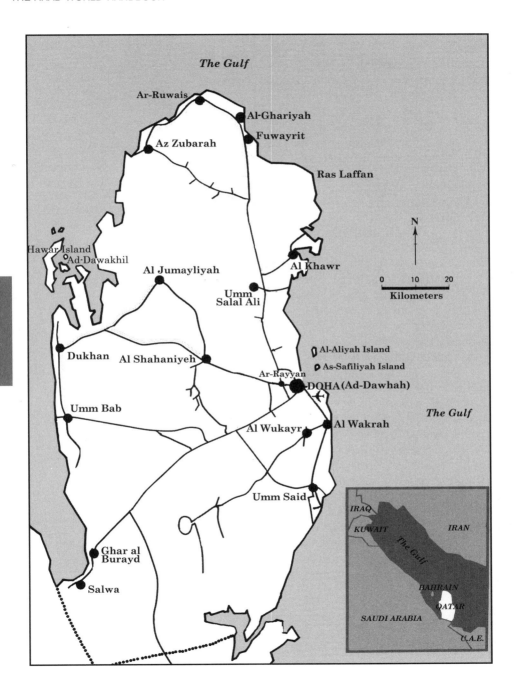

QATAR

The Gulf

Ar-Ruwais

Al-Ghariyah

Fuwayrit

Az Zubarah

Ras Laffan

N

Hawar Island
Ad-Dawakhil

Al Jumayliyah

Al Khawr

0   10   20
Kilometers

Umm
Salal Ali

Al-Aliyah Island

As-Safiliyah Island

Dukhan

Al Shahaniyeh

Ar-Rayyan

DOHA (Ad-Dawhah)

Umm Bab

The Gulf

Al Wukayr

Al Wakrah

Umm Said

Ghar al
Burayd

Salwa

IRAQ

KUWAIT

IRAN

The Gulf

BAHRAIN

QATAR

SAUDI ARABIA

U.A.E.

THE STATE OF QATAR

THE STATE OF QATAR

Geography
The Qatar Peninsula lies midway down the southern shore of the Arabian Gulf just southeast of Bahrain. The country is about 170 kms long and 90 kms wide at its widest point with a total area of 11,437 sq kms. The territory is mainly flat gravelly desert except for some low hills in the north-west and sand dunes with some marshes in the south where it borders Saudi Arabia. The capital city and commercial centre, Doha (Ad-Dawha), situated on the East coast, is a thriving modern city. It is also the location of the international airport and one of Qatar's ports. Major towns are Umm Said, south of Doha and the centre of Qatar's petrochemical industry, also with a port, and Dukhan on the west coast, the centre for the country's onshore oil production. Ras Laffan Industrial City, north of Doha is being developed as the centre for production of Qatar's liquified natural gas.

Climate
Pleasant from November to April but hot and humid from May to October. From July to September temperatures can rise to 44ºC with humidity over 85%. Sandstorms occur throughout the year especially in spring.

History
Qatar's (pronounced *Gutter*) history is associated with the Al-Thani (pronounced *Al-Thaani*) family since the country became established in the 18th century as a traditional centre for pearling. The first Emir (or Amir), Shaikh Mohammed bin Thani, came to power in the mid 19th century and Doha became the country's capital city. Qatar subsequently entered into a number of treaty relations

QATAR

first with the Turks and later in 1916 with the British until declaring independence in 1971 when the British left the region. Oil was discovered in 1939 but because of the Second World War was not commercially exploited until 1949.

Government
Executive power is vested in The Emir, His Highness Shaikh Hamad bin Khalifa Al-Thani, who rules with the assistance of an appointed Advisory Council which discusses legislation prior to promulgation.

Economy
Qatar is one of the world's wealthiest nations. Its economy is predominantly based on oil although its reserves are small in comparison with its neighbours. Its natural gas resources on the other hand, in the initial stages of exploitation, are among the world's largest. Gas constitutes Qatar's priority for economic development although it is also the Government's policy to diversify the economy where possible and this has met with some measure of success particularly in the petrochemical field.

Population
The population is estimated to be approximately 600,000 of whom about 100,000 are Qatari nationals. The remainder are foreign workers from the Indian subcontinent, Asia and other countries.

Religion
The state religion is Islam.

Official Language
Arabic, but English is widely used.

National Flag
This is divided by a vertical serrated band which is one third white on the hoist side and two thirds dark purple on the right side.

Local Time GMT + 3 hours, EST + 8 hours

Dialling Code 974

Visas
Visas are required, obtainable from Qatar Embassies abroad, and visitors must also have a local sponsor. The larger hotels will act as sponsor provided you take accommodation there and arrangements can be made to collect the visa on arrival at the airport. Visas are normally valid for one month but may be extended in country. There is an airport departure tax of QR 20.

Alcohol
The importation of alcohol is prohibited. However, it is available to non-Muslims in private bars in the larger hotels but only to guests and those who have purchased membership. Non-Muslim residents with an income above a certain level may apply for an alcohol allowance.

Public Holidays
The main Muslim festivals (*see* Chapter 1); National Day - 3 September.

Working Hours(approx.)
Government offices: Saturday to Thursday 0600-1300.
Businesses: Saturday to Thursday 0800-1300 and1600-1900.
Oil companies: half-day on Thursday. Banks: Saturday to Wednesday 0730-1100 and Thursday 0730-1130.
British Embassy: Saturday to Wednesday 0730-1430.
The working week and working hours are sometimes extensively amended during the holy month of Ramadan.

Currency
Qatar Riyal (QR) divided into 100 Dirhams, also commonly called Halalas. At the time of going to print, the exchange rate was QR 5.9103 = £1 sterling and QR 3.6410 = US$1.

Q
A
T
A
R

Electricity
220/240 volts AC. Light fittings - bayonet and screw.
Plugs 3 pin flat most common.

Transportation
Large hotels have a pick up service from the airport.
Taxis have a fixed hourly hire rate. The national airline is
Gulf Air, owned jointly by Bahrain, Abu Dhabi, Oman
and Qatar.

Tipping
No tip if service charge (normally 15%) is added. Airport
porters, 100 fils per item of baggage. Taxi drivers and
others, around 5% is customary.

Embassies
Embassy of the State of Qatar in UK
1 South Audley Street, London W1Y 5DQ
Tel: 020 7493 2200; Fax 020 7493 2819
Embassy of the State of Qatar in US
600 New Hampshire Avenue NW, Suite 1180, Washington
DC 20037. Tel: 202 338 0111
747 3rd Avenue, 22nd floor, New York, NY 10017
Tel: 212 486 9355.
British Embassy in Doha
PO Box 3 Doha, Qatar.
Tel: 00 974 421991; Fax: 00 974 438692
Commercial Section: Tel: 00 974 353543/356541-3;
Fax: 00 974 356131 E-mail: bembcomm@qatar.net.qa.
US Embassy in Doha
Intersection of Ahmed bin Ali Street and Al-Jazira Al-
Arabiya Street, Doha. Tel: 00 974 864701.

Tourist Sites
Tour companies offer tours, mainly for groups, to sites of
interest such as the National and Ethnographic and
Postal Museums, Doha Fort, The Old Police Station, Zoo
and Camel Racing.

THE KINGDOM OF SAUDI ARABIA

THE KINGDOM OF SAUDI ARABIA

Geography

Saudi Arabia occupies most of the Arabian Peninsula with an area of about 2.2 million sq kms. It consists largely of desert but there are also extensive mountainous areas in the west and southwest. The country has five regions: The Hejaz and Asir regions in the west and southwest respectively contain continuous mountain ranges of the same names running the length of the Red Sea coast. The Asir mountain region with its forests is particularly striking. These mountain ranges give way in the central region (Nejd) to the deserts of the large central plateau. The remoter northwest region is centred on the largely military town of Tabuk and the border with Jordan. The Eastern Province (Al-Hasa) is bounded by the Arabian Gulf. It takes its name from the extensive Al-Hasa oasis but otherwise consists of low lying desert with some salt flats (*sabkha*). In the north of the country lies the huge Nafud desert and in the southeast the vast desert of the 'Empty Quarter' (Rub' Al-Khali). Called 'The Sands' by the Bedu, it is the largest sand desert in the world. The Kingdom contains the two holiest cities of Islam, Makkah (Makkah Al-Mukarama) and Madinah (Al-Madina Al-Munawwara). Riyadh is the capital city, centre of Government and an increasingly important commercial centre. Jeddah, on the Red Sea coast is the principal port and main centre for private sector business. Yanbu, close to Jeddah, is a major industrial city. The other large industrial and commercial concentration and centre for the oil, gas and petrochemical industry is in the Eastern Province, based on the towns of Dammam (the country's second major port), Al-Khobar and Dhahran.

183

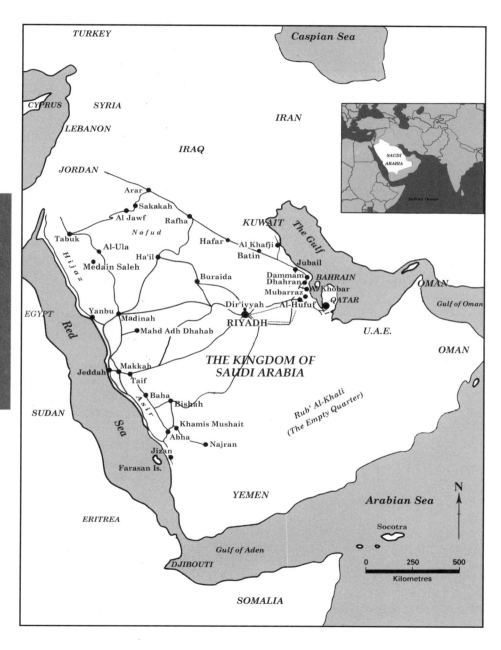

TURKEY

Caspian Sea

CYPRUS

SYRIA

IRAN

LEBANON

IRAQ

JORDAN

Arar

Sakakah

Al Jawf

Rafha

KUWAIT

The Gulf

Tabuk

Nafud

Hafar

Al Khafji

Al-Ula

Batin

Ha'il

Jubail

Medain Saleh

Buraida

Dammam

BAHRAIN

Dhahran

Mubarraz

Al Khobar

OMAN

EGYPT

Yanbu

Dir'iyyah

Al-Hufuf

QATAR

Gulf of Oman

Madinah

RIYADH

Mahd Adh Dhahab

U.A.E.

OMAN

Red

Makkah

THE KINGDOM OF
SAUDI ARABIA

Jeddah

Taif

Baha

SUDAN

Sea

Bishah

Rub' Al-Khali
(The Empty Quarter)

Khamis Mushait

Abha

Najran

Jizan

Farasan Is.

YEMEN

Arabian Sea

N

ERITREA

Socotra

Gulf of Aden

DJIBOUTI

0   250   500

Kilometres

SOMALIA

Hijaz

Asir

SAUDI ARABIA

SAUDI
ARABIA

Indian Ocean

Climate

Riyadh has a typically desert climate, very hot but dry in summer, with extremes of temperature between day and night. From April to September temperatures rise to 45°C but from December to February it is pleasant with temperatures below 20°C by day and even lower by night. Jeddah and the towns of the eastern region are hot in summer with temperatures averaging 30°C. Humidity rises to 90% particularly in September. In winter it is cooler with temperatures as in Riyadh of below 20°C. Rain storms occur in winter and spring, particularly in the coastal regions and there are occasional dust storms.

History

The history of Saudi Arabia embodies the history of the whole Peninsula. The earliest settlements in the 4th and 5th millennium BC, the Nabataean civilisation, the Arab and Bedu heritage, the home of the Arabic language and the birthplace of Islam, the rise of the House of Saud, the discovery of vast oil resources and finally, the establishment of the modern state. The magnificent remains of part of the Nabataean civilisation can be seen at Madain Salih in the northwest of Saudi Arabia. The First Saudi State was established in 1747 when Mohammed Ibn Saud formed a lasting family alliance with the great Islamic reformer Mohammed Ibn Abdul Al-Wahab, the followers of whom still predominate in Saudi Arabia today. The capital at that time was Dir'iyyah, (just outside Riyadh). The modern Kingdom of Saudi Arabia was founded in 1924/25 by one of the region's most remarkable leaders, Abdul Aziz bin Abdul Rahman Al-Saud. After a lengthy and difficult struggle, King Abdul Aziz, or Ibn Saud as he is often called, finally succeeded in capturing the cities and unifying the tribes of this vast region and establishing The Kingdom of Saudi Arabia. Although oil was discovered in the Kingdom in 1938, it was not fully exploited until the 1950s (because of the Second World War). King Abdul Aziz was succeeded in power by his sons who have

SAUDI ARABIA

185

presided over the development of the modern state in existence today.

Government

The Head of State and Supreme Religious Leader is the King, Fahd bin Abdul Aziz. He is officially entitled 'The Custodian of the Two Holy Mosques, King Fahd Bin Abdul Aziz' (and not as 'His Majesty'). The Kingdom of Saudi Arabia is a monarchy but the King rules through a Council of Ministers and a Consultative Council (*Majlis Al-Shura*) and there is also widespread consultation with the Royal family, the religious establishment and the business community over policy.

Economy

As by far the largest and most wealthy country of the region Saudi Arabia dominates the politics and the economy of the Peninsula. It is the world's leading oil exporter, with the highest GNP in the Arab world. Although the economy is dominated by oil, strenuous efforts have been made to diversify into other fields. It now has one of the world's largest petrochemical industries. Ambitious projects have emphasised industrial and urban development, defence and education as well as agriculture, mining and water development. The construction industry, although it has slowed in the last decade, nevertheless thrives. The Government is committed to privatisation starting with the telecommunication and power generation sectors and encourages joint-ventures in many areas of economic activity. Saudi Arabia is an active export market for a large range of western products.

Population

The total population is estimated at 21.2 million, of whom 14.6 million are Saudi Nationals. The balance is made up of expatriate workers from other Arab countries, the Indian sub-continent, Africa, Asia, Europe and USA. Over 50% of the population are under 15 years of age.

Religion
The State religion is Islam and the Saudi population is 100 per cent Muslim.

Official Language
Arabic, although English is widely spoken in business and official circles and by expatriates working in the service sector. All official correspondence with Government establishments must be in Arabic (and normally English as well) and carry the *Hijra* date as well as the Gregorian.

National Flag
Light green carrying the inscription in Arabic 'There is no God but God. Muhammad is His Prophet', below which is a horizontal traditional sword.

Local Time GMT + 3 hours. EST + 8 hours.

Dialling Code
966-1 (Riyadh), 966-2 (Jeddah) 966-3 (Dhahran - Eastern Province).

Public Holidays
The only festivals celebrated are the *Eid Al-Adha* and *Eid Al-Fitr* when extended holiday breaks are taken (*see* Chapter 1 for dates).

Visas
Visas are required by all except citizens of the GCC states. Application should be made to any Saudi Embassy abroad and must be accompanied by a letter of invitation from a Saudi sponsor. The expiry date of the passport must extend for six months beyond the date of the visit. There is no airport departure tax.

Alcohol and Prohihited Goods
The importation, possession and consumption of alcohol is strictly forbidden and can incur heavy penalties including imprisonment, corporal punishment and

deportation. A person arriving in the Kingdom in an inebriated state is liable to arrest and deportation. The importation of any goods with an alcoholic content, pork products, pornography and censored literature are also strictly prohibited. Magazines which depict women are likely to be confiscated or censored. Video tapes, and sometimes floppy discs and CD Roms, are likely to be inspected by customs officials before they may be imported. Finally, drug smuggling is a capital offence in Saudi Arabia and this warning is printed on every immigration form.

Working Hours
Government offices: 0830-1430 Saturday to Wednesday.
Business: Riyadh 0830-1230 and 1630-1930; Jeddah 0900-1330 and 1630-2000 both Saturday to Thursday' Eastern Province 0730-1200 and 1430-1730 Saturday to Wednesday.
Banks: 0830-1200/1700-1900 Saturday to Wednesday.
Shops: 0800 or 0830-1200 and 1600-2100/2200 Saturday to Thursday. Shops and some offices close for prayers four times a day. Prayer times, which differ each day are published in advance in local newspapers.
The British Embassy in Riyadh, the British Consulate General in Jeddah and the British Trade Office in Al-Khobar: 0700-1400 Saturday to Wednesday. The working week and working hours are sometimes extensively amended during the holy month of Ramadan.

Currency
Saudi Riyal (SR) divided into 100 Halalah. At the time of going to print, the exchange rate was SR 6.0880 = £1 sterling and SR 3.7507 = $1 US. The Saudi Riyal is pegged to the $ US at US$1 = SR 3.75. All credit cards are accepted and some major banks are linked to at least one international ATM network.

Income Tax
No income tax is imposed in Saudi Arabia, although

payment of *zakat* (*see* page 32) is obligatory for all
practicing businesses.

Electricity Suppy
A mixture of 110 volt and 220 volt, 60 cycles with two-pin
European type plugs and three-pin flat British type. Light
bulbs are both bayonet and screw fitting. Industry uses
380 volt AC 60 cycles.

Transportation
Taxis are yellow and are required to carry a meter and
visible registration details. Many taxis do not use the
meters and if so it is best to agree the fare in advance.
Hire cars are available although for a short visit local
taxis, the Saudi limousines service or a chauffeur driven
car are strongly recommended. Driving can be
hazardous, especially for a newcomer, and the
consequences of involvement in an accident are
sometimes serious. Follow the advice given in Chapter 4
on *Transportation* and *Emergencies and Car Accidents*. The
driving licences of Western countries are accepted when
hiring a car or when applying for a Saudi driving licence,
but International Driving Licences are not. Applicants for
a Saudi Driving Licence are required to donate a pint of
blood to the central blood bank. Women are not allowed
to drive. They are required to sit in the rear seat when
being driven. It is forbidden for non-Muslims to travel
within the limits of the holy cities of Makkah and
Madinah.

Tipping
Taxis are not tipped. Tips for restaurants are usual and in
the region of 10%. SR 5 to airport porters per item of
baggage.

Embassies
The Royal Embassy of Saudi Arabia in UK
30 Charles Street, Mayfair, London W1X 7PM
Tel: 020 7917 3000; Fax: 020 7917 3161.
The Royal Embassy of Saudi Arabia in US

**S
A
U
D
I

A
R
A
B
I
A**

601 New Hampshire Avenue NW, Washington DC, 20037
Tel: 202 342 3800
The British Embassy in the Kingdom of Saudi Arabia (Riyadh Diplomatic Quarter): PO Box 94351, Riyadh 11693
Kingdom of Saudi Arabia.
Tel: 00 9661 488 0077; Fax: 00 9661 4882373.
An amenity hall is available for hire (bookings one month in advance) for commercial meetings, presentations and seminars.
British Consulate General: PO Box 393, Jeddah 21411
Tel: 00966 2 6541811; Fax 0966 2 6544917
E-mail: commercial@jeddah.mail.fco.gov.uk
British Trade Office: PO Box 88 Dhahran Aiport 31932
Tel: 00 966 3 8570595; Fax: 00 966 3 8570634
E-mail: btokhobar@hotmail.com
US Embassy in the Kingdom of Saudi Arabia (Riyadh Diplomatic Quarter) Tel: 488 0077
US Consulate General in Jeddah: Falasteen Street, Ruwais District. Tel: 00 966 2 667 0080.

Tourist Sites

Tourism is being developed for Saudis and the citizens of the Arab Gulf states but not yet for other foreigners, although a few tours are arranged by the British Museum and Bales Tours. For both visitors and residents alike, Saudi Arabia offers a wealth of sites of interest. These include the Asir region, in Riyadh the ruins of Dir'iyyah, the escarpment and the Masmak Fortress. In Jeddah, the Jeddah Museum and in the north Madain Salah to mention just a few. All leading hotels have information on sites of interest and bookshops stock a number of current guides.

General Comments

Saudi Arabia, the location of the holy cities of Makkah and Madinah, is the most conservative of all Peninsula states and the Islamic code of conduct is strictly observed. Men should dress conservatively in public, wearing slacks and a shirt with sleeves. Women are required to cover their arms and legs, and although it is

not the law, a Western woman will often wear an *abaya*, the customary long black robe worn by all Muslim women, to avoid giving offence. For the same reason she may wish to wear a head scarf if, for example, she has extremely long hair, but she is certainly not required to wear a veil. In Saudi Arabia, at present, a women may not drive a car and therefore must employ a driver. She should always sit in the rear seat. Strictly speaking, apart from her driver, a woman in Saudi Arabia may not appear in public accompanied by a man other than her husband or close blood relative such as her father, brother etc. As in all Peninsula countries care should be exercised with photography. Do not photograph military bases, airports, ports, and petrochemical installations which are considered sensitive, obtain permission when photographing men and do not photograph women. Finally, you occasionally come across the Religious Police or *Mūtawwa* whose role is to monitor public behaviour in the Kingdom to ensure it conforms to Islamic norms. It is advisable for a Westerner to avoid contact with them if possible but if they make a reasonable request it is best to accede quickly and quietly. Always keep very calm and at all costs avoid a confrontation.

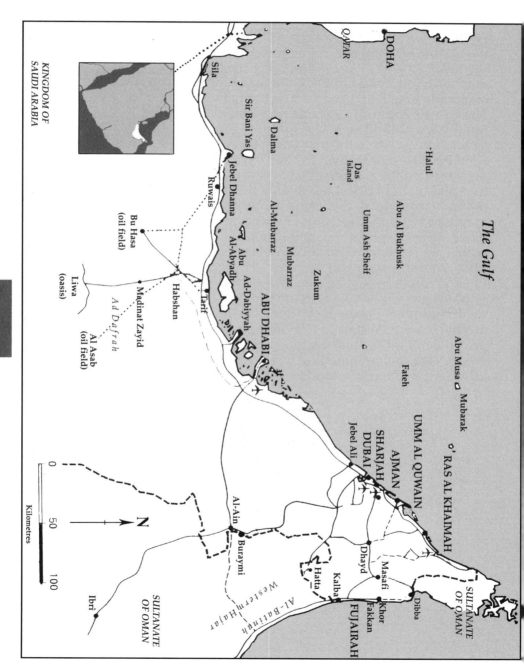

UNITED ARAB EMIRATES

THE UNITED ARAB EMIRATES

Geography

The United Arab Emirates (UAE), lies at the lower end of the Gulf and is a union of seven sovereign sheikhdoms, Abu Dhabi, Dubai, Sharjah, Fujairah, Umm Al-Quwain, Ajman and Ras Al-Khaimah, each Emirate being named after its principal town and the last five being known as the Northern Emirates. The total area is about 83,600 sq kms with some 700 kms of coastline on the Gulf and the Gulf of Oman. Abu Dhabi is the largest Emirate with 85% of the land area. Fujairah lies on the Gulf of Oman. The terrain is mainly desert with salt flats (*sabkha*), along the coast and two inland oases at Buraimi (Al-Ain) and Liwa. The Hajar Mountain range runs into the northern part of the UAE from Oman and continues into the Omani enclave of the Musamdam Peninsula. The UAE also has a number of offshore islands and coral reefs. The capital, Abu Dhabi, is a striking, modern city of towering skyscrapers interspersed with parks, mosques and considerable vegetation. It is the seat of the Federal Government and the Emirate is the centre of the country's oil, gas and petrochemical industry. The Emirate's other large city is Al-Ain, 160 kms east of Abu Dhabi, a natural oasis and the UAE's main agricultural centre. Dubai, the second largest Emirate, is situated to the northeast and is a thriving centre for commerce, the main UAE port and its principal tourist location. There is also a large free zone at Jebel Ali where more than 1,000 foreign companies (including 100 UK firms) have set up regional operations. In the Northern Emirates, Sharjah is the UAE's main manufacturing base and the remainder are establishing an increasing number of industrial plants. Ras Al-Khaimah is the main farming area and Fujairah, on the Gulf of Oman, has a developing port and expanding free trade zone.

U
A
E

193

Climate

The winter, from November to April is pleasant with temperatures between around 10-30°C and the summers are hot with temperatures up to 45°C. Humidity is high in the coastal regions. There are occasional heavy rain falls in December and January.

History

The earliest traces of settlement in the territory date from the 3rd millennium BC. Following the Islamic conquest, the region came under Portuguese and later Persian influence. In the 18th century the Qawasim and Bani Yas tribes came to prominence and the former, a seafaring race based in Sharjah and Ras Al-Khaimah, were so active that the British gave the area the name of The Pirate Coast. The Qawasim strongly opposed the rise of British naval power in the Gulf but were eventually defeated in 1820. Britain then entered into a series of treaty agreements normalising shipping in the region, which became known as The Trucial Coast. The Bani Yas tribe, on the other hand, became the main power in the Bedu hinterland, based originally on the Liwa oasis but then splitting into two branches in Abu Dhabi and Dubai; the forebears of the present ruling families. The traditional occupations at that time were fishing and pearling. In 1892 Britain entered into further 'exclusive' agreements with the tribes under which they accepted formal protection and agreed not to deal with any other foreign power. In the late 19th early 20th centuries Sharjah was the predominant Shaikhdom but Dubai then rose to prominence as a major trading centre under the Maktoum family. In recent decades, with the exploitation of immense oil reserves, Abu Dhabi has assumed prime position in the federation under the leadership of Shaikh Zayed Bin Sultan Al-Nahayan while Dubai retains its position as a major trading and commercial centre. With Britain's withdrawal from the Gulf in 1971 the Shaikhdoms assumed full independence and the present federation was formed, Ras Al-Khaimah joining in 1972. The establishment of the modern state of the UAE over

UAE

the period of the last 30 years is a truly remarkable achievement by any standards.

Government

The UAE is governed by a Supreme Council of the rulers of the seven Emirates. They elect a President who in turn appoints the Council of Ministers. The President is Shaikh Zayed Bin Sultan Al-Nahayan the ruler of Abu Dhabi and the Deputy President and Prime Minister is Shaikh Maktoum Bin Rashid Al-Maktoum the ruler of Dubai. Other posts are distributed among the Emirates. There is also a forty member Federal National Council appointed proportionately by the rulers of the Emirates which acts in a consultative and advisory role to the Supreme Council. The individual Emirates exercise internal administrative authority.

Economy

Predominantly based on oil, but also diversifying into other fields. In addition to an expanding gas and petrochemical industry, the UAE is also developing its free zones, industrial and manufacturing plants and agriculture, and undertaking major development projects in electrical power and water desalination, some of which involve a measure of privatisation. Abu Dhabi also places a strong emphasis on Offset (*see* Chapter 6 - *Background Publications; Countertrade and Offset*). The two wealthiest Emirates are Abu Dhabi and Dubai. Abu Dhabi has 9% of the world's proven oil reserves, 5% of gas reserves and its revenue from oil and gas may now be matched by its investments. Abu Dhabi contributes 75% of the Federal budget and is a generous donor of overseas development aid. Dubai, with lower oil production, has successfully diversified its economy and is also a major regional centre for trade. It has two ports, an aluminium smelter, a large free zone and an expanding tourist industry. Dubai and the Northern Emirates account for 25% of federal revenues. (*See also* Dubai and the Northern Emirates under *Geography* above). British Business Groups are established in Abu Dhabi and Dubai; contact details: Abu

U
A
E

195

Dhabi Tel: 00 971 2 457234 Fax 00 971 2 450605 and Dubai
Tel: 00 971 4 313144 Fax: 00 971 4 314155.

Population
Estimated at 2.6 million, of whom approximately 25% are
UAE nationals. The distribution is Abu Dhabi 40%, Dubai
25% and the remainder in the Northern Emirates.
Expatriates are from other Arab countries, Western
countries, and the Indian subcontinent and Asia.

Religion
The state religion is Islam. Ninety percent of the
population are Muslims. There are however, Christian
churches and Hindu temples in Abu Dhabi, Dubai and
Sharjah.

Official Language
Arabic. English is widely spoken in business and official
circles and by most expatriates in the service sector. Urdu
and Farsi are also widely spoken.

National Flag
A red vertical stripe along the hoist for a quarter of the
width of the flag and three horizontal stripes in the
remaining three quarters of green (top), white (middle)
and black (bottom).

Visas
GCC citizens and British citizens with the right of abode
in UK do not need a visa to visit UAE. Passports must be
valid for six months beyond the period of stay. A one
month stay is granted on entry which can be extended.
All other nationalities require a visa which is obtainable
from UAE embassies abroad. There is no airport
departure tax.

Alcohol
Non-Muslims are permitted to import two litres of
alcoholic beverage, except into Sharjah, where alcohol is
banned. Alcohol is available for non-Muslims in most

leading hotels (except in Sharjah) although prices are high. Non-Muslim residents can obtain a licence for a limited allocation of alcohol provided their income is above a certain level and their sponsor agrees. Visitors and residents should be warned however, that any public display of intoxication carries severe penalties and if a person is discovered to have consumed any alcohol when driving this will lead to immediate arrest and penalties of imprisonment, a fine and possible deportation.

Local Time GMT + 4 hours, EST + 9 hours

Dialling Codes
Abu Dhabi, 00 971 2; Dubai and Jebel Ali, 00 971 4; Sharjah and Ajman, 00 971 6; Ras Al-Khaimah 00 971 7; Fujairah 00 971 9.

Public Holidays
All Muslim Festivals (*see* Chapter 1), and Christian Holidays (Easter and Christmas); New Year's Day, Ruler's Accession Day 6th August, (Abu Dhabi only) and National Day on 2nd December.

U A E

Working Hours
Government offices: 0730-1430 Saturday to Wednesday.
Banks: 0700-1300 Saturday to Wednesday. Business hours: 0830-1300 and 1600-1900 Saturday to Wednesday and 0830-1200 on Thursday.
Oil companies: 0700-1500 Sunday to Wednesday.
British Embassy in Abu Dhabi and Dubai: 0730-1430 Saturday to Wednesday.
British Consulate: 0800-1300 Saturday to Wednesday. Working hours are modified during the holy month of *Rama**dan**.*

Currency
UAE Dirham (Dh/Dhs) divided into 100 fils. The Dirham is officially linked to the US$. At the time of going to print, the exchange rate was Dh 5.9622 = £1 sterling and (Dh 3.6730) = US$1. Credit cards are widely accepted and

197

most major banks are linked to at least one international ATM network.

Income Tax
There is no personal taxation in UAE.

Electricity Supply
240 volts in Abu Dhabi and 220 volts in Dubai and the Northern Emirates. Plugs are three-pin flat or round.

Transportation
Most hotels have an airport pick up service. Taxis are numerous and inexpensive. Taxis have meters in both Abu Dhabi and Dubai. Cars can be hired on production of an international driving licence but chauffeur-driven limousines are reasonably priced and often considered more convenient for visitors on business. In the border areas of the Northern Emirates or Buraimi, drivers should ensure they have vehicle insurance cover for Oman if there is any likelihood that they will cross the Omani border, however briefly. National airlines are Gulf Air owned jointly by Abu Dhabi, Bahrain, Oman and Qatar and Emirates airline owned by Dubai.

Tipping
Taxis are not tipped. Hotels and restaurants normally add a service charge although this goes to the restaurant, not to the waiter. The rate for airport porters is up to Dhs 5 depending on the number of pieces of baggage.

Embassies
Embassy of the United Arab Emirates in UK
30 Princes Gate, London SW7 1PT
Tel: 0171 581 1281/4113; Fax: 0171 581 9616
Embassy of the United Arab Emirates in US
600 New Hampshire Avenue NW, Washington DC 20037
Tel: (202) 338 6500.
British Embassies in the United Arab Emirates
Abu Dhabi (Resident Ambassador), PO Box 248, Abu Dhabi Tel: 00 971 2 326600 Fax: 00 971 2 341744;

U
A
E

Commercial Section Tel: 00 971 2 3216600
E-mail: commercial@abudhabi.mail.fco.gov.uk
Dubai (Resident Consul-General) British Embassy, Al-Seef Road, PO Box 65. Dubai.
Tel: 00 971 4 521070 Fax 00 971 4 525750 Commercial Section Tel: 00 971 4 521893/524993; Fax: 00 971 4 527095
E-mail: commercial@dubai.mail.fco.gov.uk
US Embassy in the United Arab Emirates
Sudan Street, Abu Dhabi. Tel: 00971 2 436 691

Tourist Sites and Activities

The many sites of interest in Abu Dhabi include the Al-Husn Palace (The Old Fort), the oldest building in the city, excellent restaurants in the large hotels, on the breakwater, in the port or aboard a dhow, some of which have live entertainment. There is also fishing, ice skating, scuba diving, camel racing and a polo club. There are a number of topical events of interest such as the annual boat race and if time permits, a visit to Al-Ain and Buraimi is well worthwhile. In Dubai which caters more widely for tourists there are again first class hotels, international class golf clubs, horse racing, water sports, excellent restaurants and live evening entertainment. Among the tourist sites are the excellent Dubai museum, Shaikh Saeed's House (the grandfather of the present ruler), the *souq*, the traditional buildings with their wind towers, the creek crossing on an *abra* boat (meaning 'across' in Arabic) or hiring an *abra* for a short tour of the waterfront. There are also numerous sites of interest in the Northern Emirates, the mountains and beaches of which are popular picnic spots.

General Comments

The UAE is among the most relaxed of the Peninsula states for a Westerner to visit. Thoroughly modern and catering for many tastes it nevertheless retains its very distinctive Arab culture, and the underlying society is conservative, well-ordered and always in accordance with the tenets of Islam. Western visitors are, of course, expected to fully respect the Islamic culture in their general behaviour and in such matters as dress.

U
A
E

199

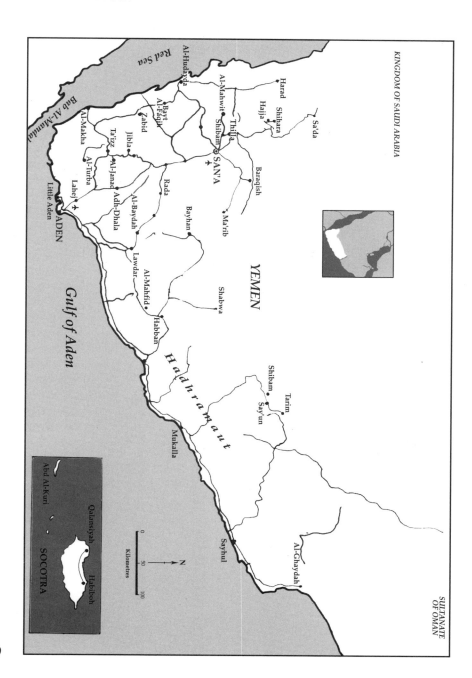

THE REPUBLIC OF YEMEN

THE REPUBLIC OF YEMEN

Geography

The Republic of Yemen occupies the southwestern corner of the Arabian Peninsula and covers an area of about 530,000 sq kms. The topography is mainly mountainous. Beyond the Tihama, a semi-desert strip up to 50 kms wide along the Red Sea coast, lies the western mountain region which rises to over 3000m above sea level in places. This in turn gives way to fertile plateaus at around 2000m before reaching the eastern mountain region. The eastern mountains slowly descend to about 1000 m on the border with Oman. The Yemen's capital city and international airport, San'a, is situated inland in the San'a Basin at around 2000m above sea level. It has over a million inhabitants. Aden, the second city and main port, also with an international airport and the location of the Aden Free Zone, lies on the southern coast. Its population is around 425,000. Aden is 363 kms from San'a. Other major towns include Al-Hudaidah, the country's main Red Sea port and Tai'z, one time the capital of north Yemen, 256 kms south of San'a and Yemen's most industialised city with about 500,000 inhabitants. In the eastern governorates of the Hadhramaut are the ancient city of Shabwa and the Arabian Sea port of Al-Mukalla.

Climate

The Tihama and the southern coastal strip is generally hot, humid and dusty with daytime temperatures averaging 36°C in winter and 40°C and above in summer. Rainfall is low. The highlands have a mild climate with daytime temperatures between 25 and 30°C. The winters can be cold, particularly at night when temperatures fall to 0°C. Most rain falls in the western mountains, mainly in July and August.

History

Home to a number of civilisations and kingdoms since the 11th century BC, the region prospered until the 4th Century AD because of the development of overland trade routes to the north and also because of its agriculture, as the main source of frankincense and myrrh. This was the land described by the Romans as Arabia Felix and the country of the Queen of Sheba. In the 7th century the area came under Persian control and converted to Islam. There followed a series of Yemeni rulers and dynasties, prominent among them the Zaydi and the Kathirid, until the arrival of the Portuguese in the region. They were supplanted by the Ottoman Turks in the 16th Century who were in turn ousted by the Zaydi Imams (religious leaders of the Zaydi dynasty). From 1839 Britain, anxious to protect its strategic route to India, eventually colonised Aden and entered into protectorate relations with the adjacent Shaikhdoms (the area previously known as South Yemen). The Ottomans returned to occupy the Yemeni highlands (the north Yemen) until at the end of World War I they were finally ousted by the Zaydi Imams. In 1962 an army coup overthrew the Imamate in a revolution and established the Yemen Arab Republic (YAR). There followed a bitter eight-year civil war between Republican and Royalist Forces in which Egypt and Russia supported the Republicans. However, in 1967 the Egyptians withdrew and in 1970 the conflict was resolved. Meanwhile in the south, a nationalist (Marxist) movement in Aden and the surrounding Protectorates fomented the outbreak of a guerrilla war which led to the withdrawal of the British in 1967 and the formation in 1970 of the People's Democratic Republic of Yemen (PDRY). In 1990 the two Yemeni states, north and south, were unified and the Republic of Yemen (ROY) was declared.

Government

Under a power-sharing arrangement on unification, the President of the former YAR, Ali Abdallah Saleh, took over as President of the ROY and the President of the former PDRY, Haidar Abu Bakr Al-Attas became the Prime Minister. Elections in 1997 confirmed these

appointments and a new government. Despite some continued internal opposition, the Government is committed to a major development programme.

Economy

The Republic of Yemen is in the initial stages of a programme of economic reform and infrastructure development. The economy is dependent on the hydrocarbons sector, agriculture, industry and mining. Oil was discovered in 1980 but production revenues are as yet low. However, anticipated increased production and refining, the establishment of the Aden Free Zone and the economic reforms, including a measure of privatisation, are among the measures being taken to improve economic prospects for the future.

Conduct of Business

Although not legally required in all cases, it is generally advisable for Western businessmen exporting to the Republic of Yemen to appoint a reliable local agent or distributor. Franchising has also become an accepted practice.

Population

The population is estimated at 17 million with an annual growth rate of 3.7%. It is a strongly tribal society. The tribes and a number of ethnic groups influence the political groupings and Government policy.

Religion

The state religion is Islam. Almost all Yemenis are Muslims, fairly evenly divided between followers of the Zaydis, a Shia Grouping, predominant in the former YAR and the Shafi, a Sunni grouping predominant in the former PDRY.

Official Language

Arabic. English is the second language and is widely spoken in business circles.

National Flag
Divided into three horizontal stripes - red (top), white and black.

Visas
Visas are required by all visitors and are normally valid for a stay of one month. Application is made to Yemeni Embassies abroad and if the passport contains evidence of a visit to Israel an enquiry should be made with the Embassy prior to application. There is an airport departure tax of US$10 on international flights and US$3 on domestic flights.

Alcohol
The importation of alcohol is prohibited, as are goods from Israel.

Local Time GMT + 3 hours, EST + 8 hours

Dialling Code
00 967. Area codes are: San'a 1, Aden 2, Hodeidah 3, Tai'z 4, Mukalla 5.

Public Holidays
All Muslim Festivals (*see* Chapter 1), Al-Isra Eva - 27 Rajab, New Year's Day, Labour Day - 1 May, Unification Day - 22 May, Victory Day - 7 July, September Revolution - 26 September, October Revolution - 14 October and Independence Day - 30 November.

Working Hours
Government offices: 0800-1200 Saturday to Wednesday and 0800-1130 on Thursday. Banks: 00830-1200 Saturday to Wednesday and 0800-1130 Thursday.
Business: 0800-1200 Saturday to Wednesday and 0800-1130 Thursday.
Shops: 0800-1300 and 1600-2100 Sunday to Thursday.
British Embassy: 0730-1430 Sunday to Thursday. Working hours are modified during the Holy month of Ramadan.

Currency
The Yemeni Riyal (YR) is divided into 100 fils. At the time of going to print, the exchange rate was YR 240.485 = £1 sterling and YR 148.150 = US$1. Credit cards are only accepted in the largest hotels.

Health
Advice on health should be sought prior to travel. Medical facilities in Yemen are limited and in cases of urgent need Westerners are advised to seek advice from their Embassy in San'a. It is also advisable to drink bottled water.

Security
The Foreign and Commonwealth Office (FCO) London cautions visitors to the Yemen of 'the risk of random kidnapping throughout the country, including the capital San'a, although abductees are generally treated well and have eventually been released unharmed'. The armed theft of vehicles, particularly four wheel drive is also commonplace. For these and other reasons it is important that prior to their visit, British visitors to the Yemen seek advice from the FCO and in the case of other nationalities the appropriate national authority.

Personal Taxation
There is an upper income tax level for non-residents of 22%.

Electricity Supply
220/230 volts AC, 50 Hz, with 2-pin plugs.

Transportation
Taxis do not have meters and the fare should be negotiated before each journey. The fare from San'a and Aden airports to each of the city centres costs up to US$10. It is recommended to either hire a taxi for a day or half day or to hire a car with a driver. The national airline, Yemenia, flies twice weekly direct to Yemen from Gatwick Airport in London.

Tipping

Although service is included in hotel and restaurant bills it is customary to tip between 10% to 15%. This is also the case with taxis.

Embassies

Embassy of the Republic of Yemen in UK
57 Cromwell Road, London SW7 2ED
Tel: 0171 584 6607 Fax 0171 584 3350
Embassy of the Republic of Yemen in US
Suite 860, Watergate Six Hundred, 600 New Hampshire Avenue NW, Washington, DC 20037
Tel: (202) 965 4760/1, 865 4781.
United Nations, 8th Floor, 747 3rd Avenue, New York, NY 10017 Tel: (212) 355 1730/1.
British Embassy in the Republic of Yemen
129 Haddah Road, SAN'A. Postal Address PO Box 1287 SAN'A, Republic of Yemen.
Tel: 0 967 1 264081-4; Fax: 00 967 1 263059;
Email: Abu Dhabi & Dubai: hhtp://www.britain.uae.org
British Consulate-General in the Republic of Yemen
28 Shara Ho Cho Minh, Aden. Postal Address PO Box 6304, Aden, Republic of Yemen.
US Embassy in the Republic of Yemen
Sa'wan Street SAN'A. Tel: 00 967 1 238842/52.

Tourist Sites

Tourism is in its infancy but increasing. Visitors are likely to be fascinated by the Yemen's ancient culture and enthralled by its architecture, from the low painted houses of the Tihama to the famous tower houses built of stone, mud or mud brick of the highlands, each floor with its own function as home for the animals, *majlis*, bedrooms, etc. Sites of interest in San'a include the Old City, the National Museum and the mosques. Also the Souq Al-Milh, meaning Salt Souq but actually a collection of around forty different souqs. Outside San'a the sites include the fertile Wadi Dahr, Shibam (not to be confused with Shibam in the Hadhramaut), and Kawkaban. Further afield, Ta'iz and in the Hadhramaut, the ancient

cities of Shabwa, Shibam and Al-Mukalla. Further information can be obtained from the office of the General Tourist Corporation in San'a at the western end of Maidan At-Tahir. Tourists should bear in mind the advice under *Security* above.

General Comments

Visitors to Yemen will hear mention of a mild 'national' narcotic *qat*. This is a leaf from the evergreen tree or bush, the *catha edulis* which is grown at altitudes above 1500m and traditionally chewed (in the cheek) but not swallowed, at weekly social gatherings.

Y
E
M
E
N

207

FCO CONSULAR ASSISTANCE ABROAD

UK FOREIGN AND COMMONWEALTH (FCO) - CONSULAR ASSISTANCE ABROAD AND TRAVEL ADVICE

General

The FCO publish information on their Consular Services abroad which sets out:

- What a British Consulate can do for you
- What it cannot do for you
- What you should do for youself

The Travel Advice Unit provides general advice on individual countries. Full contact details for British Embassies are also given.

British Consuls

British Consuls will do everything they properly can to help British people in difficulty abroad. Details of how to avoid trouble abroad and what help you can expect from a British Consul are given below:

- issue emergency passports
- contact relatives and friends and ask them to help you with money or tickets
- tell you how to transfer money
- in an emergency, cash you a sterling cheque worth up to £100 if supported by a valid banker's card
- as a last resort, and as long as you meet certain strict rules, give you a loan to get you back to the UK.... they must be sure there is no one else who can help you
- help you get in touch with local lawyers, interpreters and doctors
- arrange for next of kin to be told of an accident or a death and advise on procedures

F
C
O

- visit you if you have been arrested or put in prison
- give guidance on organisations who help trace missing persons
- speak to local authorities for you, in certain circumstances

UK law obliges them to charge for some services. Consulates display the standards of service you can expect under the Citizen's Charter.

What a British Consulate cannot do for you

- intervene in court cases
- get you out of prison
- give legal advice or start court proceedings for you
- get you better treatment in hospital or prison than is given to local nationals
- investigate a crime
- pay your hotel, legal, medical or any other bills
- pay your travel costs, except in special circumstances
- do work normally done by travel agents, airlines, banks or motoring organisations
- get you somewhere to live, a job or work permit
- formally help you if you are a dual national in the country of your second nationality. (You should read the FCO's Dual Nationality leaflet for more information.)

What you should do for yourself

The FCO advises contacting the Travel Advice Unit either on the FCO website or by telephoning the Travel Advice Unit on 020 7238 4503/4504 for the latest advice on the country you are visiting.

Their advice includes the purchase of tickets, money, insurance, health, avoiding trouble spots, security, obeying the law, drugs, acohol, driving and what to do if you are arrested, have something stolen, and if someone should die. It advises noting the address and telephone

number of the British Embassy or Consulate.

FCO contact details are:

Consular Information Internet: http://www.fco.gov.uk/text
Travel Advice Unit: Tel: 020 7238 4503/4504: Fax: 020 7238
4545; Internet: http://www.fco.gov.uk/travel.

F
C
O

COMMERCIAL SUPPORT FOR US COMPANIES

COMMERCIAL SUPPORT IN THE PENINSULA FOR UNITED STATES COMPANIES

General Information
For general information about US Government export promotion programmes, contact the Trade Information Center which provides information on Federal programmes and activities that support US exports, information on overseas markets and industry trends, as well as a computerised calendar of US Government sponsored domestic and overseas trade events. The Center's nationwide toll-free number is: 1-800-USA-TRADE(1-800-872-8723).

Specific Information and Support
The specific start point for any US company wishing to consider doing business in the countries of the Peninsula would be to approach their local US Export Assistance Center of the International Trade Administration, US and Foreign Commercial Service of theUS Department of Commerce. (*See* directory below.)

US Foreign Commercial Service
The US Foreign Commerical Service is represented in the US Embassies of all important market locations. They pull together local information and undertake basic commercial research in local markets in support of US-Arab trade. Much of this research information is provided to US companies free of charge, unless they have incurred significant expense in the process, in which case a nominal charge is made. In addition, the Foreign Commercial Service offer a direct market service, support the various Economic Development Groups and Trade Promotion Missions and provide a Gold Key Service to individual US small- to medium-sized companies under

213

which, on payment of a fee, the Foreign Commercial Service will advise on specific markets, support a company visit and make appointments in-country.

Contact details for US Embassies in the Peninsula states are given in the relevant Country Annexes.

Directory of Export Assistance Centers

The list of US Department of Commerce, Export Assistance Centers is given below. (Cities in capital letters are centres which combine the export promotion and trade finance service of the Department of Commerce, the Export-Import Bank, the Small Business Administration and the Agency for International Development.)

ALABAMA
Birmingham, Alabama - George Norton, Director
950 22nd Street North, Room 707, ZIP 35203
Tel : (205) 731-1331, Fax: (205) 731-0076

ALASKA
Anchorage, Alaska - Charles Becker, Director
550 West 7th Ave., Suite 1770, ZIP: 99501
Tel: (907) 271-6237, Fax: (907) 271-6242

ARIZONA
Phoenix, Arizona - Frank Woods, Director
2901 N. Central Ave., Suite 970, ZIP 85012
Tel: (602) 640-2513, Fax: (602) 640-2518

CALIFORNIA - LONG BEACH
Joseph F Sachs, Director
Mary Delmege, CS Director
One World Trade Center, Ste. 1670, ZIP: 90831
Tel: (562) 980-4550, Fax: (562) 980-4561

CALIFORNIA - SAN JOSE
101 Park Center Plaza, Ste. 1001, ZIP: 95113
Tel: (408) 271-7300, Fax: (408) 271-7307

COLORADO - DENVER
Nancy Charles-Parker, Director
1625 Broadway, Suite 680, ZIP: 80202
Tel: (303) 844-6623, Fax: (303) 844-5651

CONNECTICUT
Middletown, Connecticut - Carl Jacobsen, Director
213 Court Street, Suite 903 ZIP: 06457-3346
Tel: (860) 638-6950, Fax: (860) 638-6970

DELAWARE
Served by the Philadelphia, Pennsylvania U.S. Export
AssistanceCenter

FLORIDA - MIAMI
John McCartney, Director
P.O. Box 590570, ZIP: 33159
5600 Northwest 36th St., Ste. 617, ZIP: 33166
Tel: (305) 526-7425, Fax: (305) 526-7434

GEORGIA - ATLANTA
Samuel Troy, Director
285 Peachtree Center Avenue, NE, Suite 200, ZIP: 30303-
1229
Tel: (404) 657-1900, Fax: (404) 657-1970

HAWAII
Honolulu, Hawaii - Greg Wong, Manager
1001 Bishop St.; Pacific Tower; Suite 1140, ZIP: 96813
Tel: (808) 522-8040, Fax: (808) 522-8045

IDAHO
Boise, Idaho - James Hellwig, Manager
700 West State Street, 2nd Floor, ZIP: 83720
Tel: (208) 334-3857, Fax: (208) 334-2783

ILLINOIS - CHICAGO
Mary Joyce, Director
55 West Monroe Street, Suite 2440, ZIP: 60603
Tel: (312) 353-8045, Fax: (312) 353-8120

US SUPPORT

215

INDIANA
Indianapolis, Indiana - Dan Swart, Manager
11405 N. Pennsylvania Street, Suite 106
Carmel, IN, ZIP: 46032
Tel: (317) 582-2300, Fax: (317) 582-2301

IOWA
Des Moines, Iowa - Allen Patch, Director
601 Locust Street, Suite 100, ZIP: 50309-3739
Tel: (515) 288-8614, Fax: (515) 288-1437

KANSAS
Wichita, Kansas - George D. Lavid, Manager
209 East William, Suite 300, ZIP: 67202-4001
Tel: (316) 269-6160, Fax: (316) 269-6111

KENTUCKY
Louisville, Kentucky - John Autin, Director
601 W. Broadway, Room 634B , ZIP: 40202
Tel: (502) 582-5066, Fax: (502) 582-6573

LOUISIANA - DELTA
Patricia Holt, Acting Director
365 Canal Street, Suite 1170
New Orleans ZIP: 70130
Tel: (504) 589-6546, Fax: (504) 589-2337

MAINE
Portland, Maine - Jeffrey Porter, Manager
c/o Maine International Trade Center
511 Congress Street, ZIP: 04101
Tel: (207) 541-7400, Fax: (207) 541-7420

MARYLAND - BALITMORE
Michael Keaveny, Director
World Trade Center, Suite 2432
401 East Pratt Street, ZIP: 21202
Tel: (410) 962-4539. Fax: (410) 962-4529

US SUPPORT

MASSACHUSETTS - BOSTON
Frank J. O'Connor, Director
164 Northern Avenue
World Trade Center, Suite 307, ZIP: 02210
Tel: (617) 424-5990, Fax: (617) 424-5992

MICHIGAN - DETROIT
Neil Hesse, Director
211 W. Fort Street, Suite 2220, ZIP: 48226
Tel: (313) 226-3650, Fax: (313) 226-3657

MINNESOTA - MINNEAPOLIS
Ronald E. Kramer, Director
45 South 7th St., Suite 2240, ZIP: 55402
Tel: (612) 348-1638, Fax: (612) 348-1650

MISSISSIPPI
Mississippi - Harrison Ford, Manager
704 East Main St., Raymond, MS, ZIP: 39154
Tel: (601) 857-0128, Fax: (601) 857-0026

MISSOURI - ST LOUIS
Randall J. LaBounty, Director
8182 Maryland Avenue, Suite 303, ZIP: 63105
Tel: (314) 425-3302, Fax: (314) 425-3381

MONTANA
Missoula, Montana - Mark Peters, Manager
c/o Montana World Trade Center
Gallagher Business Bldg., Suite 257, ZIP: 59812
Tel: (406) 243-2098, Fax: (406) 243-5259

NEBRASKA
Omaha, Nebraska - Meredith Bond, Manager
11135 "O" Street, ZIP: 68137
Tel: (402) 221-3664, Fax: (402) 221-3668

NEVADA
Reno, Nevada - Jere Dabbs, Manager
1755 East Plumb Lane, Suite 152, ZIP: 89502
Tel: (702) 784-5203, Fax: (702) 784-5343

US SUPPORT

217

NEW HAMPSHIRE
Portsmouth, New Hampshire - Susan Berry, Manager
17 New Hampshire Avenue, ZIP: 03801-2838
Tel: (603) 334-6074, Fax: (603) 334-6110

NEW JERSEY
Trenton, New Jersey - Rod Stuart, Director
3131 Princeton Pike, Bldg. #4, Suite 105, ZIP: 08648
Tel: (609) 989-2100, Fax: (609) 989-2395

NEW MEXICO
New Mexico - Sandra Necessary, Manager
c/o New Mexico Dept. of Economic Development
P.O. Box 20003, Santa Fe, ZIP: 87504-5003
FEDEX:1100 St. Francis Drive, ZIP: 87503
Tel: (505) 827-0350, Fax: (505) 827-0263

NEW YORK - NEW YORK
John Lavelle, Acting Director
6 World Trade Center, Rm. 635, ZIP: 10048
Tel: (212) 466-5222, Fax: (212) 264-1356

NORTH CAROLINA - CAROLINAS
Roger Fortner, Director
521 East Morehead Street, Suite 435, Charlotte, ZIP: 28202
Tel: (704) 333-4886, : (704) 332-2681

NORTH DAKOTA
Served by the Minneapolis, Minnesota Export
AssistanceCenter

OHIIO - CLEVELAND
Michael Miller, Director
600 Superior Avenue, East, Suite 700, ZIP: 44114
Tel: (216) 522-4750, Fax: (216) 522-2235

OKLAHOMA
Oklahoma City, Oklahoma - Ronald L. Wilson, Director
301 Northwest 63rd Street, Suite 330, ZIP: 73116
Tel: (405) 608-5302, Fax: (405) 608-4211

OREGON - PORTLAND
Scott Goddin, Director
One World Trade Center, Suite 242
121 SW Salmon Street, ZIP: 97204
Tel: (503) 326-3001, Fax: (503) 326-6351

PENNSYLVANIA - PHILADELPHIA
 Rod Stuart, Acting Director
615 Chestnut Street, Ste. 1501, ZIP: 19106
Tel: (215) 597-6101, Fax: (215) 597-6123

PUERTO RICO
San Juan, Puerto Rico (Hato Rey) - Vacant, Manager
525 F.D. Roosevelt Avenue, Suite 905, ZIP: 00918
Tel: (787) 766-5555, Fax: (787) 766-5692

RHODE ISLAND
Providence, Rhode Island - Vacant, Manager
One West Exchange Street, ZIP: 02903
Tel: (401) 528-5104, Fax: (401) 528-5067

SOUTH CAROLINA
Columbia, South Carolina - Ann Watts, Director
1835 Assembly Street, Suite 172, ZIP: 29201
Tel: (803) 765-5345, Fax: (803) 253-3614

SOUTH DAKOTA
Siouxland, South Dakota - Cinnamon King, Manager
Augustana College, 2001 S. Summit Avenue
Room SS-44, Sioux Falls, ZIP: 57197
Tel: (605) 330-4264, Fax: (605) 330-4266

TENNESSEE
Memphis, Tennessee - Ree Russell, Manager
Buckman Hall, 650 East Parkway South, Suite 348 ZIP:
38104. Tel: (901) 323-1543, Fax: (901) 320-9128

TEXAS - DALLAS
 LoRee Silloway, Director
P.O. Box 420069, ZIP: 75342-0069

US SUPPORT

2050 N. Stemmons Fwy., Suite 170, ZIP: 75207
Tel: (214) 767-0542, Fax: (214) 767-8240

UTAH
Salt Lake City, Utah - Stanley Rees, Director
324 S. State Street, Suite 221, ZIP: 84111
Tel: (801) 524-5116, Fax: (801) 524-5886

VERMONT
Montpelier, Vermont - Susan Murray, Manager
National Life Building, Drawer 20, ZIP: 05620-0501
Tel: (802) 828-4508, Fax: (802) 828-3258

VIRGINIA
Richmond, Virginia - Helen D. Lee Hwang, Manager
400 North 8th Street, Suite 540, ZIP: 23240-0026
P.O. Box 10026
Tel: (804) 771-2246, Fax: (804) 771-2390

WASHINGTON - SEATTLE
David Spann, Director
2001 6th Ave, Suite 650, ZIP: 98121
Tel: (206) 553-5615, Fax: (206) 553-7253

WEST VIRGINIA
Charleston, West Virginia - Harvey Timberlake, Director
405 Capitol Street, Suite 807, ZIP: 25301
Tel: (304) 347-5123, Fax: (304) 347-5408

WISCONSIN
Milwaukee, Wisconsin - Paul D. Churchill, Director
517 E. Wisconsin Avenue, Room 596, ZIP: 53202
Tel: (414) 297-3473, Fax: (414) 297-3470

WYOMING
Served by the Denver, Colorado U.S. Export Assistance
Center

GLOSSARY

abaya Traditional long black cloak worn by Muslim women in the Peninsula.

Abdul 'Servant of', e.g. Abdul-Rahmaan - 'Servant of the Merciful' (*see* page 82).

Abu 'Father of' (*see* page 82).

Ad-Din 'Of the faith' (*see* page 82).

Akhee 'My brother'. Traditional way of referring to a friend.

Al or *El* Definite article.

aqaal Head rope, originally double-looped used for hobbling camels.

Allah The Muslim word for God, which means 'the God'.

Amir Ruler (Bahrain, Kuwait and Qatar).

baksheesh A tip.

Bedu Sing. *Bedouin,* 'a nomadic desert dweller'.

bisht Kuwaiti and Saudi term for the traditional outer robe or cloak. Also called a *mishlah* and often trimmed with gold when worn by distinguished citizens, shaikhs, etc.

bin 'Son of', used with the father's and grand-father's name, e.g. Mohammed bin Ahmed bin Abdullah. Also written *ibn.*

bint 'Girl' or 'daughter'. Used in a name in the same way as *bin* or *ibn.*

221

birka	Veil covering the whole of a Muslim woman's face, except for the eyes. Also called *hijab*.
burga	Mask covering lower part of face of a veiled Muslim woman.
Caliph	Literally, 'successor'. Title adoped by leaders of the Muslim community after the death of the Prophet Muhammad.
dinar	Unit of currency in Kuwait and Bahrain.
dirham	Unit of currency in the UAE.
dishdasha	Kuwaiti term for the full length, long cotton robe worn throughout the Peninsula. Also called a *thobe* in Saudi Arabia and the Gulf.
Eid Al-Adha	The festival celebrating the end of the Pilgrimage at which all pilgrims offer a sacrifice to God.
Eid Al-Fitr	The festival celebrating the end of the month-long fast of Ramadan.
fatwa	Religious edict issued by the *Ulema* (religious scholars).
ghūtra	One term used for the headcloth worn in Saudi Arabia and the Gulf. Also called a *shemaag*.
Hadith	Authenticated teachings, sayings and acts of the Prophet Muhammad and his Companions.
Hajj	The Pilgrimage to Makkah which, in accordance with the Five Pillars of Islam, must be made by every Muslim if he can afford it. The *Hajj* is made in the pilgrimage month which ends *Eid Al-Adha*.

Hajji (fem. *Hajja*)	Pilgrim. Title given to someone who has completed the pilgrimage to Makkah.
halaal	'Permitted'. Used to describe food which is allowed to Muslims, including animals slaughtered in the prescribed Islamic manner.
hijab	Veil covering the whole face of Muslim women, except the eyes - also called a *birka*.
Hijra	The 'migration 'in AD 622 when Muhammad fled to Medina. The official start of the Muslim era and calendar, described as Anno Hijra (AH).
ibn	'Son of', *see bin*.
(Al-)Ikhwaan	A collective term meaning 'Brothers', given to fervent Islamic believers.
Iqaama	Residence permit.
Imaam	'He who goes before'. One who leads Muslims in prayer. In Iran the term is used to describe the ruling religious hierarchy.
In-sha'Allah	'If God wills', often proclaimed by a Muslim to demonstrate his belief that every occurrence on earth is ordained by God.
Jihad	Holy War. Used to cover any large-scale action, including war and economic sanctions, in which a whole Muslim community endeavours to achieve a religiously sanctified objective.
Ka'aba	The large cube-shaped monument in the Grand Mosque in Makkah, which is the focal point to which all Muslims pray. It is revered as the House of God built by Abraham. The Ka'aba is about 50 feet high and draped in rich black and gold hangings, which are renewed each year.

G
L
O
S
S
A
R
Y

223

Koran	*see Quran (Holy).*
kūfeeya	Small, white skullcap worn under the *gūtra/shemaag.*
majlis	Reception or meeting in an Arab house or palace. From the verb *jalas,* 'he sits down'.

Majlis As-Shura Consultative Council.

masjid	Mosque.
minaara	Minaret.
minbar	Pulpit in mosque from which the oratory is given at Friday prayers.
mihraab	Niche in mosque wall indicating the direction of Makkah.
mishlah	*See bhisht.*
muezzin	Caller to prayer.
nargeela	Hubble-bubble. Smokers' pipe, burning various flavours of tobacco. The smoke is drawn through water along a long pipe.
Nasrani	Christian. Lit. 'a follower' of the man from Nazareth.
Qadi	Judge
qūbba'a	Small, round, woven hat in a variety of decorative colours, worn in Oman.
Quran (Holy)	Also spelt Koran. The Muslim holy book containing God's revelation to the Prophet Muhammad, set out in 114 *Suras* (*qv*). (*See* Chapter 1.)

G
L
O
S
S
A
R
Y

Ramadan	The holy month of fasting *(Sawm)*, one of the Five Pillars of Islam. Commemorates the revelation of the Holy Quran by Allah to the Prophet Muhammad. Between dawn and dusk Muslims abstain from food, drink and all pleasurable pursuits.
riyal	Unit of currency in Saudi Arabia, Qatar and Yemen.
Rub' Al-Khali	The Empty Quarter. Derives from the term 'the barren lands', used by the Bedu to describe the immense desert in the south of Saudi Arabia.
rūkhsa	Leave or holiday.
Sawm	Fasting. One of the Five Pillars of Islam.
Salaa	Prayer. One of the Five Pillars of Islam.
Shahaada	The Declaration of Faith. Lit. 'bearing witness'. One of the Five Pillars of Islam.
Shaikh	Hereditary title used by members of the ruling families of the Arab Gulf states. Also a title given to leaders of tribes, senior members of leading families, religious leaders and judges. Lit. 'old and revered person'.
Shari'a	Islamic law.
shemaag	See *gūtra*.
Shia	Classification within Islam. *(See* page 30.)
sooq	Market.
Sultan	Ruler (Oman).
Sunna	Lit. 'customary procedure'.
Sunni	Classification within Islam. The Sunni, or 'orthodox',

G
L
O
S
S
A
R
Y

follow the succession of the elected caliphate. The great majority of Arabs in the Arabian Peninsula are Sunni.

Sura   Chapter in the Holy Quran.

tafaddal   Used when offering someone something.
                  Lit. 'be pleased to'.

thobe   *See dishdasha*

Ulema   A grouping of Islamic scholars and/or dignatories who hold an important position in Islam in most Islamic countries.

Umm   Mother. Also traditionally used to describe a woman as the mother of her eldest son, e.g. 'Umm Mohammed'.

wosta   Influence.

wadi   Dry, stony river bed (except in the rainy season).

wūdooh   Minor ablution.

Zakat   Alms giving to the poor. A religious duty on all Muslims. One of the Five Pillars of Islam.

BASIC VOCABULARY

about	*howl*	back	***dhahr***
above	*foqe*	bad	*batt**aal***
accident	***haa**dith*	bag (paper)	*kees (ay**kaas**)*
	*(ha**waa**dith)*	bag (suitcase)	*shan**ta***
across	*aber*	Bahrain	*Al-Bah**rayn***
adviser	*mūsta**shaar***	baker	*khab**baaz***
	*(mūtashaa**reen**)*	bananas	*mooz*
after	*ba'ad*	bank	*baank*
afternoon/this	*ba'ad adh-**dhū**hr*	bar	*baar*
afternoon		barber	*hal**laaq***
again	*murra* or	bazaar	*sooq*
	***thaa**neeya*	bathroom	*ham**maam***
against	*did*	beautiful	*jameel*
he agrees (on)	*yū**waa**faq ala*	because	*lee**yan***
he agreed (on)	***waa**faq ala*	bed	*fi**raash***
air conditioner	*mū**kayyif***	beer	***beera***
aircraft	*tei**yaara***	before	*qobl*
air force	*sillah al-jow*	behind	*wora*
airport	*mat**aar***	belly dancer	***raa**qisa sharqeeya*
all	*kūll*	beneath	*taht*
also	*ei**dan***	beside	*jamb*
always	*deiman*	better	*ahsan*
ambassador	*safeer (sū**fara'a**)*	between	*bayn*
America	*Amreeka*	big	*ka**beer***
and	*wa*	bill (restaurant)	*hi**saab***
angy	*za'**laan***	bird	*tayr (tū**yoor**)*
animal	*heiya**waan***	black	*aswad*
	*(heiyawaa**naat**)*	blue	*azraq*
answer	*jow**aab***	boat/ship	*mar**kab***
antiques	*antee**qaat***		*(ma**raa**kib)*
apples	*tūf**fah***	boiled	*mas**looq***
apricots	*mishmish*	book	*kitaab (kū**tub**)*
April	*Nee**saan***	bookshop	***mak**taba*
Arab	*Arabee (Arab)*	bowling	***boo**ling*
Arab Gulf	*Al-Kha**leej***	box	*sūn**dook***
	*Al-**Arab**ee*		*(sana**adeek**)*
army	*jeysh (jū**yoosh**)*	boy	*wulud (aw**laad**)*
assistant	*mū**aa**win*	brass	*nū**haas***
	*(mūaawi**neen**)*	bread	*khūbz*
at	*eind*	bread (local)	*khūbz bala**di***
attack	*hū**joom***	breakfast	*fū**toor***
August	*Aab*	bring me	*jee**blee***

VOCABULARY

Britain	*Bareetaaneeya*	he cleaned	**nodhdhaf**
British	*Bareetaanee*	he cleans	*yūnnadhif*
broken	*mak**soor***	clever	**shaatir**
brother	*akh (ikhwa)*	clock/hour	**saa'a (saa'aat)**
brown	*asmar*	closed	*m'sukkar*
brush	*fūrsha (fūrash)*	close (to)	**qoreeb** (*min*)
bus	*bus (busaat)*	clothing	**libaas**
bus stop	*ma**hatt**at al-bus*	club	**naadee**
businessman	*raj**ūl a'**maal*	coast	**saahil**
but	**laa**kin or wa**laa**kin	coffee	**qahwa**
butter	*zibda*	coffee-house	**maqha**
he buys	*yash**taree***	cold	**baarid**
he bought	*ish**taraa***	college	*kūleeya*
by	*bi*	colour	**lone** (*alwaan*)
by car	*bi se**iyaara***	commerce/trade	**tijaara**
		complaint	**shakwa**
cake	*kaa'k*	concerning	*bikhūsoos*
Cairo	*Al-**Qaa**hira*	congratulations	**mabrook**
camel	*jamal (jimaal)*	Consulate	*Consūleeya*
camera	*aalat at-tasweer*	contract	*aqd (ūqood)*
capital city	*aa**sima***	cook	**tabbaakh**
car	*se**iyaara***	correct	**saheeh**
	*(se**iyaaraat*)*	cost	**qeema**
card	*bi**taaqa***	country	*bi**laad** (b**ū**ldaan)*
carpet	*saj**jaada***	crime	*ja**reema** (jaraa'im)*
he carried	*hamal*	cross (n)	**saleeb**
he carries	*yah**mil***	crowd	*jūm**hoor***
case (legal)	*da'wa*		*(jamaahir)*
case (luggage)	**shanta**	cup	**finjaan**
castle/palace	*qal'a*		*(fanaajeen)*
centre	*markaz (maraakiz)*	custom	*aada (aadaat)*
certainly	*ma'**loom***	customs (at	*jūmrūk or*
certificate	*sha**haada***	airport)	*jamaarik*
chair	*kūrsee (ka**raasee)***		
cheap	*rakhees*	Damascus	*Dimashq*
cheaper	*ar**khas***	dancing	*raqs*
cheese	*jubna*	danger	**khatar**
chemist shop	*seidal**leeya***	date	**taareekh**
cheques	see *travellers'*	date (edible)	*tamar (tūmoor)*
	cheques	dawn	*fajar*
chief	*ra'ees (ru'asaa)*	day (in a day)	**yome** (*ayaam*)
chicken	*dūjaaja*	day before	*awal ams*
Christian	*Maseehee*	yesterday	
	*(maseehee**yeen**)*	day after	*ba'**ad** b**ūk**ra*
church	*kaneesa*	tomorrow	
cigarette	*si**gaara***	daytime	*nahaar*
circle	*daa'ira*	December	*Kaanoon Al-Awwal*
city	*ma**deena** (mūdūn)*	defence	*difaa'*
clean	*nodheef*	delicious	*lodheedh*

dentist	*tobeeb al-asnaan*	envelope	*dharf (dhūroof)*
department	*daa'ira (dawaa'ir)*	equipment (piece of)	*jihaaz (ajhiza)*
desert	*baadia*		
deputy	*wokeel (wūkalaa)*	equipment (military)	*ūdd (ūdad)*
dictionary	*qaamoos*		
the difference between	*al-farq bayn*	especially	*khūsoosan*
		essential	*jawharee*
difficult	*sa'ab*	evening	*masaa*
direction	*jiha or ittijaah*	evening entertainment	*sahra*
director	*mūdeer (mūdara)*		
dirty	*wasakh*	every	*kūll*
distance	*musaafa*	exactly	*tamaaman bidopt*
district	*mintaqa (manaatiq)*	for example	*mathalan*
division, part	*qism (aqsaam)*	except	*illa*
he did	*amil or sawwa*	excellent	*mūmtaaz*
he is doing	*ya'mal*	exhibition	*ma'rid (ma'aarid)*
doctor	*tobeeb*	it existed	*wajad*
dog	*kalb (kilaab)*	it exists	*yoojad*
donkey	*himaar*	exit	*makhraj*
door	*baab (abwaab)*	expense	*masroof (massaareef)*
dress (general)	*libaas*		
dress (woman)	*fūstaan (fasaateen)*	expensive	*ghaalee*
drink	*mashroob (mashroobaat)*	experiment	*tajriba (tajaarib)*
		expert (in)	*khabeer (bi)*
driver	*saa'iq (suwwaaq)*	explosion	*infijaar*
dry	*naashif*	exports	*saadiraat*
during	*khilaal*	external	*khaarijee*
dust	*tūraab*	eye	*'ein ('ūyoon)*
duty	*waajib (waajibaat)*		
		face	*wajh*
each of	*kūl min*	family	*aa'ila*
early	*bakeer*	far...from	*ba'eed ...'an*
earth	*ardh*	fare (taxi)	*ūjra*
east	*sharq*	fat (adj)	*sameen*
easy	*sahul*	Feast at end of Ramadan	*Eid Al-Fitr*
he ate	*akal*		
he eats	*yaakūl*	February	*Shūbaat*
egg	*bayda (bayd)*	festival	*eid*
Egypt	*Musr*	Festival of the Sacrifice	*Eid Al-Adha*
electricity	*kahraba*		
embassy	*sifaara*	few	*qoleel*
employee	*mūwadhaf (mūwadhdhafeen)*	figs	*teen*
		film	*film (aflaam)*
empty	*farrigh*	finally	*akheeran*
end	*nihaaya*	finger	*ūsbū (asaabi')*
engineer	*mūhandis (mūhandiseen)*	finish	*khalas*
		fire	*naar (fem)*
England	*Inglaterra*	fish	*samak*
English	*Ingleezee*	fishing	*sayd as-samak*

VOCABULARY

V
O
C
A
B
U
L
A
R
Y

flag	*a'lam*	he goes out	*yakhrūj*
it flew	*taar*	he went out	*kharaj*
it flies	*yateer*	goat	*ma'z*
floor	*ardh*	God	*Allah*
floor (stony)	*taabūq*	gold	*dhahab*
floor show	*cabaaray*	golf	*goolf*
flower	*zahar (zūhoor)*	good	*teiyyib*
food	*akl*	government	*hūkooma*
foot	*qadam (aqdaam)*	green	*akhdhar*
for	*li*	group	*jamaa'a*
forbidden	*mamnoo'a*	guard (collective)	*haras*
foreign/foreigner	*ajnabee (ajaanib)*	guard	*haaris (hūrraas)*
he forgot/I forgot	*nasa/nasat*	(watchman)	
		guest	*dhayf (dhūyoof)*
he forgets	*yansa*	guide	*daleel*
France	*Faransa*	guidebook	*kitaab daleel*
free	*hūrr (ahraar)*	gulf	*khaleej*
free (of charge)	*majaanee*	gun	*madfa' (madaafi')*
French	*Fransaawee*		
Friday	*Yome al-Jūmaa*	hair	*sha'r*
friend	*sodeeq (asdiqaa)*	half	*nūss*
fried/roasted	*maqlee*	hand	*yad (aydin)*
from	*min*	handkerchief	*mandeel*
frontier	*hūdood*	happy	*fūrhaan*
fruit (pl)	*fawaakih*	harbour	*meena*
fuel	*wūqood*	hard	*sa'b*
full	*malyaan*	hat	*qūbba-a*
future	*mūstaqbil*	head	*raas*
		headcloth	*kūfeeyya*
gallon	*gaaloon*	headquarters	*qeeyaada*
garden	*būstaan or hadeeqa*	health	*sahha*
garment	*thawb (theeyaab)*	heart	*qolb*
gate	*baab (abwaab)*	heat	*haraara*
general (adj)	*aam*	heavy	*thaqeel*
generous	*kareem*	help	*awn or mūsaa'ada*
Germany	*Almaaneeya*	he helped	*saa'ad*
gift	*hadeeya (hadaayaa)*	he helps	*yūsaa'id*
		here	*hina*
girl	*bint (banaat)*	high	*aalee*
he gave	*a'taa*	hire	*eejaar*
he gives	*ya'atee*	he hired	*ista'jar*
glad	*farhaan*	he hires	*yasta'jir*
glass (drinking)	*kūbaaya*	holiday	*'ūtla*
glasses (spectacles)	*nadhaaraat*	honest	*ameen*
		horizontal	*ūfqee*
(go)he goes	*yarooh*	hors d'oeuvres	*mezza*
he went	*raah*	horse	*hisaan (husn)*
he goes in	*yadkhūl*	hot	*haar*
he went in	*dakhal*	hotel	*fūndūq (fanaadiq)*

hour	*saa'a (saa'aat)*	June	*Huzayraan*
house	*bayt (būyoot)*		
housewife	*sitt*	key	*miftaah*
how?	*kayf?*		*(mafaateeh)*
how many?	*kam?*	kilogram	*keelo*
how much?	*bi-kam?*	kilometre	*keelomitre*
hubble bubble	*nargeela*		*(keeloomitraat)*
hungry	*jo'aan*	kind (thoughtful)	*loteef*
hurry (in a)	*musta'jil*	king	*malik (mūlook)*
hunting	*sayd*	kingdom	*mamlaka*
husband	*zawj*	knife	*sikeen (sakaakeen)*
		he knew	*'araf*
ice	*thalj*	he knows	*ya'rif*
identity card	*hūweeya*	knowledge	*ilm*
if	*idha*		
ill	*mareedh*	last (adj)	*aakhir*
immediately	*haalan*	last week	*al-ūsboo'a al-*
important	*mūhim*		*maadhey*
imports	*waaridaat*	last year	*al-sana al-*
he imported	*istawrad*		*maadheeya*
he imports	*yastawrid*	late	*mūta'akhkhir*
in	*fee*	lately	*akheeran*
incident	*haadith*	law	*qaanoon*
	(hawaadith)		*(qawaaneen)*
India	*Al-Hind*	lazy	*kaslaan*
he informed	*khabir*	leader	*qaa'id (qūwaad)*
he informs	*yūkhbir*	Arab League	*Al-Jaami'a Al-*
information	*khabar*		*Arabeeya*
influence	*hibr*	left (opp. right)	*yesaar*
ink	*wosta*	leg	*rijl (arjul)*
inside	*daakhil*	lemon	*laymoon*
international	*dūwalee*	to let	*lil-eejaar*
invitation	*da'wa*	letter	*maktoob*
invitation card	*bitaaqat da'wa*	library	*maktaba*
is there?	*fee?*	life	*heiyaat*
island	*jazeera (jazaa'ir)*	lift (n)	*mas'ad*
			(masaa'id)
jacket	*jaaket or sūtra*	light (opp. dark)	*noor*
January	*Kanoon Ath-*	light (opp. heavy)	*khafeef*
	Thaani	like, as: such as	*mithl*
jewels	*jawaahir or*	he liked/loved	*habb*
	mūjawharaat	he likes/loves	*yahibb*
Jordan	*Al-Ūrdun*	little	*qoleel*
job	*wadheefa*	he looked around	*tafaaraj*
	(wadhaa'if)	he looks around	*yatafarraj*
journalist	*sahaafee*	love	*hūbb*
	(sahaafeeyeen)	lunch	*ghada*
July	*Tammooz*	machine	*makeena*
juice	*aseer*	mad	*majnoon*

magazine	*majalla*	mistake	*ghalat (aghlaat)*
man	*rajūl (rijaal)*	modern	*hadeeth*
manager	*mūdeer*	moment	*lahdha (lahdhaat)*
many	*katheer*	Monday	*Yome al-Ithnayn*
map	*khaarita/khareeta*	money	*feloos*
March	*Aadhaar*	month	*shahr (shūhoor)*
marine (or naval)	*bahree*	moon	*qamr*
market	*sooq*	morning	*sabaah*
married	*mutazowwaj*	Morocco	*Al-Maghrib*
matches (pl. n)	*kabreet*	mosque	*masjid*
May	*Ayaar*	most of	*aghlab min*
meat	*lahm*	mountain	*jebal (jebaal)*
meat spiced and	*shawurma*	Mr	*seiyyid or meester*
grilled		much	*katheer*
meeting	*ijtimaa'*	music	*moozeeqa*
	(ijtimaa'aat)	Muslim	*Mūslim*
melon	*botteekh*		*(Muslimeen)*
merchant	*taajir (tujjaar)*		
message	*risaala (rasaa'il)*	name	*ism (asmaa)*
metre	*mitar (amtaar)*	navy	*bahreeya*
middle	*wost*	near (to)	*qareeb (min)*
Middle East	*Ash-Sharq Al-*	necessary	*dharooree*
	Owsat	neighbour	*jar (jeeraan)*
military (adj)	*difaa'ee*	never	*abadan*
(*lit.* defence)		new	*jadeed*
milk	*haleeb*	news	*khabar (akhbaar)*
million	*milyoon*	newspaper	*jareeda*
minaret	*manaara*	next week	*al-ūsboo'a al-jaiy*
minister	*wozeer (wuzaraa)*	next year	*as-sana al-jaiy*
ministry	*wizaara*	night	*layl (layaali)*
Ministry of	*Wizaarat...*	no	*laa*
Agriculture	*Az-Ziraa'a*	noise	*sawt*
Aviation	*At-Teiyaaraan*	noon	*dhuhr*
Commerce	*At-Tijaara*	north	*shimaal*
Communications	*Al-Mūwaasillaat*	notebook	*daftar (dafaatir)*
Education	*At-Tarbeeya*	November	*Tishreen ath-*
Defence	*Ad-Difaa*		*Thaanee*
Development	*Al-I'maar*	now	*alaan*
Finance	*Al-Maaleeya*	number	*raqm (arqaam)*
Foreign Affairs	*Al-Khaarijeeya*		
Health	*As-Sahha*	October	*Tishreen Al-Awwal*
Industry	*As-Sinaa'a*	office	*maktab (makaatib)*
Interior	*Ad-Daakhileeya*	oil (petroleum)	*naft*
Labour	*Al-Amal*	oil (vegetable or	*zayt*
Marine	*Al-Bahreeya*	lubricating)	
(Public) Works	*Al-Ashghaal (Al-*	old	*qodeem*
	Aamma)	olives	*zaytoon*
Transport	*An-Naqleeyaat*	on	*ala*
minute	*daqeeqa (daqaa'iq)*	onions	*basal*

on the subject of	*bi-khūsoos*	porter	*hammaal*
only	*foqot/bass*	possible	*mūmkin*
open	*maftooh*	post	*bareed*
opportunity	*fūrsa*	post office	*maktab al-bareed*
or	*aw*	potatoes	*bataata*
oranges	*būrtūqaal*	pound (money)	*jūnayh*
other	*aakhar (fem.ūkhra)*	pound (weight)	*ratl*
outside	*kharij*	present (adj)	*haalee*
over	*ala/foqe*	present/gift	*hadeeya*
			(hadaayaa)
pain	*waj'a*	Prime Minister	*Ra'ees al-Wūzara*
palace	*qala*	press (n)	*sahaafa*
Palestine	*filasteen*	principal (main)	*ra'eesee*
paper (piece of)	*woroqa (awraaq)*	problem	*mūshkila*
park	*būstaan*		*(mashaakil)*
Parliament	*barlamaan*	prohibited	*mamnoo'a*
part (of)	*juz (ajzaa) (min)*		
party	*hafla (haflaat)*	qualification	*salaaheeya*
political party	*hizb (ahzaab)*		*(salaaheeyaat)*
passenger	*raakib (rūkkaab)*	queen	*malika*
passport	*jawaaz*	question	*su'aal (as'ila)*
	(jawaazaat) Safar	quickly	*bisir'a*
past	*maadee*	quiet	*haadee*
the past	*al-maadee*	Quran, the Holy	*Al-Qūraan Al-*
peace	*silm* or *salaam*		*Kareem*
pen	*qolum hibr*		
pencil	*qolum rūsaas*	rain	*matar*
people (collect.)	*naas*	razor blades	*moos hallaaka*
the (or a)	*(ash-)sha'b*	ready	*haadhir*
people		reason	*sabab (asbaab)*
pepper	*filfil*	recent	*akheer*
perhaps/possibly	*yimkin*	red	*ahmar*
period	*mūdda*	Red Sea	*Al-Bahr Al-Ahmar*
permission/	*rūkhsa*	religion	*deen*
permit		rent	*eejaar*
person	*shakhs (ashkhaas)*	repair	*tasleeh*
petrol	*benzeen*	he repaired	*sallah*
photography	*soora (suwar)*	he will repair	*yūssalih*
pills	*hūboob*	reply	*jawaab (ajwiba)*
place	*mahal (mahallat)*	report (of	*taqreer (taqaareer)*
please	*mindfudlak*	committee)	
police	*shūrta/boolees*	request	*talab (talabaat)*
policeman	*shūrtee*	requested	*matloob*
police station	*mahattat ash-*	he requested	*talab*
	shūrta/boolees	he requests	*yatlūb*
poor	*faqeer (fūqaraa)*	reservation	*hajz*
pork	*lahm khanzeer*	he reserved	*hajaz*
port	*meena*	he reserves	*yahjaz*
	(mawaanee)	responsible (for)	*mas'ool (an)*

233

responsiblity	*mas'ooleeya*	at your service	*fee khidmatak*
rest (ease)	*raaha*	sheep (coll.)	*ghanam*
the rest of	*al-baaqee min*	Shaikh	*Shaykh (Shūyookh)*
restaurant	*mat'am (mataa'im)*	ship	*markab*
result (of)	*nateeja (min) (nataa'ij)*	shirt	*qomees*
		shoes	*ahdheeya* or *jazma (jizaam)*
he returned	*raja'*		
he returns	*yirja'*	shop	*dūkkaan (dakaakeen)*
rice	*ruz*		
rich	*ghanee*	shore	*shatt*
rifle	*būndūqeeya (banaadiq)*	short	*qaseer*
		shut	*mūsakkar*
right (opp. of left)	*yameen*	silver	*fidhdha*
		simple	*boseet*
river	*nahr*	since (time)	*mūndh*
room	*ghūrfa (ghūraf)*	slow (adj.)	*būtee'*
round (circular)	*mūdawwar*	small	*sagheer*
ruins	*aathar*	soldier	*jūndi (jūnood)*
ruler	*haakim*	some of	*ba'd min*
roast/fried	*maglee*	sometimes	*ihyaanan*
		soon (after a while)	*ba'd qaleel*
sad	*hazeen*		
safe (adj)	*saalim*	soup	*shoorba*
safe (n)	*khazna*	south	*jūnoob*
safety	*salaama*	he spoke	*takullum or haka*
salad	*salaata*	he speaks	*yatakallum or yihkee*
salt	*milh*		
sand	*raml*	specialist	*ikhsaa'ee*
Saturday	*Yome As-Sabt*	sport	*reeyaadha*
sauce/gravy	*salsa*	square (adj.)	*mūrubb'a*
Saudi Arabia	*Al-Mamlaka Al-Arabeeya As Sowdeeya*	stairs	*daraj*
		stamp (postage)	*taabi' (tawaabi'a)*
		star (lit. and fig.)	*najm (nūjoom)*
he said	*qaal*	station	*mahatta*
he says	*yaqool*	Sterling	*Isterleeney*
school	*madrassa (madaaris)*	step	*daraja*
		stomach	*botn*
sea	*bahr*	stone	*hajar (ahjaar)*
seat (chair)	*kūrsee*	street	*sharri' a*
secret (n.)	*sirr (asraar)*	strong	*qowee*
secret (adj.)	*sirree*	student	*taalib (tūllaab)*
secretary	*sikriteer (fem. sikriteera)*	sugar	*sūkkar*
		summer	*sayf*
he saw	*shaaf*	sun	*shams*
he sees	*yashoof*	Sunday	*Yome Al-Ahad*
September	*Aylool*	sweet	*hiloo*
servant	*khaadim (khūddaam)*	he swam	*sabah*
		he swims	*yasbah*
service	*khidma*	swimming pool	*masbaha*

VOCABULARY

table	*taawūla*	he travels	*yūsaafir*
tailor	*khayyaat*	travellers' cheques	*cheeqaat seeyaaha*
he talked	*takullum or haka*	tree	*shajara (ashjaar)*
he talks	*yatakullum or*	tribe	*qobeela (qabaa'il)*
	yakhee	trousers	*bantaloon*
target	*hadaf (ahdaaf)*	true	*saheeh*
tax	*dareeba (daraaib)*	truth	*haqq*
tea	*shei*	Tuesday	*Yome Al-Thalaatha*
teacher	*mūdarris*	type (mark)	*tiraaz*
	(mūdarriseen) or		
	mū'allim	under	*taht*
	(mū'allimeen)	he understood	*fahim*
technical (adj.)	*fannee*	he understands	*yafham*
technique	*fann (fūnoon)*	university	*jaami'a*
telegram	*telegraaf*	until	*hatta*
telephone	*telefoon*	up useful	*foqe*
temperature	*darajat al-haraara*	usual	*mūfeed*
tent	*khayma*	usually	*'aadi or 'aadatan*
there is/are	*fee*		
there was/were	*kaan fee*	valid	*jayyid*
that	*dhaalik*	valley (dry)	*waadee*
theatre	*masrah*	value	*qeema*
there	*hinaak*	valuable	*thameen*
thing	*shee (ashyaa)*	vegetables	*khūdra*
thirsty	*atshaan*	vertical	*amoodee*
this	*haadha*	very	*jiddan*
this morning	*haadha as-sabah*	village	*qoriya (qūraa)*
this afternoon	*ba'ad adh-dhūhr*	he visited	*zaar*
thousand	*elf (aalaaf)*	he visits	*yazoor*
Thursday	*Yome Al-Khamees*		
time (period)	*woqt (awqaat)*	he waited	*intadhar*
time (occasion)	*murra (murraat)*	he waits	*yantadhir*
tired	*taa'baan*	he walked	*mashaa*
to	*ila*	he walks	*yimshee*
tobacco	*tombak*	wallet	*mahfaza*
today	*al-yome*	he wants	*yūreed*
toilet	*hammaam*	water	*moya/maa*
tomato	*tamaata*	weak	*da'eef*
tomorrow	*būkra*	weapon	*silaah (asliha)*
tomorrow night	*būkra fee-layl*	weather	*toqs*
toothbrush	*fūrsha lil-asnaan*	Wednesday	*Yome Al-Arba'a*
toothpaste	*ma'joon lil-asnaan*	week	*ūsboo'a*
tourism	*seeyaaha*	weight	*wazn*
tourist	*saa'ih (sūyaah)*	west	*gharb*
tourist office	*maktab as-*	what?	*aysh? or shoo?*
	seeyaaha	when?	*aymta? or matta?*
towel	*manshafa*	where?	*wayn? or fayn?*
town	*balad*	which?	*ay?*
he travelled	*safar*	while	*baynamaa*

235

white	*abyad*
who?	*meen?*
whole	*kul*
why?	*laysh?*
wind	*howa*
window	*shūb**baak***
wine	***nbeedh***
winter	***shita***
with	*ma*
without	*bi**doon***
wireless	*la-**silkee***
woman	***hurma** (ha**reem**)*
word	***kalima** (kali**maat**)*
work	*shogl/amal*
worker	*'aamil/('aamal**leen***
	or *'ūm**maal**)*
world	***aalam***
he wrote	***katab***
he writes	***yak**tūb*
writing paper	***woroq** al-ki**taaba***
wrong (n.)	***gha**lat (agh**laat**)*
wrong (adj.)	*ghal**taan***
year	*sana (si**neen**)*
yellow	***as**far*
Yemen	*Al-**Yeman***
yes	*ei**wa** or naam*
yesterday	*ams*
yoghurt	***laban***
young	*sa**gheer***
zero	*sifr*
zoological	*ha**dee**qat al-*
gardens	*heiya**waa**naat*

INDEX

I
N
D
E
X

INDEX

DATE DUE

239